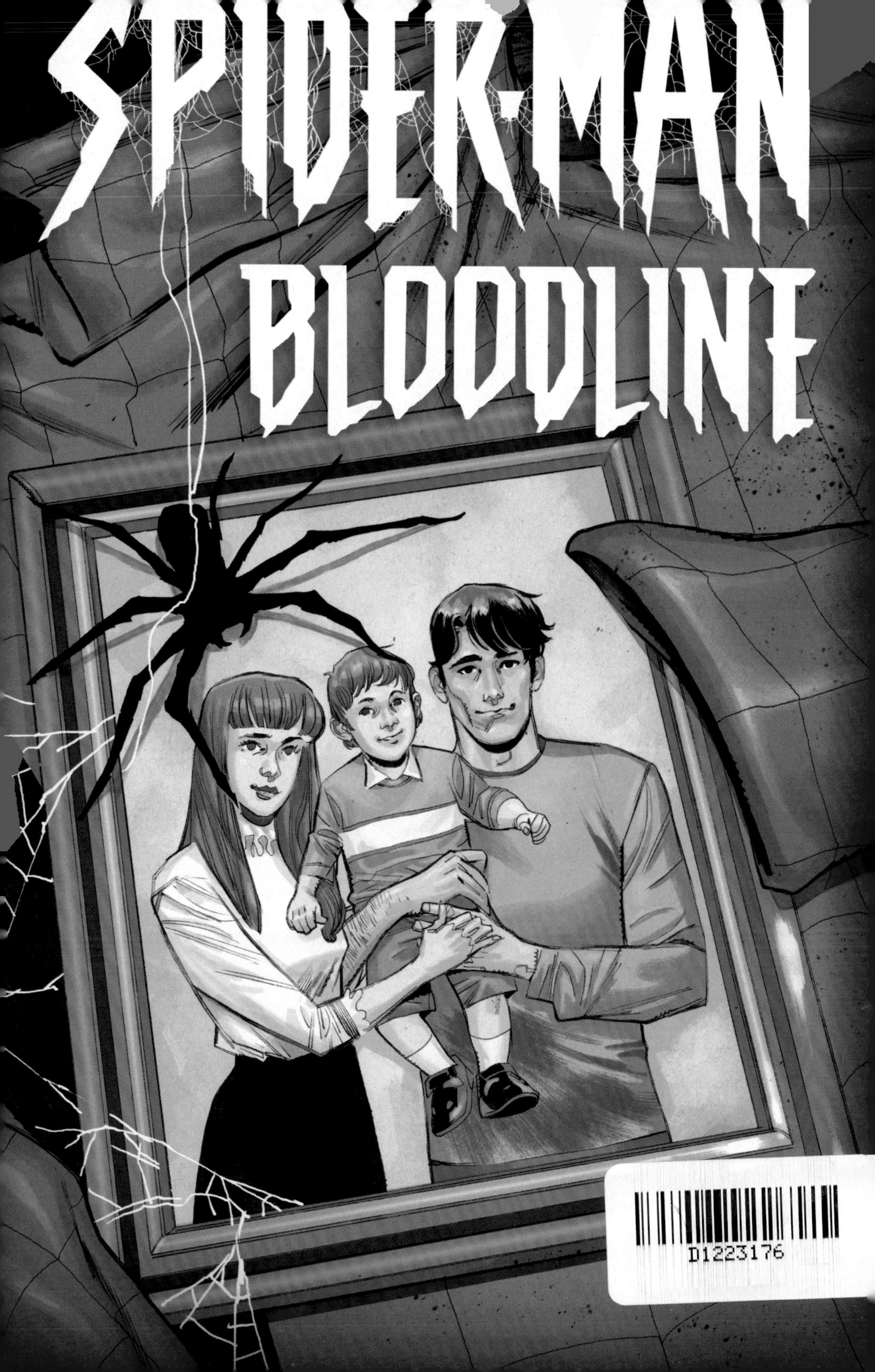
SPIDER-MAN
BLOODLINE

SPIDER-MAN CREATED BY **STAN LEE** & **STEVE DITKO**

JENNIFER GRÜNWALD
COLLECTION EDITOR

DANIEL KIRCHHOFFER
ASSISTANT EDITOR

MAIA LOY
ASSISTANT MANAGING EDITOR

LISA MONTALBANO
ASSISTANT MANAGING EDITOR

JEFF YOUNGQUIST
VP PRODUCTION & SPECIAL PROJECTS

ADAM DEL RE WITH **ANTHONY GAMBINO**
BOOK DESIGNERS

DAVID GABRIEL
SVP PRINT, SALES & MARKETING

C.B. CEBULSKI
EDITOR IN CHIEF

SPIDER-MAN: BLOODLINE. Contains material originally published in magazine form as SPIDER-MAN (2019) #1-5. First printing 2020. ISBN 978-1-302-91788-3. Published by MARVEL WORLDWIDE, INC., a subsidiary of MARVEL ENTERTAINMENT, LLC. OFFICE OF PUBLICATION: 1290 Avenue of the Americas, New York, NY 10104. © 2021 MARVEL No similarity between any of the names, characters, persons, and/or institutions in this magazine with those of any living or dead person or institution is intended, and any such similarity which may exist is purely coincidental. Printed in Canada. KEVIN FEIGE, Chief Creative Officer; DAN BUCKLEY, President, Marvel Entertainment; JOE QUESADA, EVP & Creative Director; DAVID BOGART, Associate Publisher & SVP of Talent Affairs; TOM BREVOORT, VP, Executive Editor; NICK LOWE, Executive Editor, VP of Content, Digital Publishing; DAVID GABRIEL, VP of Print & Digital Publishing; JEFF YOUNGQUIST, VP of Production & Special Projects; ALEX MORALES, Director of Publishing Operations; DAN EDINGTON, Managing Editor; RICKEY PURDIN, Director of Talent Relations; JENNIFER GRÜNWALD, Senior Editor, Special Projects; SUSAN CRESPI, Production Manager; STAN LEE, Chairman Emeritus. For information regarding advertising in Marvel Comics or on Marvel.com, please contact Vit DeBellis, Custom Solutions & Integrated Advertising Manager, at vdebellis@marvel.com. For Marvel subscription inquiries, please call 888-511-5480. Manufactured between 1/1/2021 and 2/2/2021 by SOLISCO PRINTERS, SCOTT, QC, CANADA.

10 9 8 7 6 5 4 3 2 1

SPIDER-MAN
BLOODLINE

J.J. ABRAMS & **HENRY ABRAMS**
WRITERS

SARA PICHELLI
ARTIST

ELISABETTA D'AMICO
INKING ASSISTANT

DAVE STEWART
COLOR ARTIST

VC's JOE CARAMAGNA
LETTERER

OLIVIER COIPEL & **DAVE STEWART**
COVER ART

TOM GRONEMAN & **DANNY KHAZEM**
ASSISTANT EDITORS

KATHLEEN WISNESKI
ASSOCIATE EDITOR

NICK LOWE
EDITOR

1

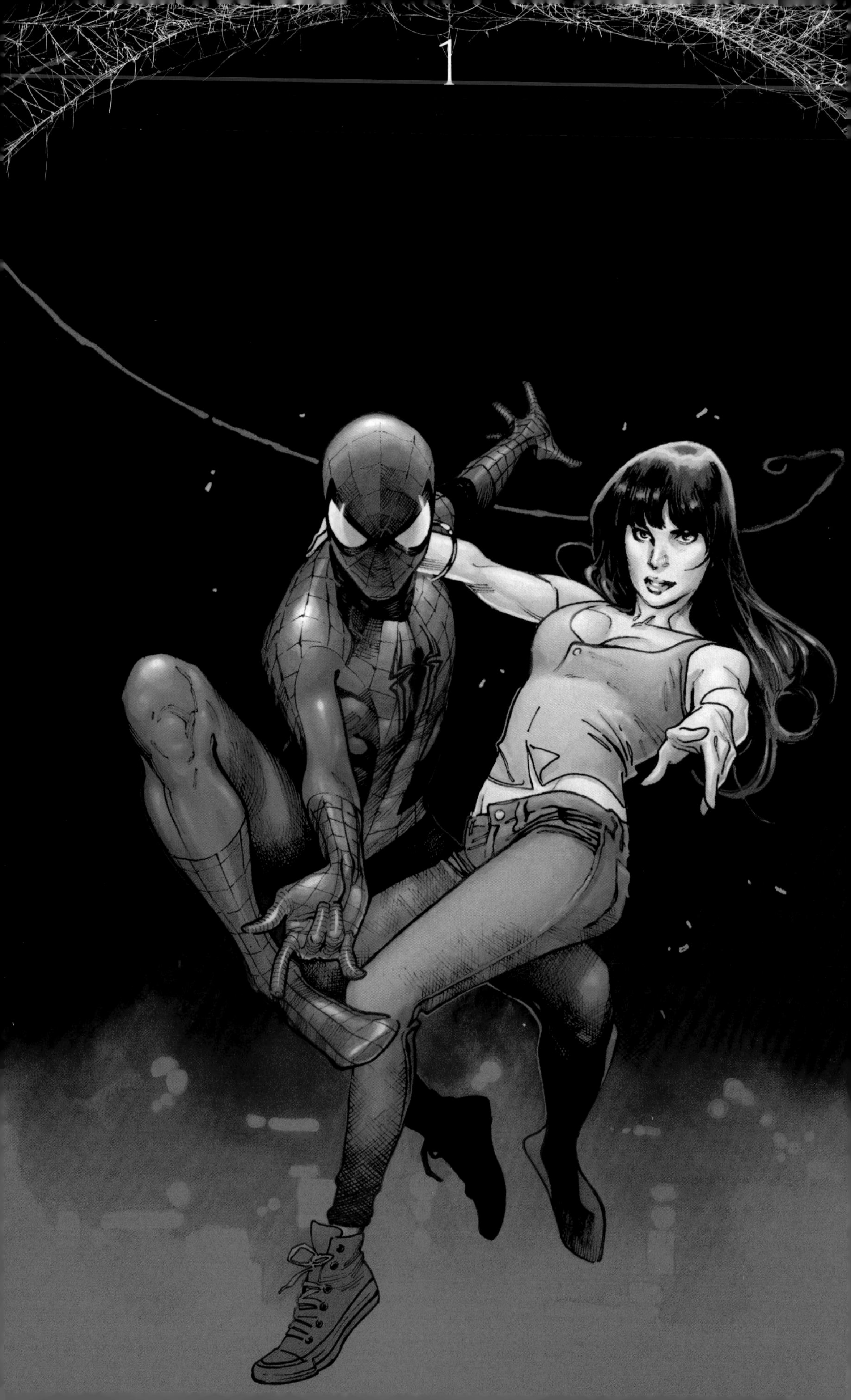

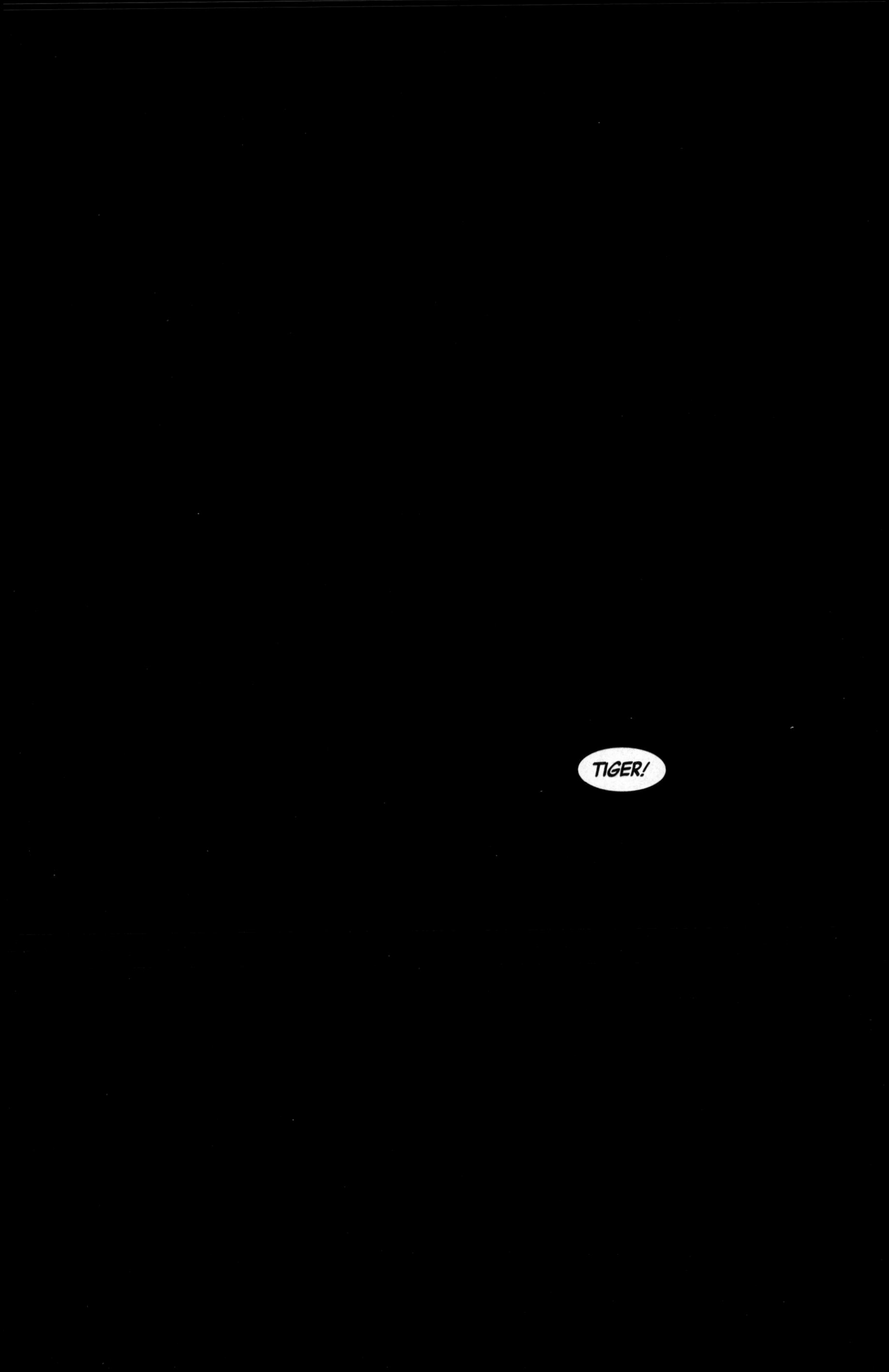
TIGER!

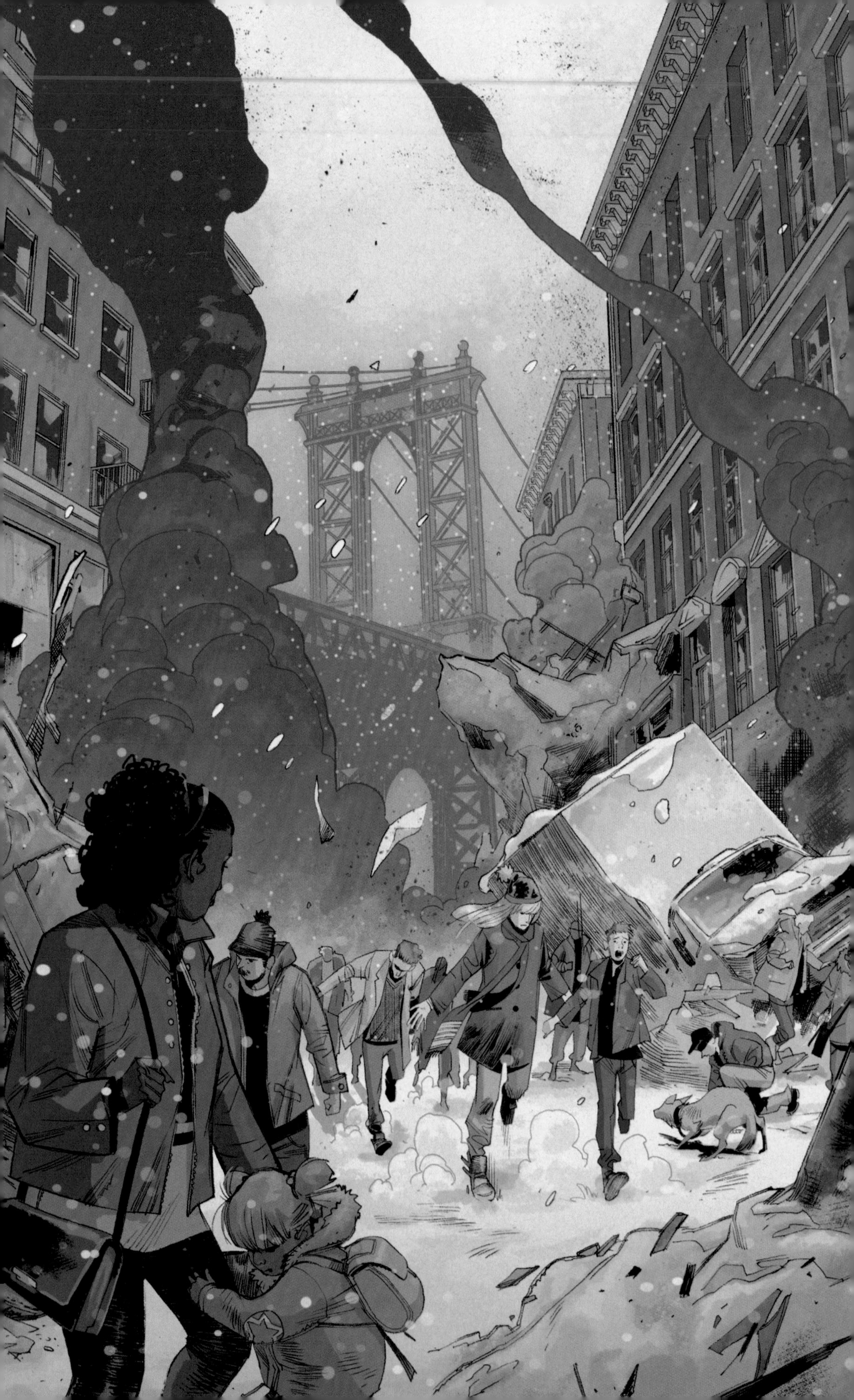

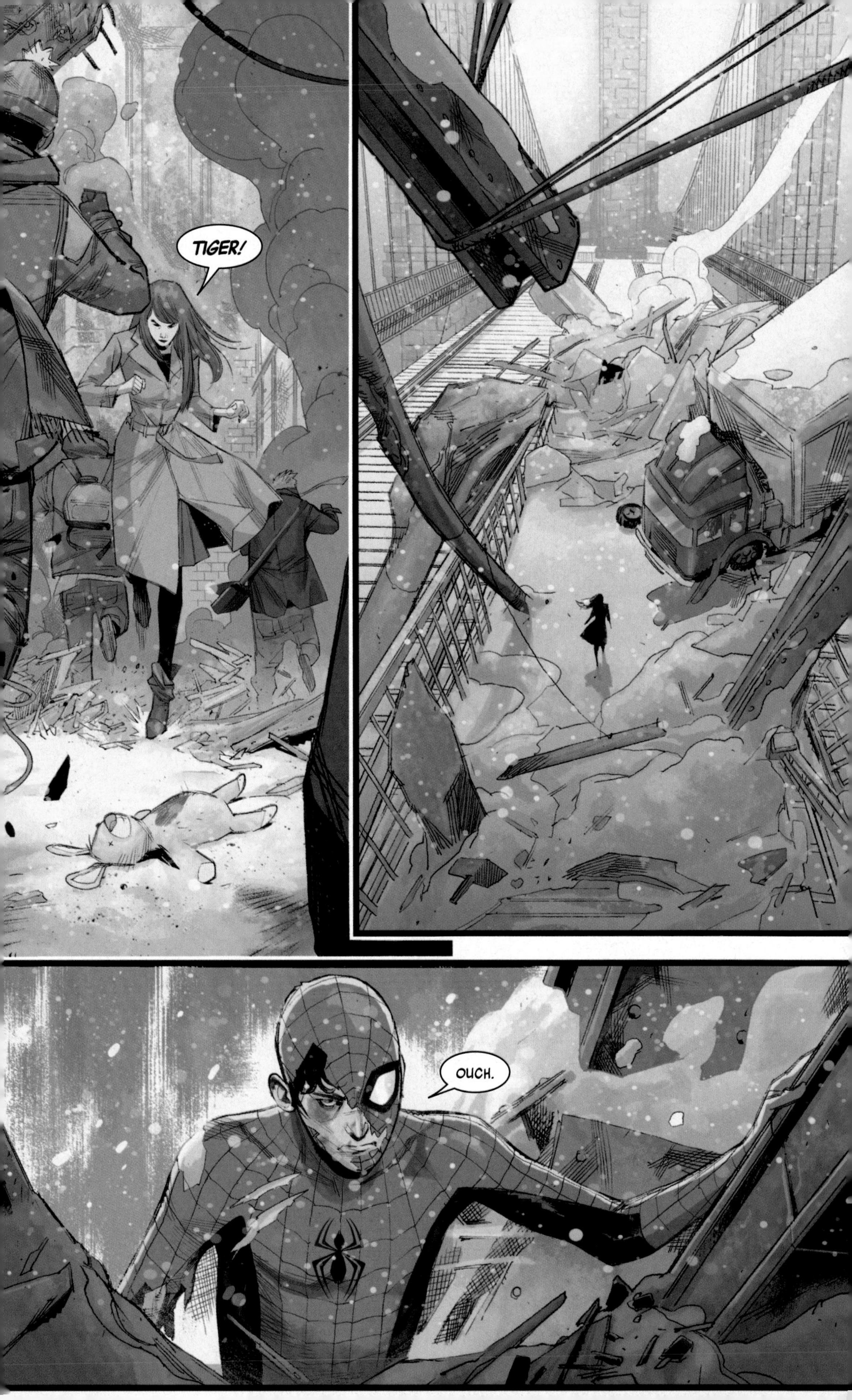
TIGER!
OUCH.

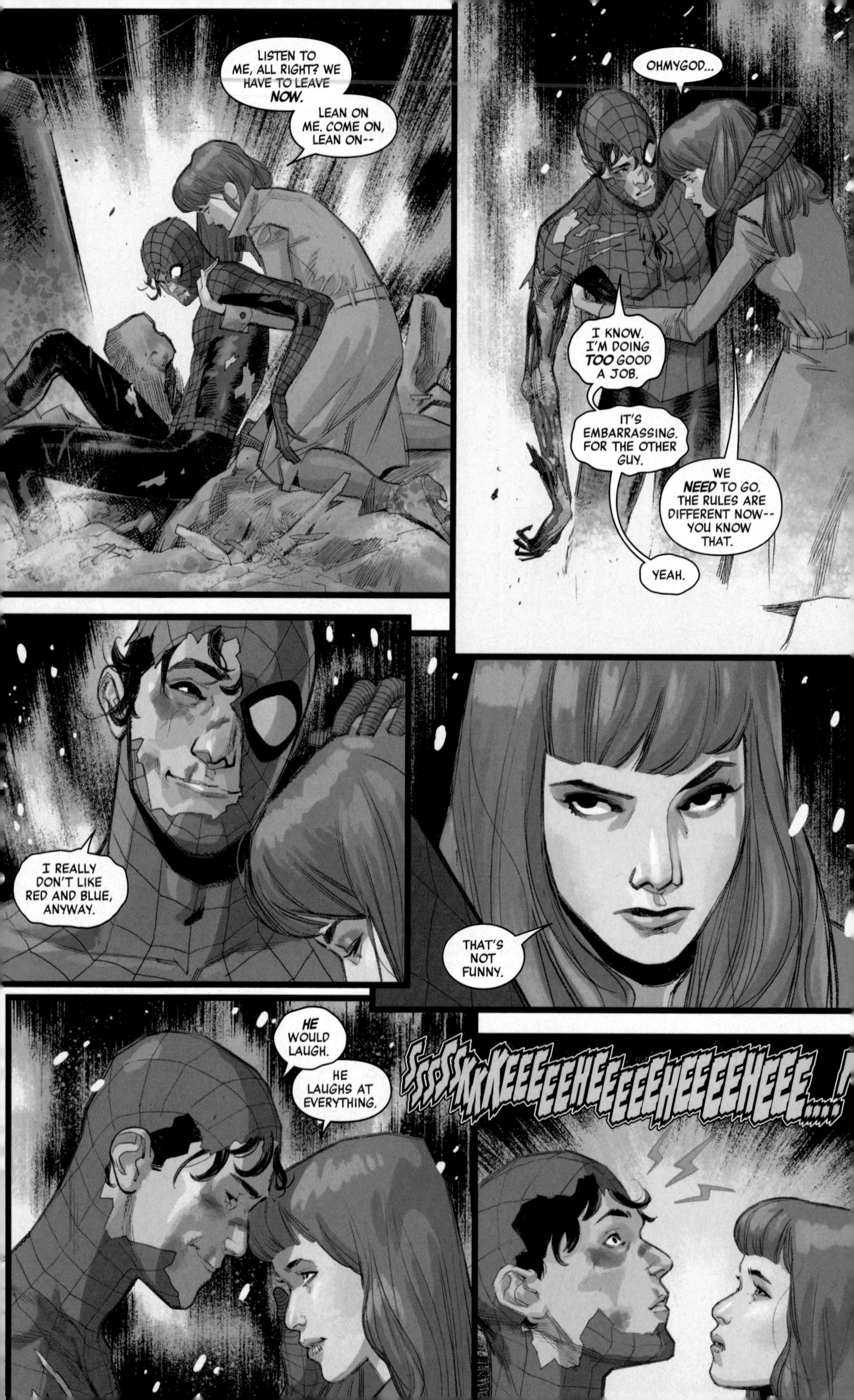
LISTEN TO ME, ALL RIGHT? WE HAVE TO LEAVE NOW.
LEAN ON ME. COME ON, LEAN ON--
OHMYGOD...
I KNOW. I'M DOING TOO GOOD A JOB.
IT'S EMBARRASSING. FOR THE OTHER GUY.
WE NEED TO GO. THE RULES ARE DIFFERENT NOW-- YOU KNOW THAT.
YEAH.
I REALLY DON'T LIKE RED AND BLUE, ANYWAY.
THAT'S NOT FUNNY.
HE WOULD LAUGH.
HE LAUGHS AT EVERYTHING.
SSSSKKKEEEEEHEEEEEEHEEEEHEEE...!

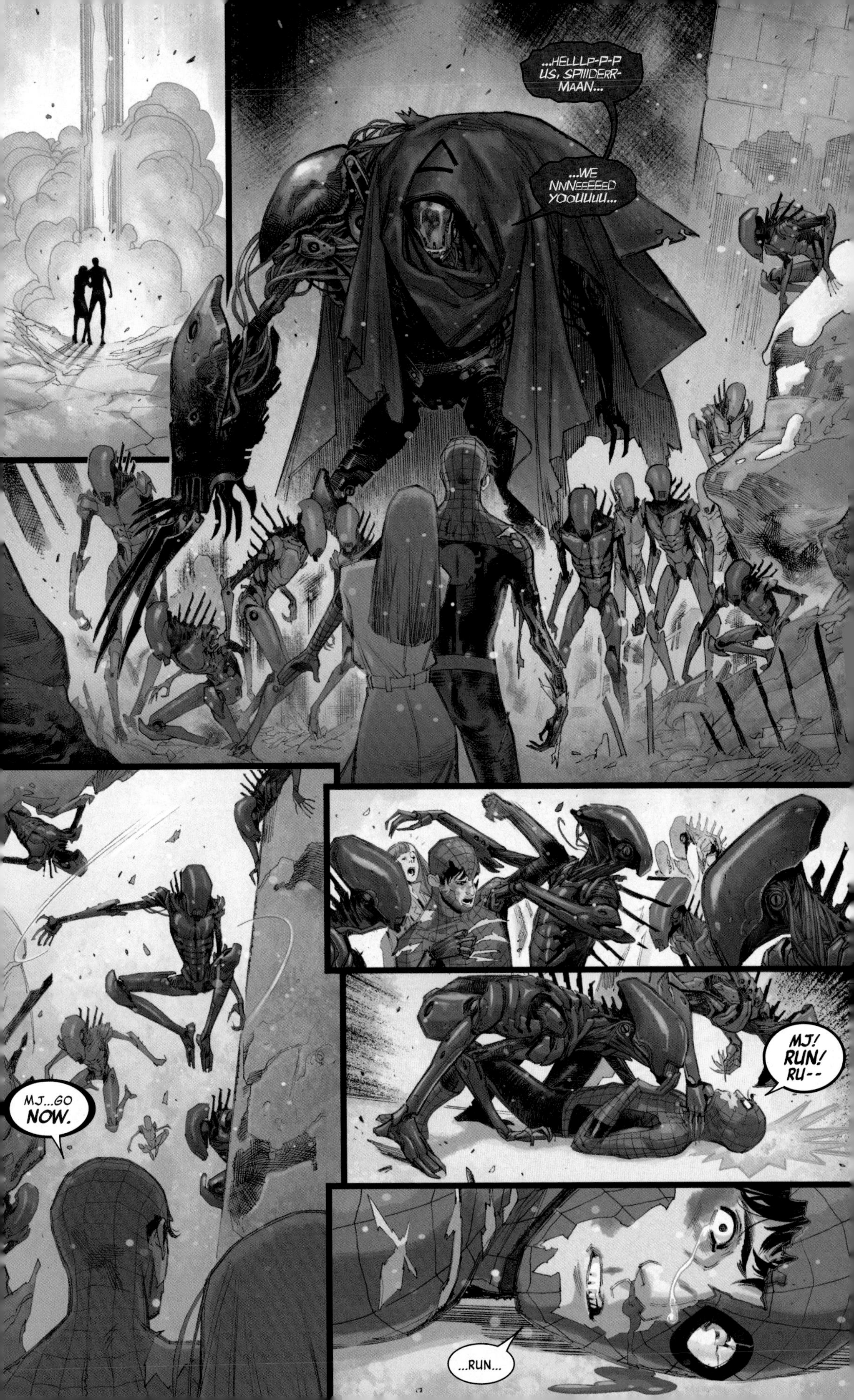
...HELLLP-P-P US, SPIIIDERR-MAAN...
...WE NNNEEEEED YOOUUUU...
MJ...GO NOW.
MJ! RUN! RU--
...RUN...

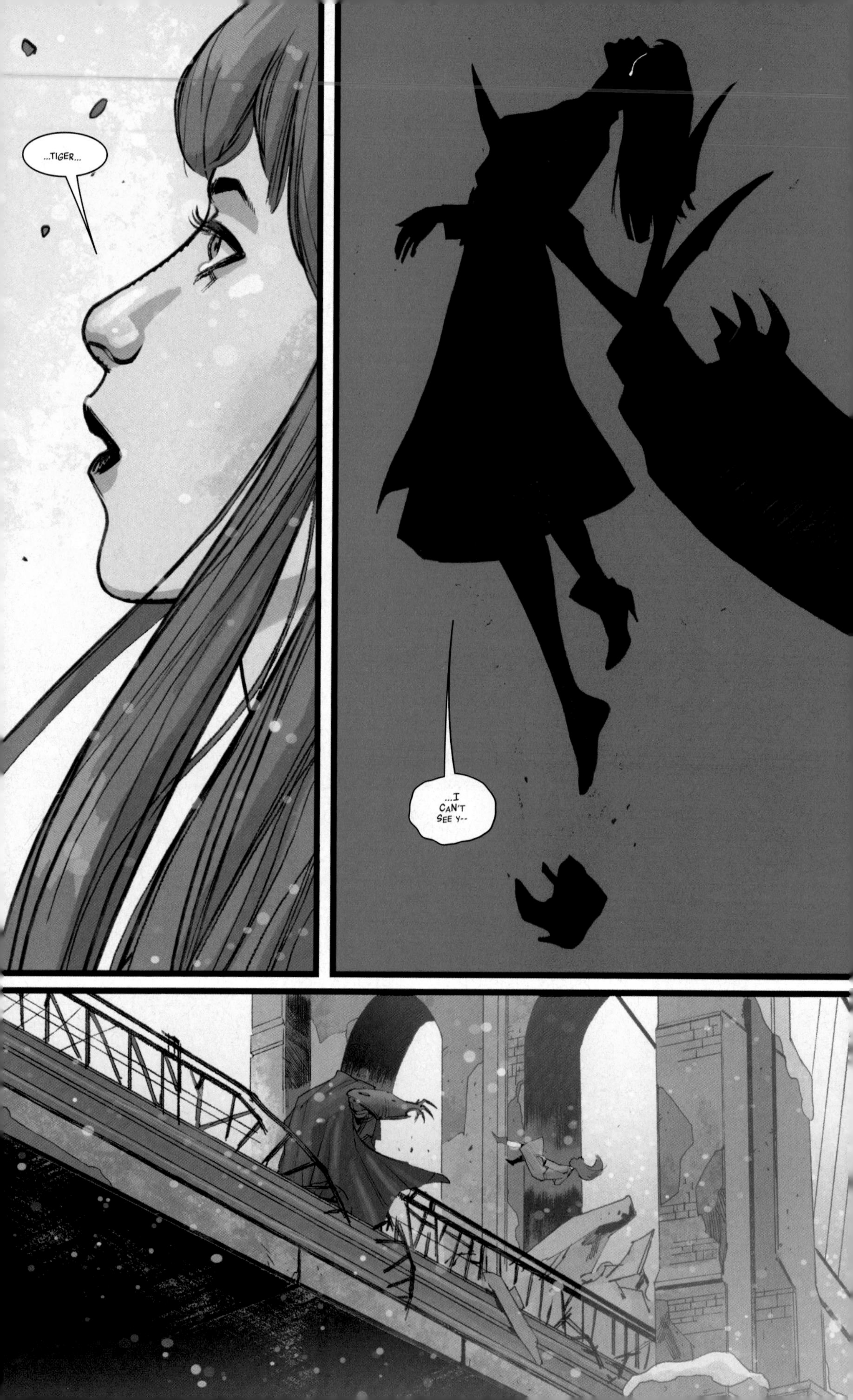
...TIGER...
...I CAN'T SEE Y--

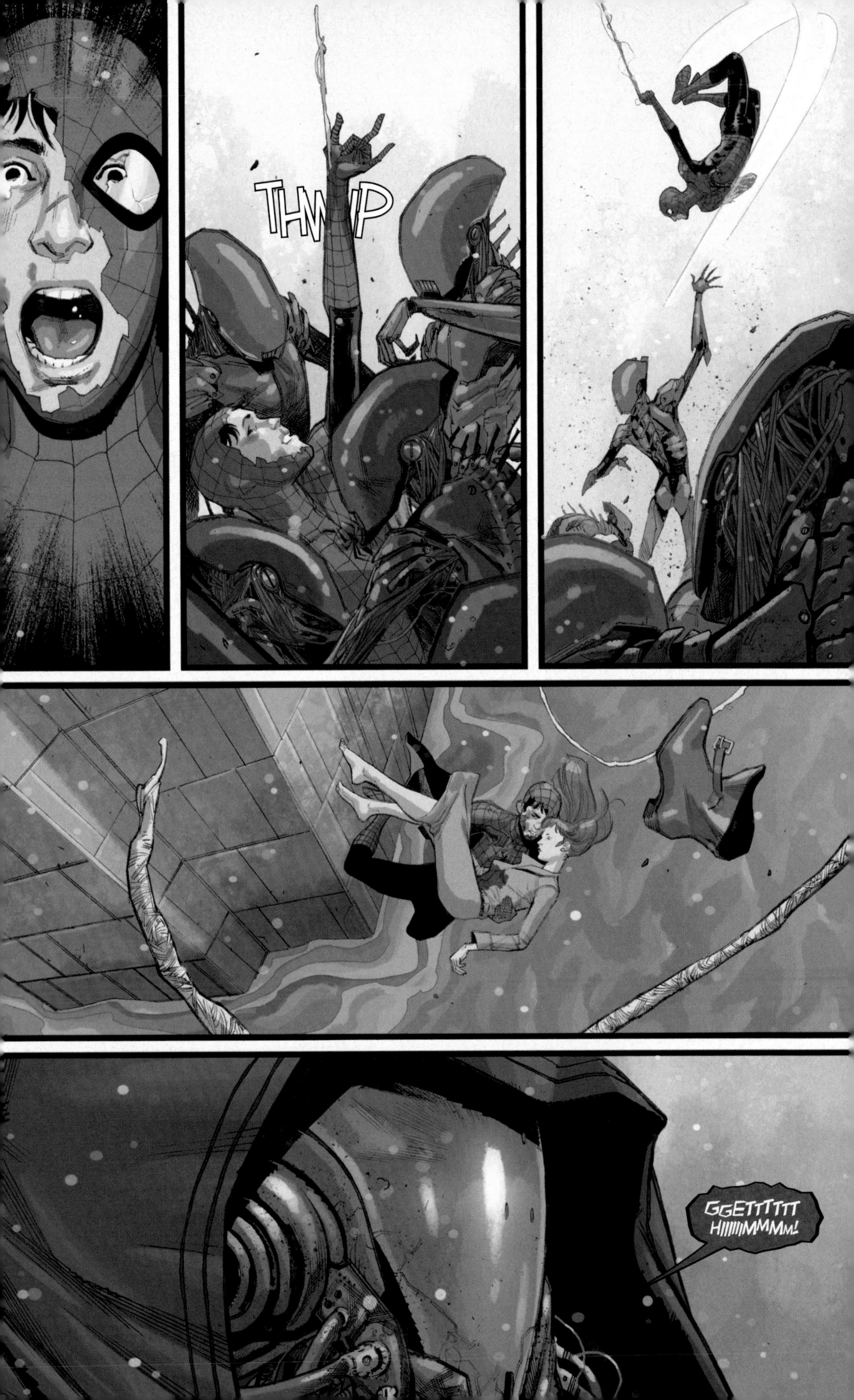
THWIP
GGETTTTTT
HIIIIIIMMMM!

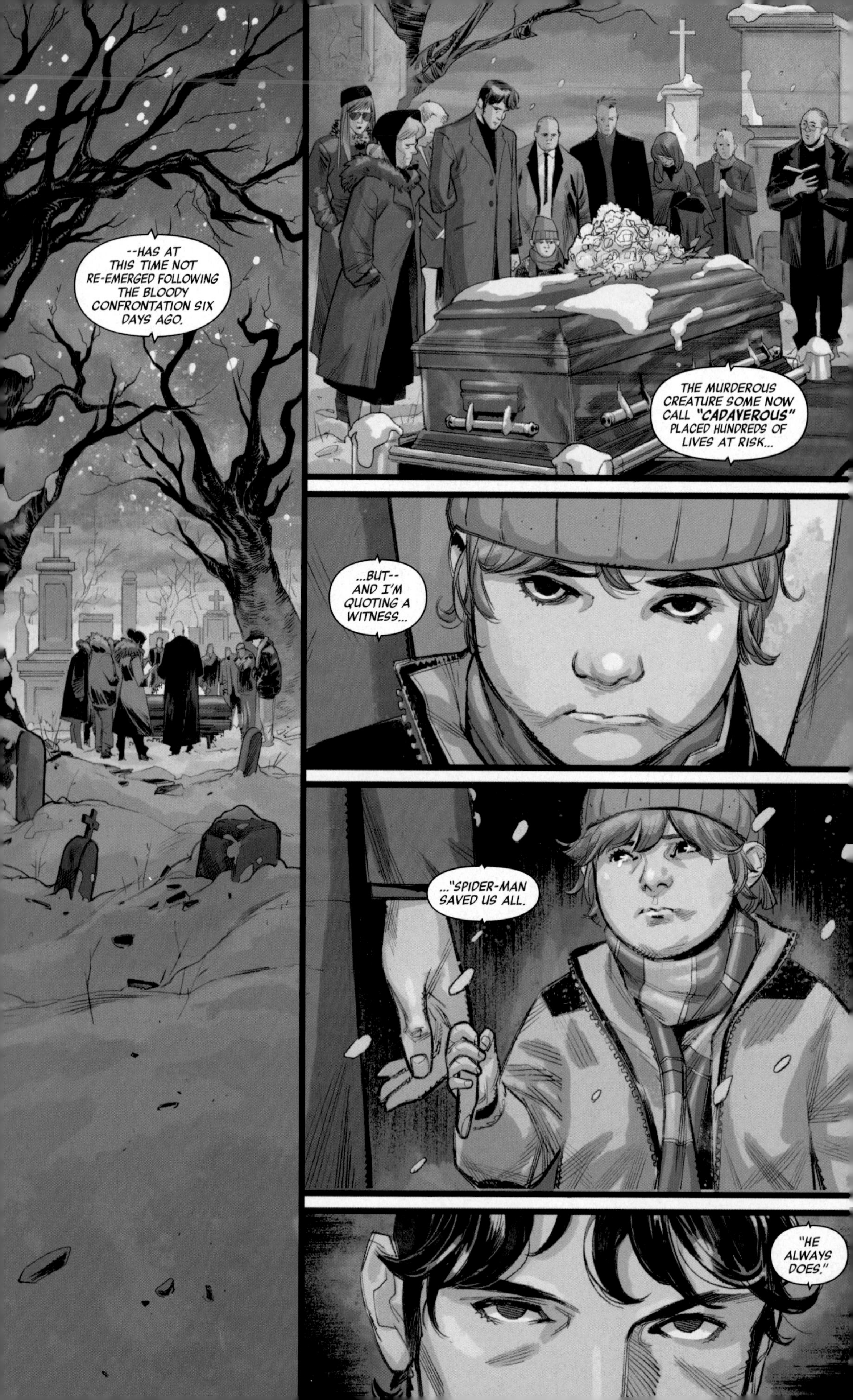
--HAS AT THIS TIME NOT RE-EMERGED FOLLOWING THE BLOODY CONFRONTATION SIX DAYS AGO.
THE MURDEROUS CREATURE SOME NOW CALL "CADAVEROUS" PLACED HUNDREDS OF LIVES AT RISK...
...BUT--AND I'M QUOTING A WITNESS...
..."SPIDER-MAN SAVED US ALL.
"HE ALWAYS DOES."

TWELVE YEARS LATER...

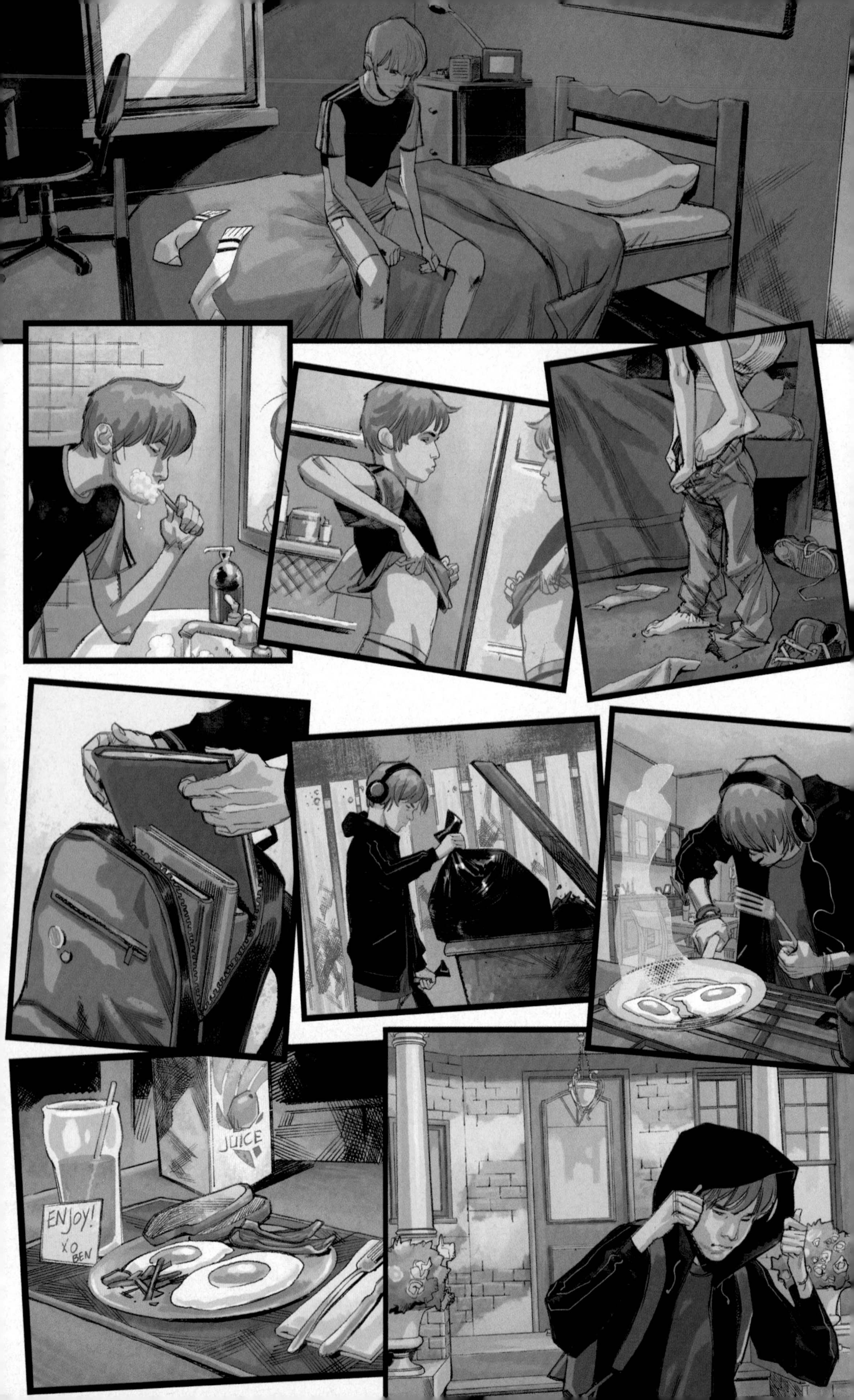
JUICE
ENJOY!
X O
BEN

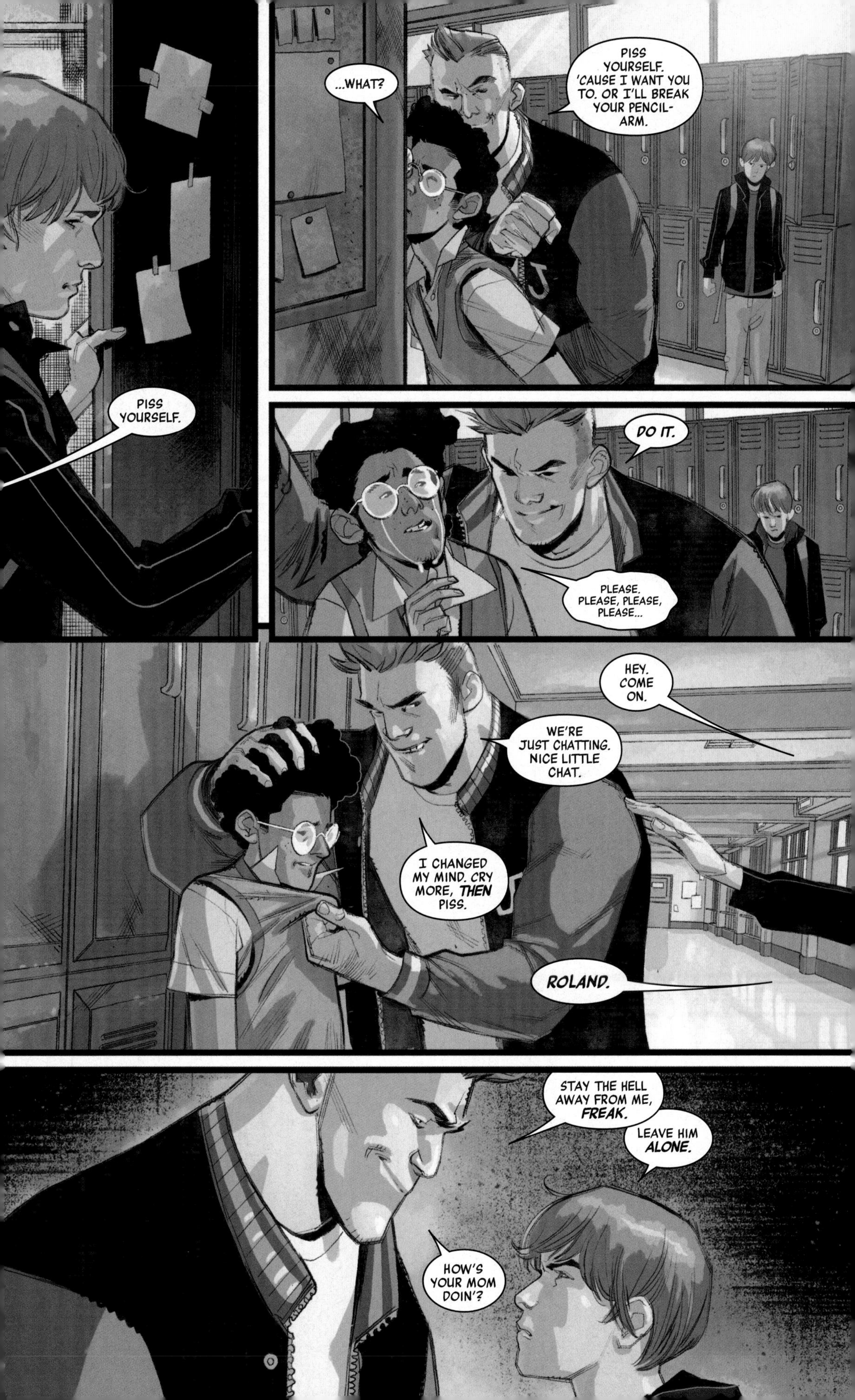
...WHAT?
PISS YOURSELF. 'CAUSE I WANT YOU TO. OR I'LL BREAK YOUR PENCIL-ARM.
PISS YOURSELF.
DO IT.
PLEASE. PLEASE, PLEASE, PLEASE...
HEY. COME ON.
WE'RE JUST CHATTING. NICE LITTLE CHAT.
I CHANGED MY MIND. CRY MORE, THEN PISS.
ROLAND.
STAY THE HELL AWAY FROM ME, FREAK.
LEAVE HIM ALONE.
HOW'S YOUR MOM DOIN'?

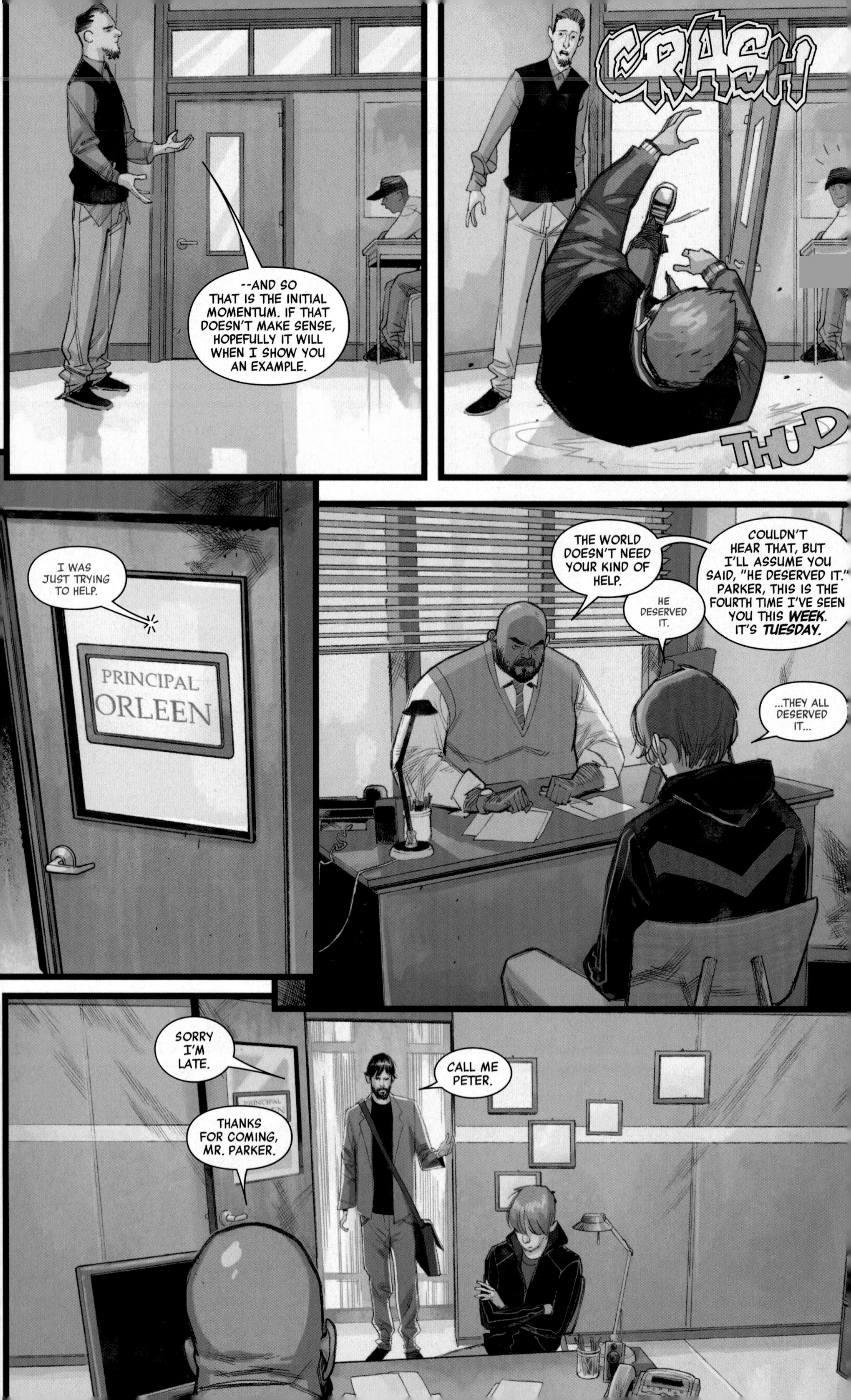
--AND SO THAT IS THE INITIAL MOMENTUM. IF THAT DOESN'T MAKE SENSE, HOPEFULLY IT WILL WHEN I SHOW YOU AN EXAMPLE.
CRASH
THUD
I WAS JUST TRYING TO HELP.
PRINCIPAL ORLEEN
THE WORLD DOESN'T NEED YOUR KIND OF HELP.
HE DESERVED IT.
COULDN'T HEAR THAT, BUT I'LL ASSUME YOU SAID, "HE DESERVED IT." PARKER, THIS IS THE FOURTH TIME I'VE SEEN YOU THIS WEEK. IT'S TUESDAY.
...THEY ALL DESERVED IT...
SORRY I'M LATE.
CALL ME PETER.
THANKS FOR COMING, MR. PARKER.

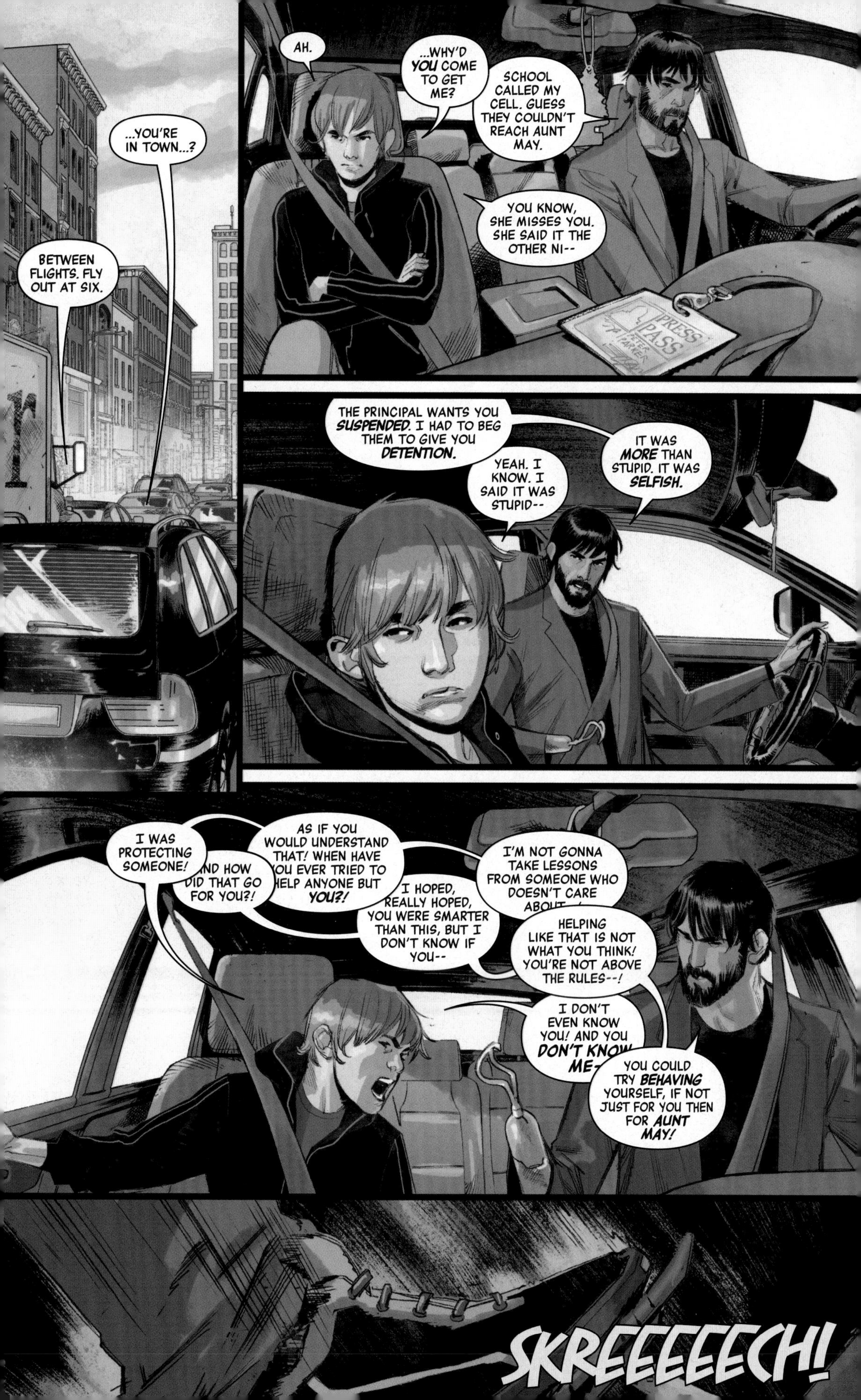
...YOU'RE IN TOWN...?
BETWEEN FLIGHTS. FLY OUT AT SIX.
AH.
...WHY'D YOU COME TO GET ME?
SCHOOL CALLED MY CELL. GUESS THEY COULDN'T REACH AUNT MAY.
YOU KNOW, SHE MISSES YOU. SHE SAID IT THE OTHER NI--
PRESS PASS
PETER PARKER
THE PRINCIPAL WANTS YOU SUSPENDED. I HAD TO BEG THEM TO GIVE YOU DETENTION.
YEAH. I KNOW. I SAID IT WAS STUPID--
IT WAS MORE THAN STUPID. IT WAS SELFISH.
I WAS PROTECTING SOMEONE!
AND HOW DID THAT GO FOR YOU?!
AS IF YOU WOULD UNDERSTAND THAT! WHEN HAVE YOU EVER TRIED TO HELP ANYONE BUT YOU?!
I HOPED, REALLY HOPED, YOU WERE SMARTER THAN THIS, BUT I DON'T KNOW IF YOU--
I'M NOT GONNA TAKE LESSONS FROM SOMEONE WHO DOESN'T CARE ABOUT
HELPING LIKE THAT IS NOT WHAT YOU THINK! YOU'RE NOT ABOVE THE RULES--!
I DON'T EVEN KNOW YOU! AND YOU DON'T KNOW ME--
YOU COULD TRY BEHAVING YOURSELF, IF NOT JUST FOR YOU THEN FOR AUNT MAY!
SKREEEEEECH!

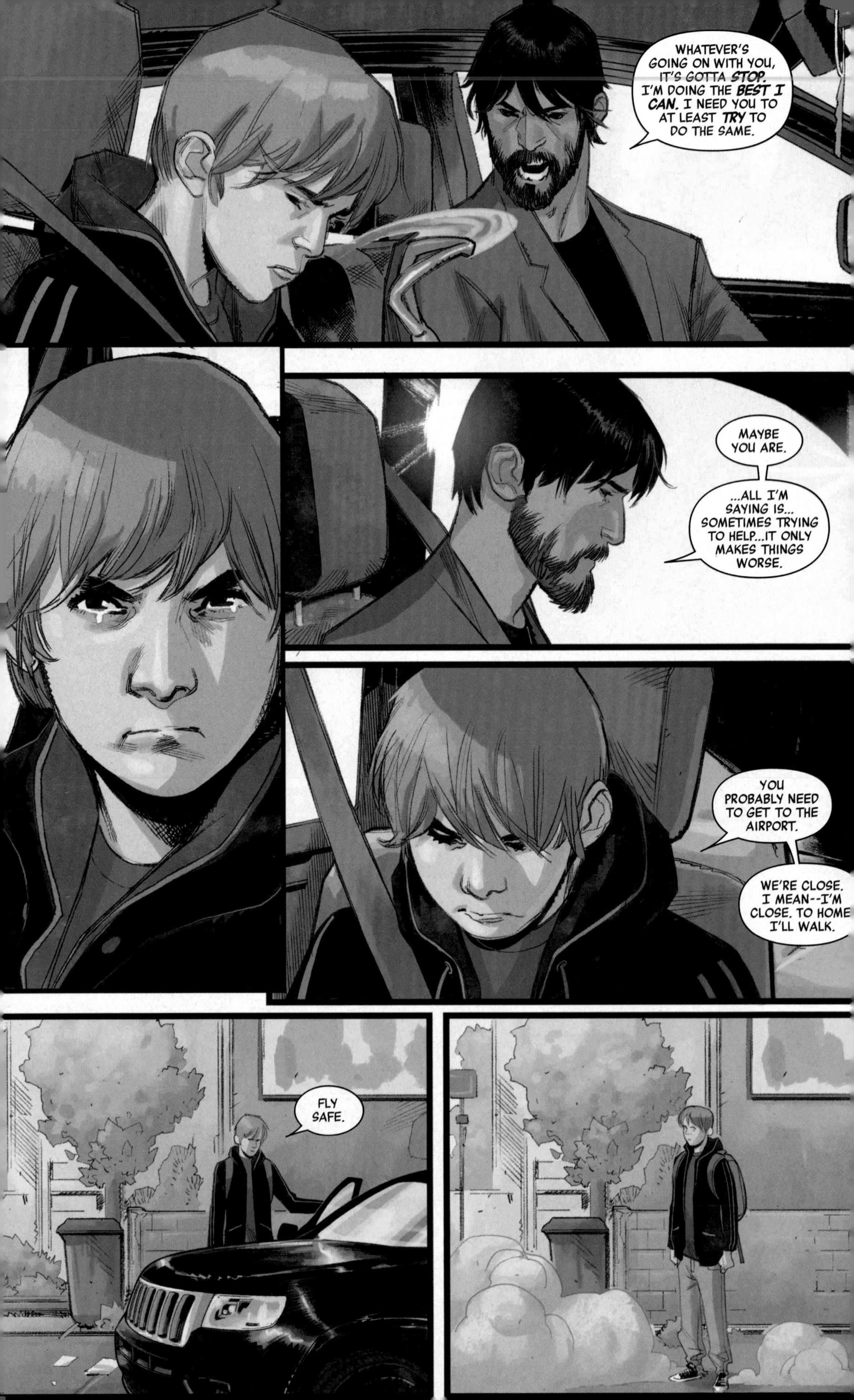
WHATEVER'S GOING ON WITH YOU, IT'S GOTTA STOP. I'M DOING THE BEST I CAN. I NEED YOU TO AT LEAST TRY TO DO THE SAME.
MAYBE YOU ARE.
...ALL I'M SAYING IS... SOMETIMES TRYING TO HELP...IT ONLY MAKES THINGS WORSE.
YOU PROBABLY NEED TO GET TO THE AIRPORT.
WE'RE CLOSE. I MEAN--I'M CLOSE. TO HOME I'LL WALK.
FLY SAFE.

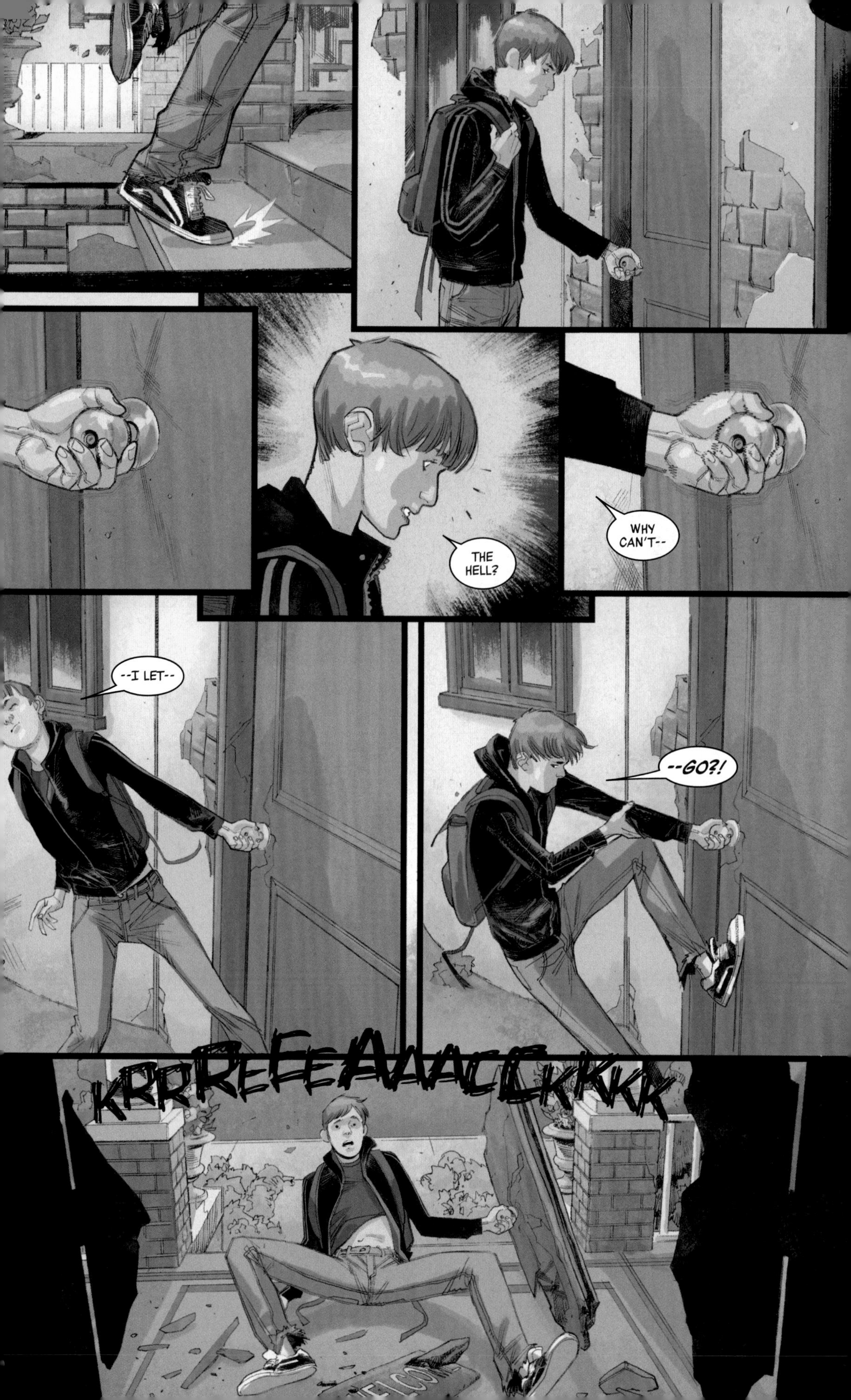
THE HELL?
WHY CAN'T--
--I LET--
--GO?!
KRRRREEEAAAACCKKKK

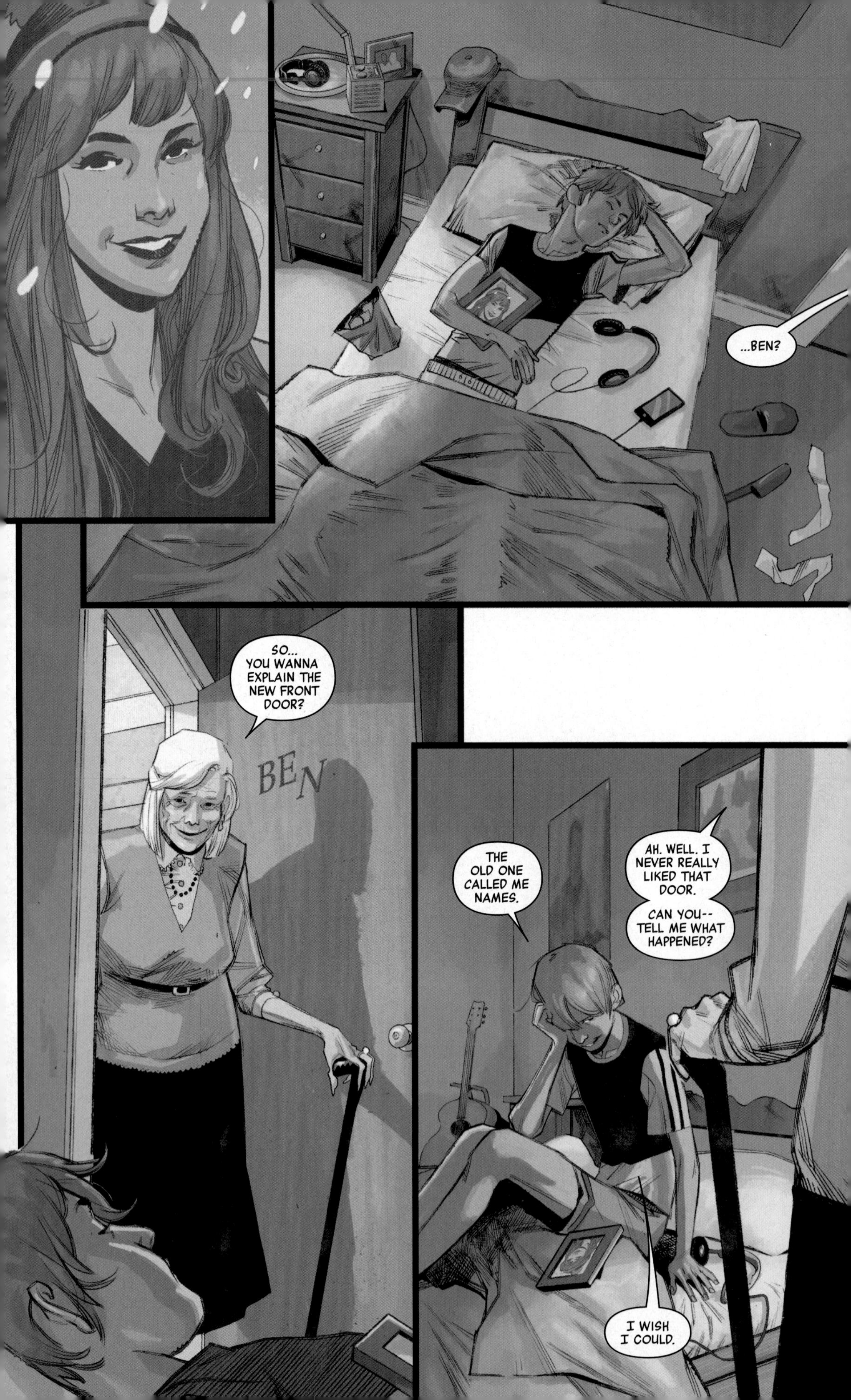
...BEN?
SO... YOU WANNA EXPLAIN THE NEW FRONT DOOR?
BEN
THE OLD ONE CALLED ME NAMES.
AH. WELL. I NEVER REALLY LIKED THAT DOOR.
CAN YOU-- TELL ME WHAT HAPPENED?
I WISH I COULD.

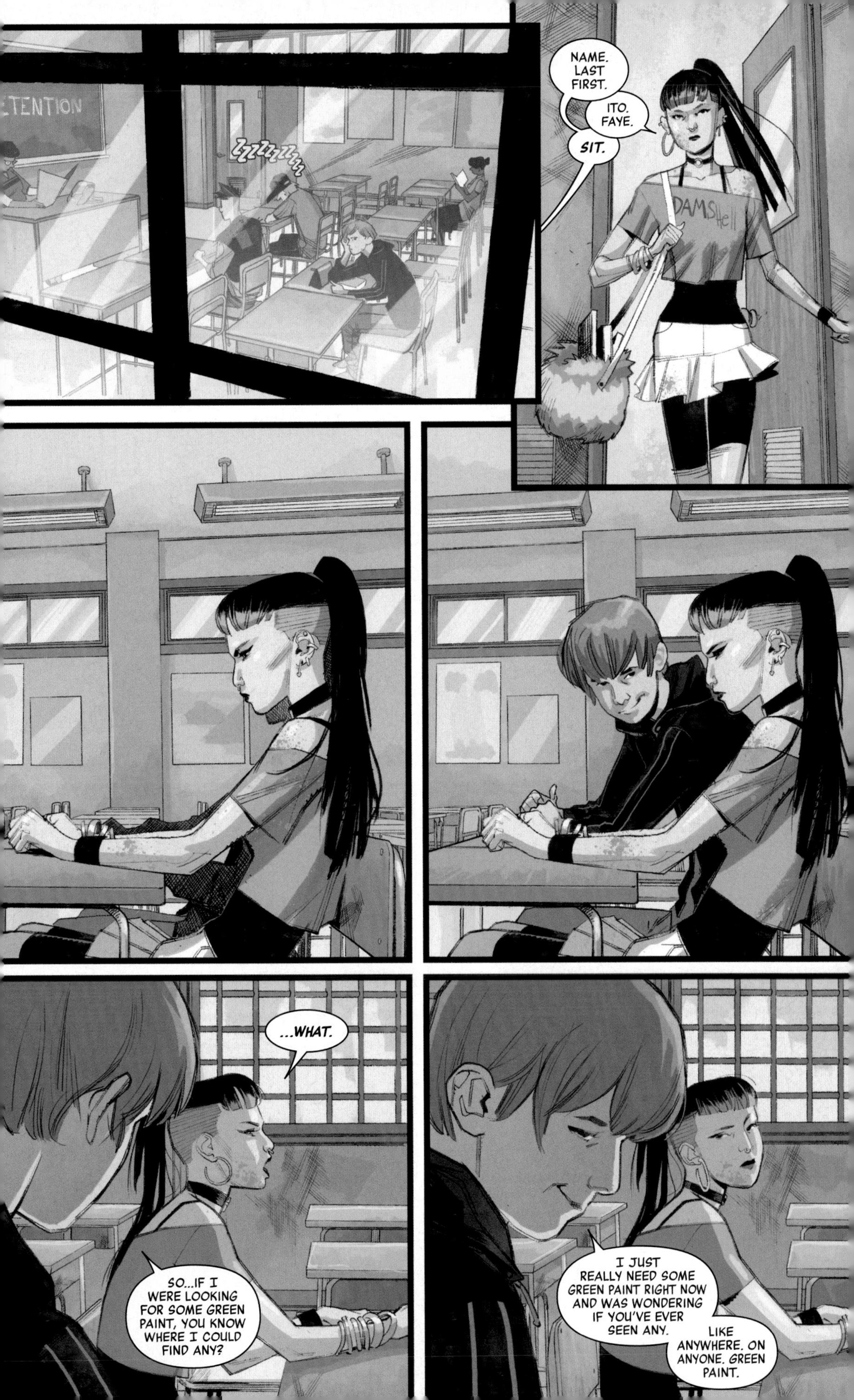
DETENTION
ZZZZZZZZZ
NAME. LAST FIRST.
ITO. FAYE.
SIT.
DAMSHell
...WHAT.
SO...IF I WERE LOOKING FOR SOME GREEN PAINT, YOU KNOW WHERE I COULD FIND ANY?
I JUST REALLY NEED SOME GREEN PAINT RIGHT NOW AND WAS WONDERING IF YOU'VE EVER SEEN ANY.
LIKE ANYWHERE. ON ANYONE. GREEN PAINT.

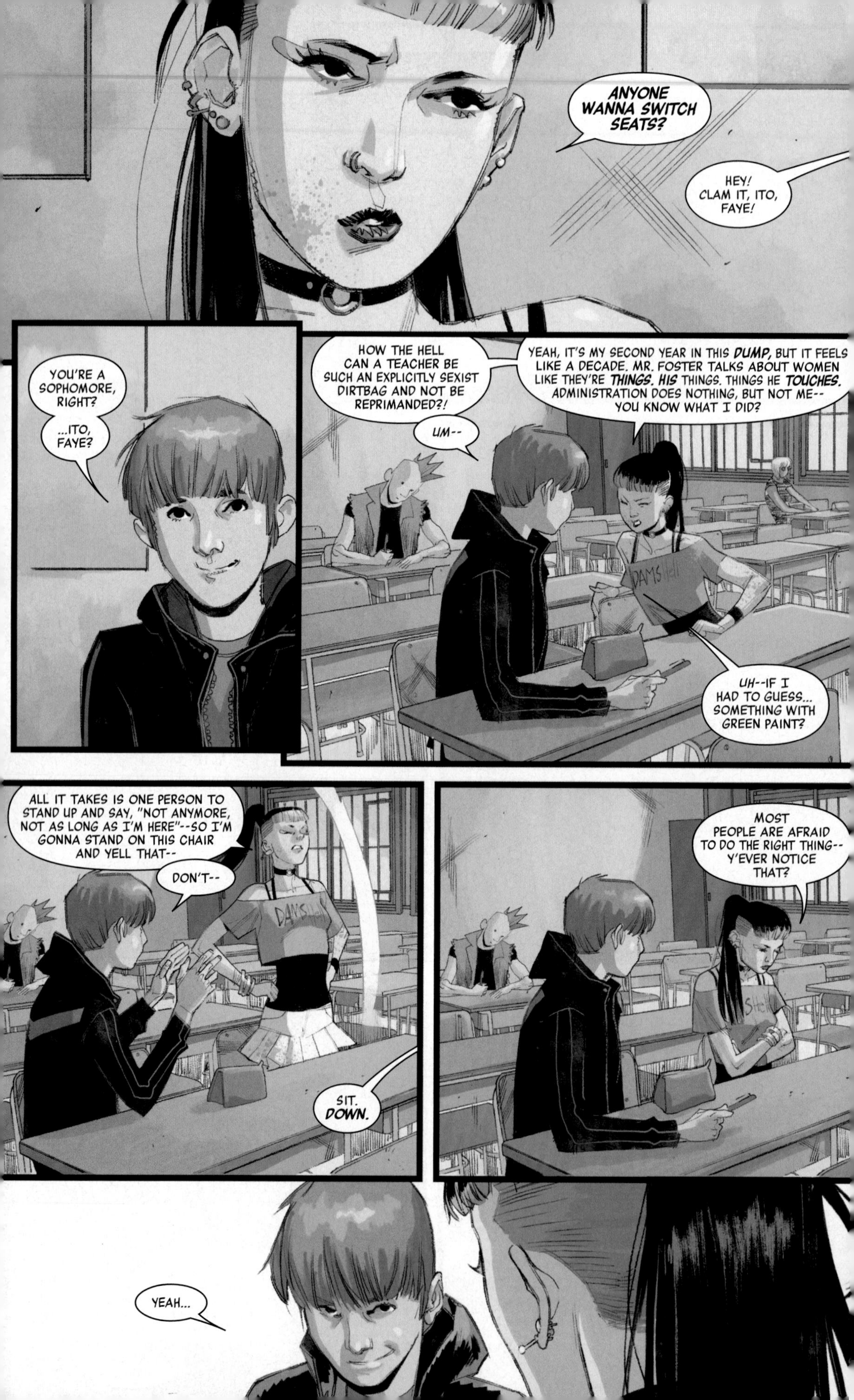

ANYONE WANNA SWITCH SEATS?
HEY! CLAM IT, ITO, FAYE!
YOU'RE A SOPHOMORE, RIGHT?
...ITO, FAYE?
HOW THE HELL CAN A TEACHER BE SUCH AN EXPLICITLY SEXIST DIRTBAG AND NOT BE REPRIMANDED?!
UM--
YEAH, IT'S MY SECOND YEAR IN THIS DUMP, BUT IT FEELS LIKE A DECADE. MR. FOSTER TALKS ABOUT WOMEN LIKE THEY'RE THINGS. HIS THINGS. THINGS HE TOUCHES. ADMINISTRATION DOES NOTHING, BUT NOT ME-- YOU KNOW WHAT I DID?
UH--IF I HAD TO GUESS... SOMETHING WITH GREEN PAINT?
ALL IT TAKES IS ONE PERSON TO STAND UP AND SAY, "NOT ANYMORE, NOT AS LONG AS I'M HERE"--SO I'M GONNA STAND ON THIS CHAIR AND YELL THAT--
DON'T--
SIT. DOWN.
MOST PEOPLE ARE AFRAID TO DO THE RIGHT THING-- Y'EVER NOTICE THAT?
YEAH...

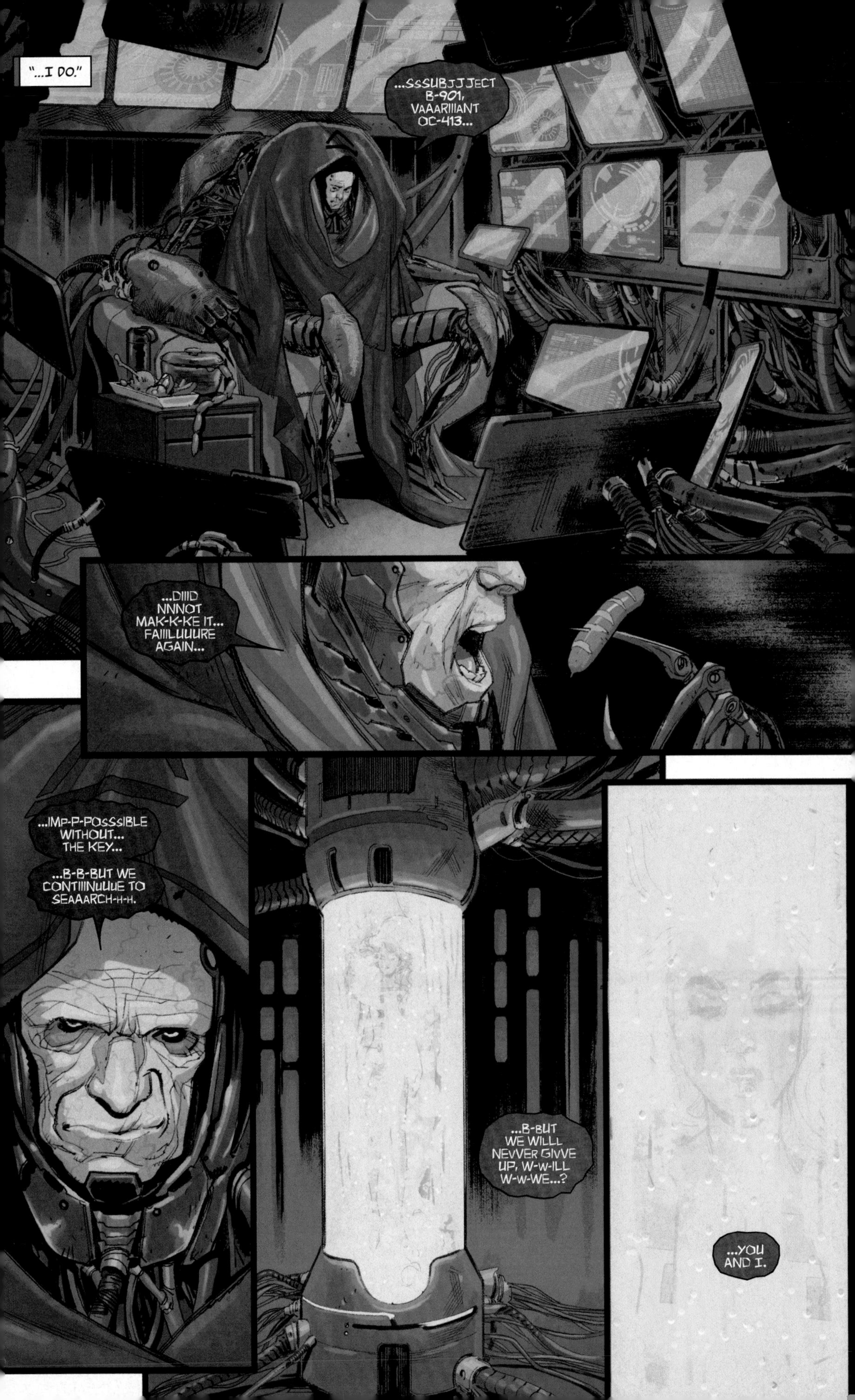
"...I DO."
...SSSUBJJJECT B-901, VAAARIIIANT OC-413...
...DIIID NNNOT MAK-K-KE IT... FAIIILUUURE AGAIN...
...IMP-P-POSSSIBLE WITHOUT... THE KEY...
...B-B-BUT WE CONTIIINUUUE TO SEAAARCH-H-H.
...B-BUT WE WILLL NEVVER GIVVE UP, W-W-ILL W-W-WE...?
...YOU AND I.

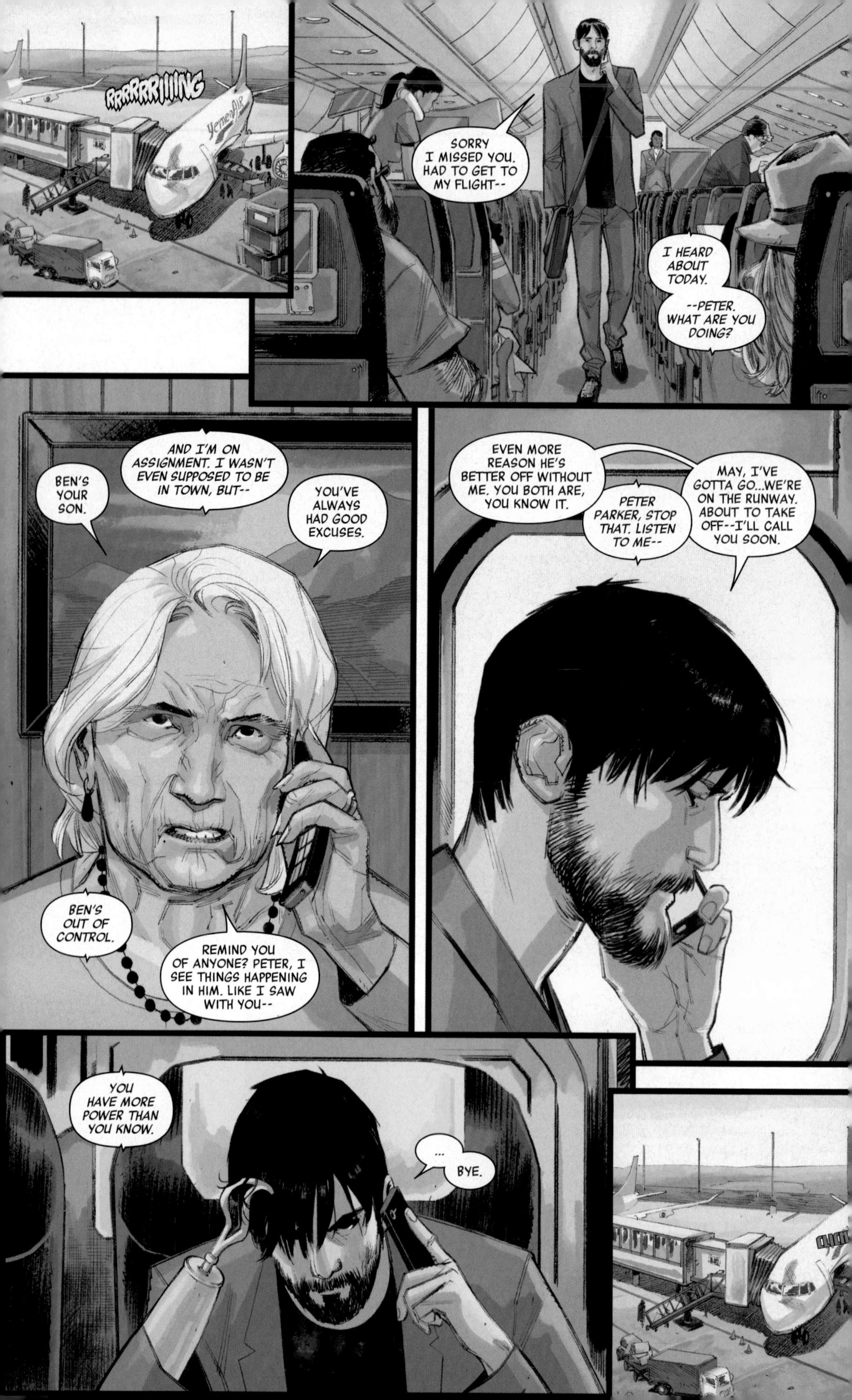
RRRRRRIIIING
Yemen AIR
SORRY I MISSED YOU. HAD TO GET TO MY FLIGHT--
I HEARD ABOUT TODAY.
--PETER. WHAT ARE YOU DOING?
BEN'S YOUR SON.
AND I'M ON ASSIGNMENT. I WASN'T EVEN SUPPOSED TO BE IN TOWN, BUT--
YOU'VE ALWAYS HAD GOOD EXCUSES.
BEN'S OUT OF CONTROL.
REMIND YOU OF ANYONE? PETER, I SEE THINGS HAPPENING IN HIM. LIKE I SAW WITH YOU--
EVEN MORE REASON HE'S BETTER OFF WITHOUT ME. YOU BOTH ARE, YOU KNOW IT.
PETER PARKER, STOP THAT. LISTEN TO ME--
MAY, I'VE GOTTA GO...WE'RE ON THE RUNWAY. ABOUT TO TAKE OFF--I'LL CALL YOU SOON.
YOU HAVE MORE POWER THAN YOU KNOW.
... BYE.

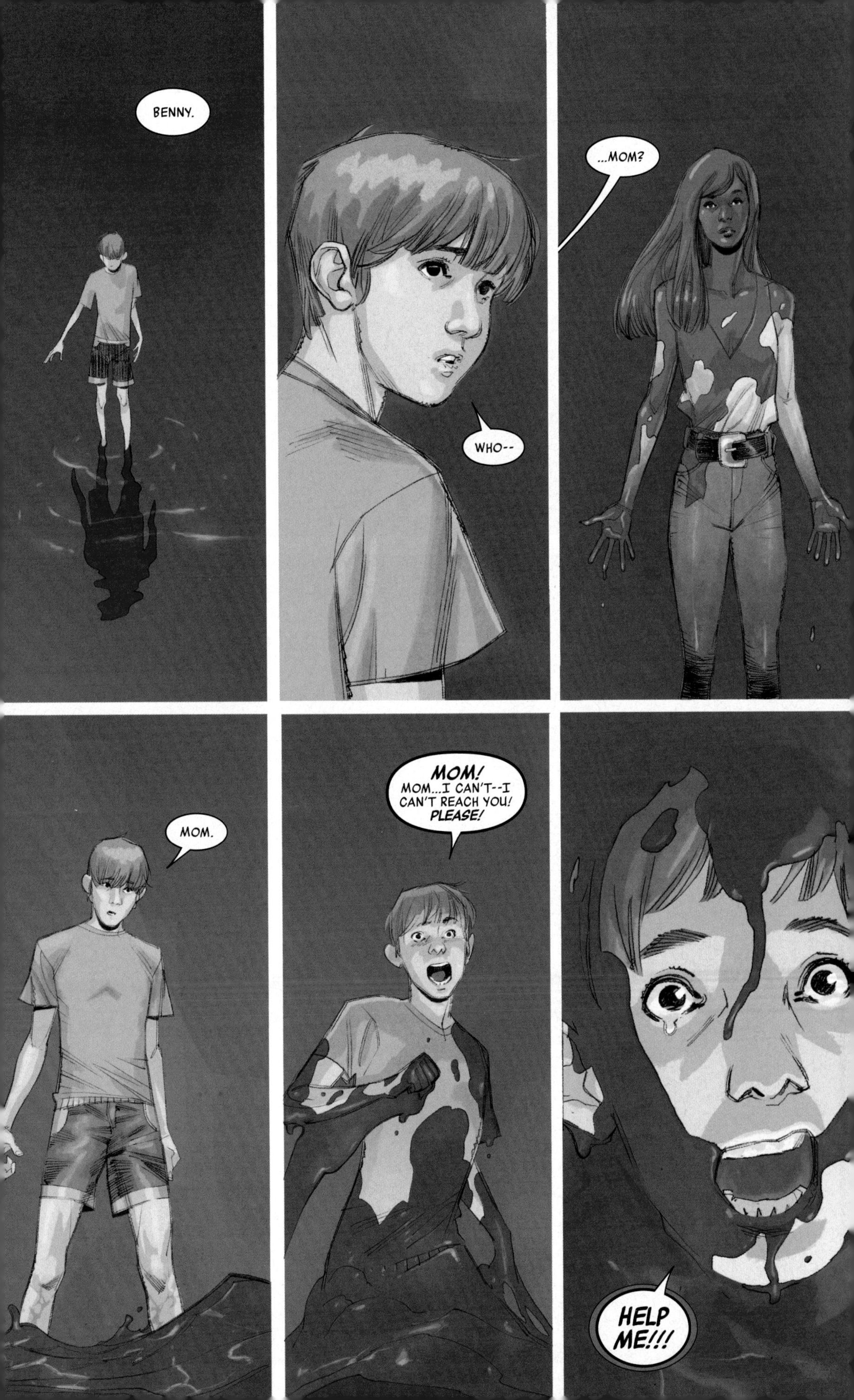
BENNY.
WHO--
...MOM?
MOM.
MOM!
MOM...I CAN'T--I CAN'T REACH YOU! PLEASE!
HELP ME!!!

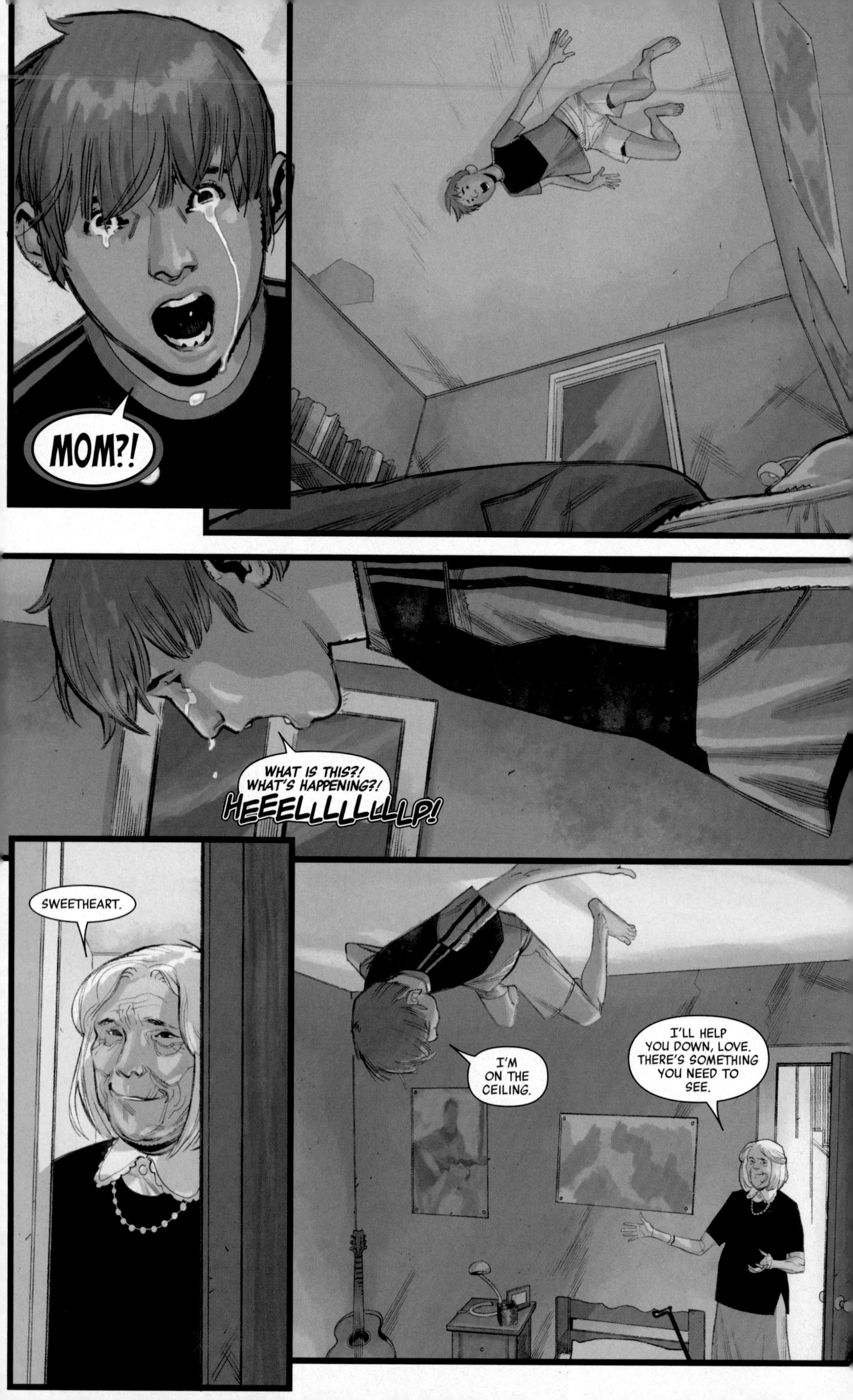
MOM?!
WHAT IS THIS?! WHAT'S HAPPENING?!
HEEELLLLLLLLP!
SWEETHEART.
I'M ON THE CEILING.
I'LL HELP YOU DOWN, LOVE. THERE'S SOMETHING YOU NEED TO SEE.

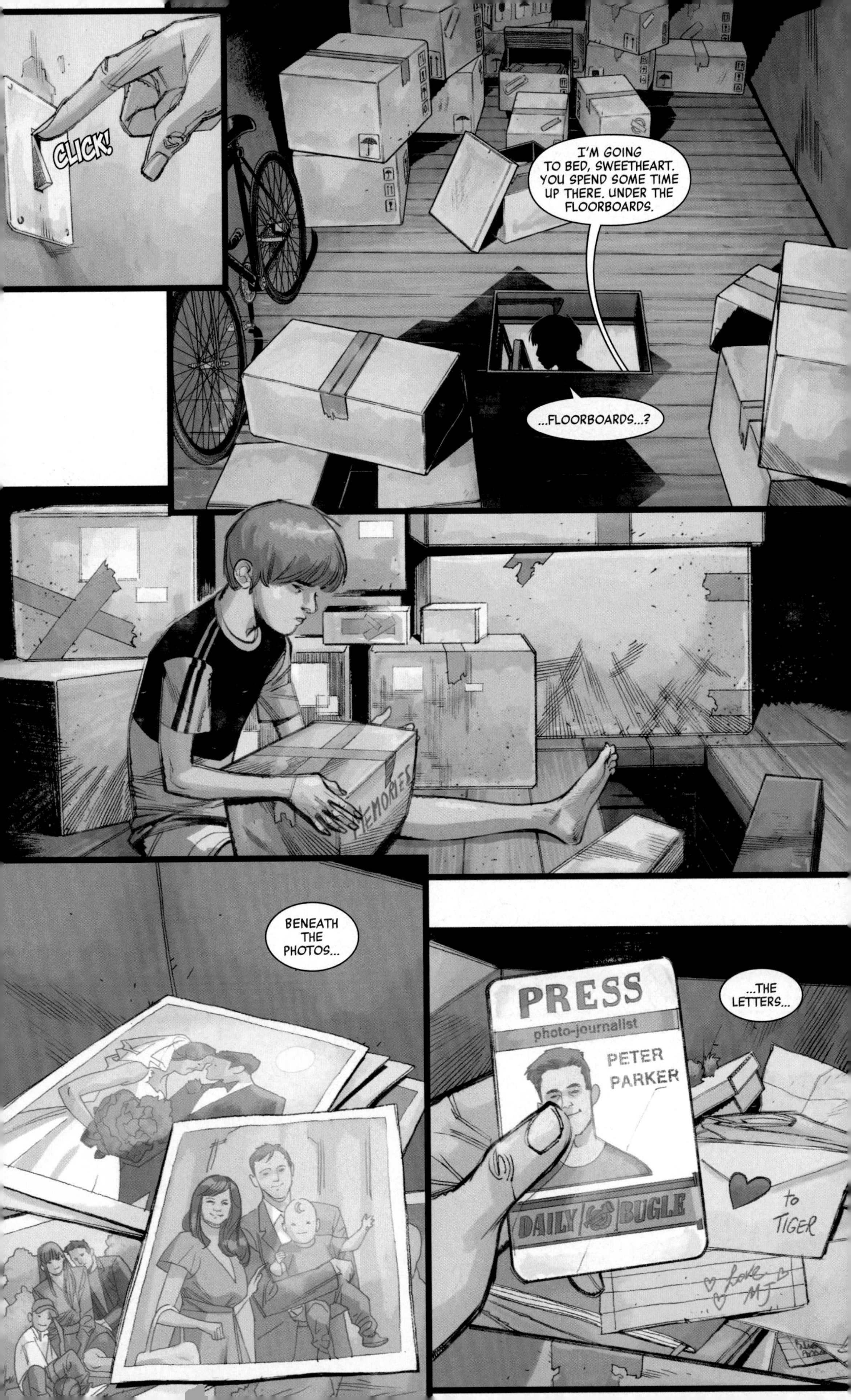
CLICK!
I'M GOING TO BED, SWEETHEART. YOU SPEND SOME TIME UP THERE. UNDER THE FLOORBOARDS.
...FLOORBOARDS...?
MEMORIES
BENEATH THE PHOTOS...
...THE LETTERS...
PRESS
photo-journalist
PETER PARKER
DAILY BUGLE
to TIGER
Love MJ

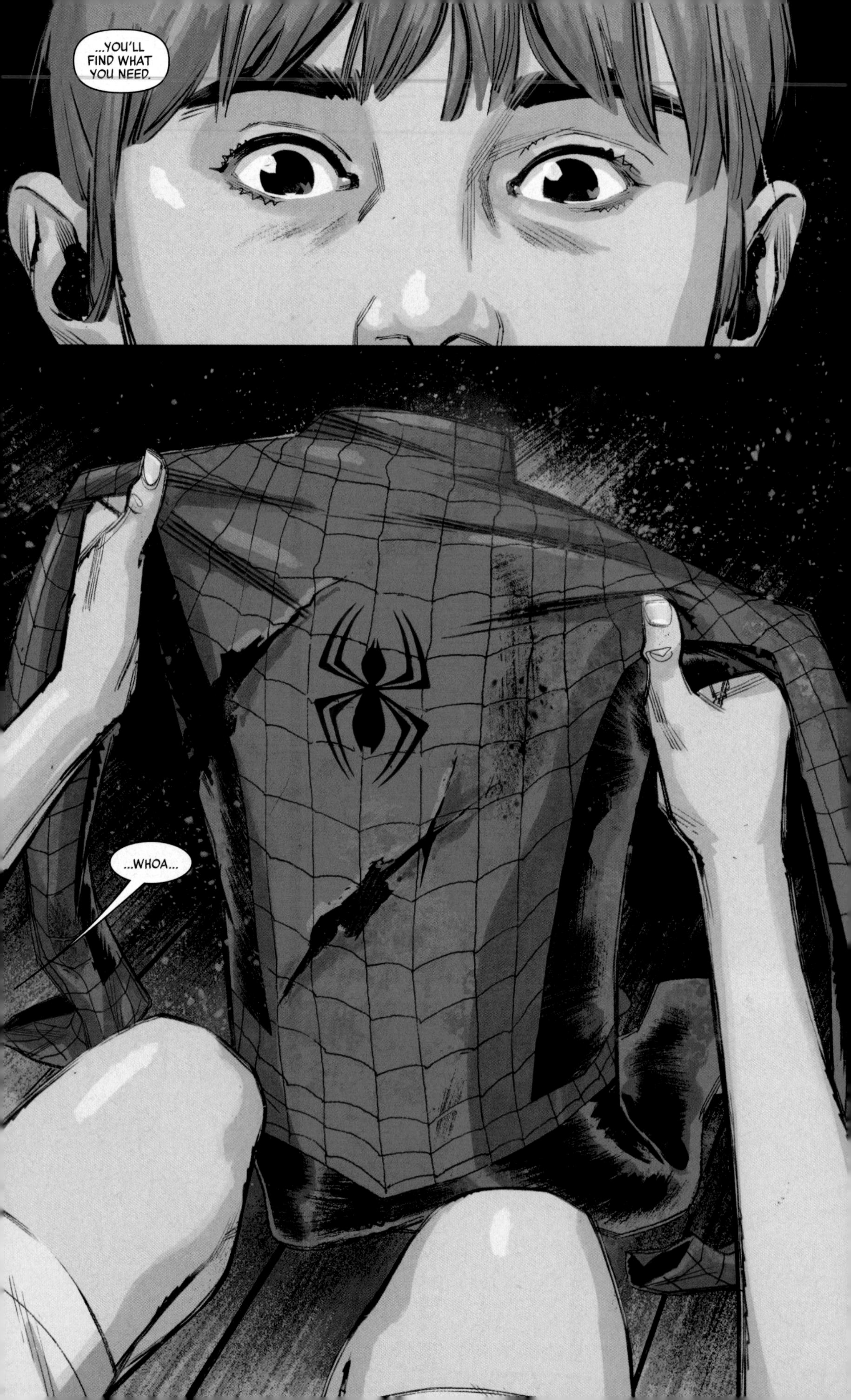
...YOU'LL FIND WHAT YOU NEED.
...WHOA...

2

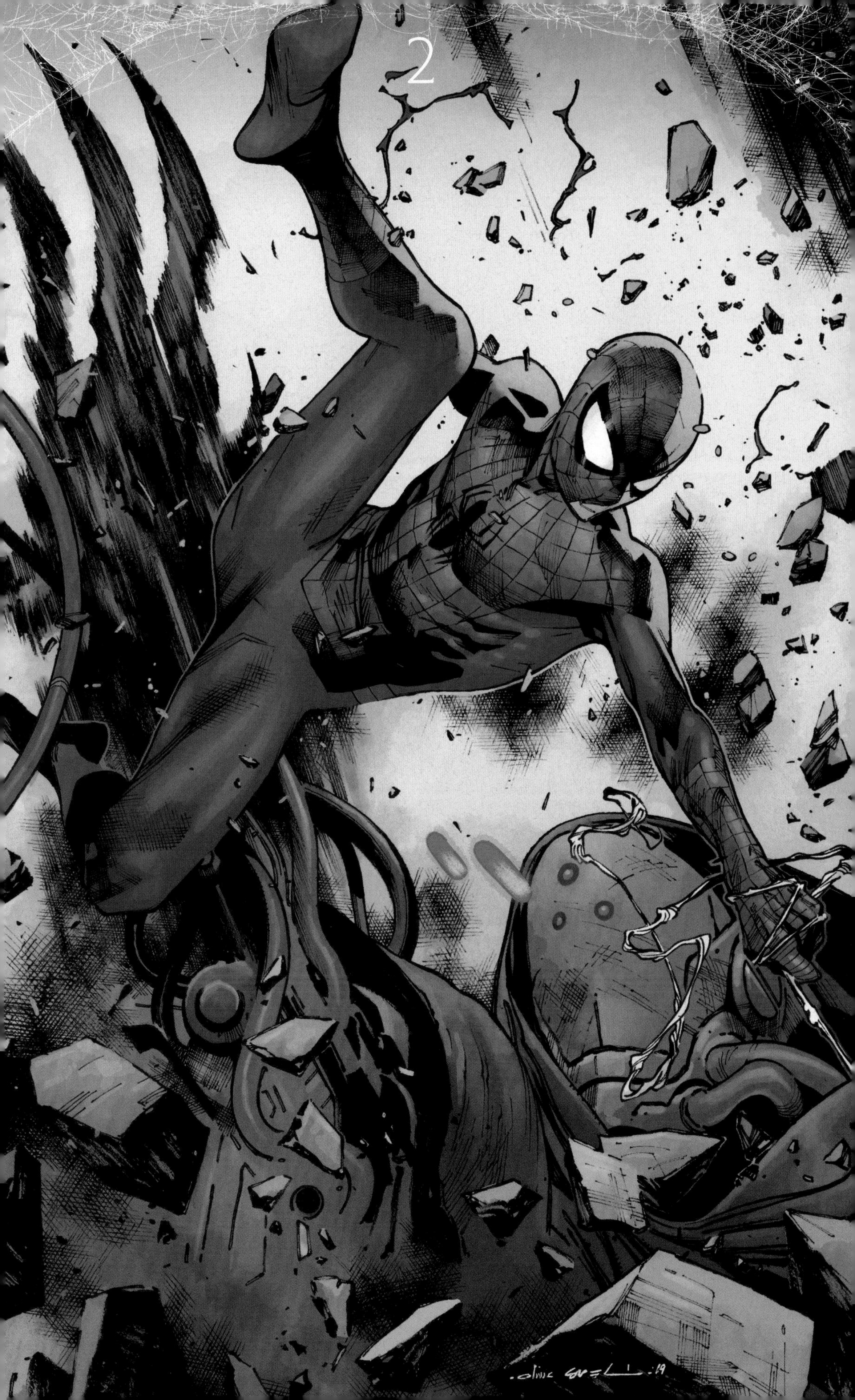

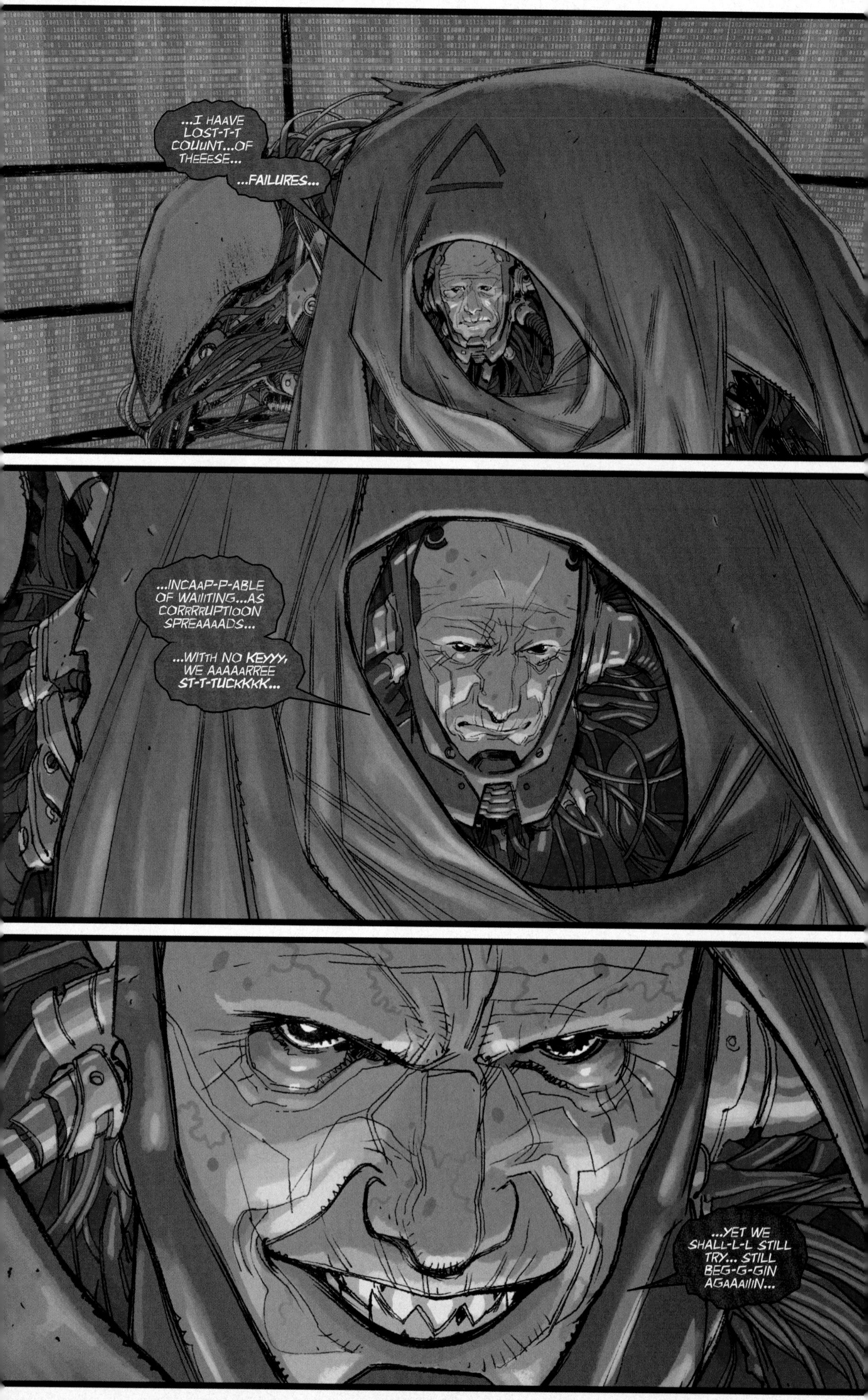
...I HAAVE LOST-T-T COUUNT...OF THEEESE...
...FAILURES...
...INCAAP-P-ABLE OF WAIIITING...AS CORRRRUPTIOON SPREAAAADS...
...WITTH NO KEYYY, WE AAAAARREE ST-T-TUCKKKK...
...YET WE SHALL-L-L STILL TRY... STILL BEG-G-GIN AGAAAIIIN...

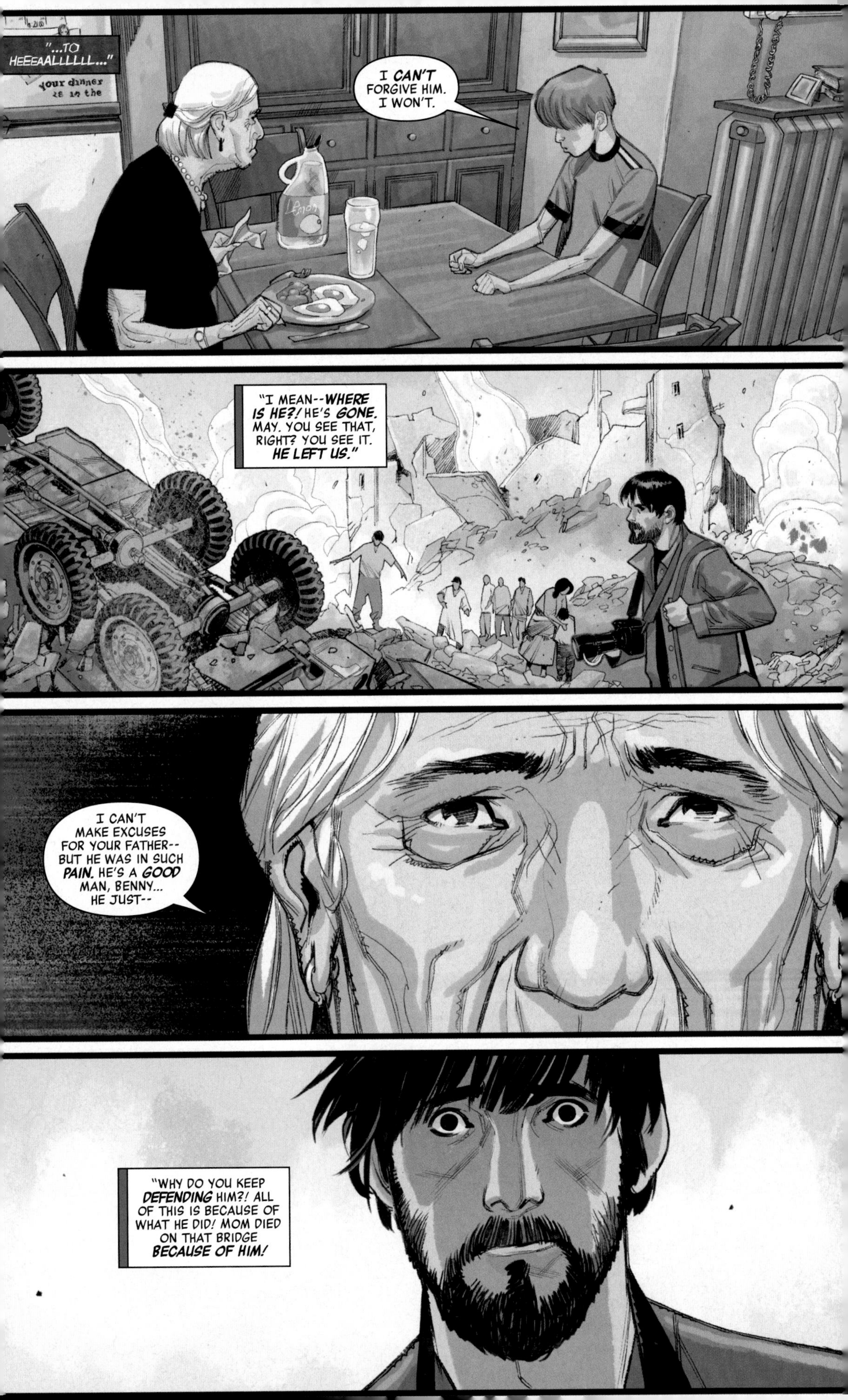
"...TO HEEEAALLLLLL..."
your dinner is in the
I CAN'T FORGIVE HIM. I WON'T.
"I MEAN--WHERE IS HE?! HE'S GONE. MAY. YOU SEE THAT, RIGHT? YOU SEE IT. HE LEFT US."
I CAN'T MAKE EXCUSES FOR YOUR FATHER--BUT HE WAS IN SUCH PAIN. HE'S A GOOD MAN, BENNY... HE JUST--
"WHY DO YOU KEEP DEFENDING HIM?! ALL OF THIS IS BECAUSE OF WHAT HE DID! MOM DIED ON THAT BRIDGE BECAUSE OF HIM!

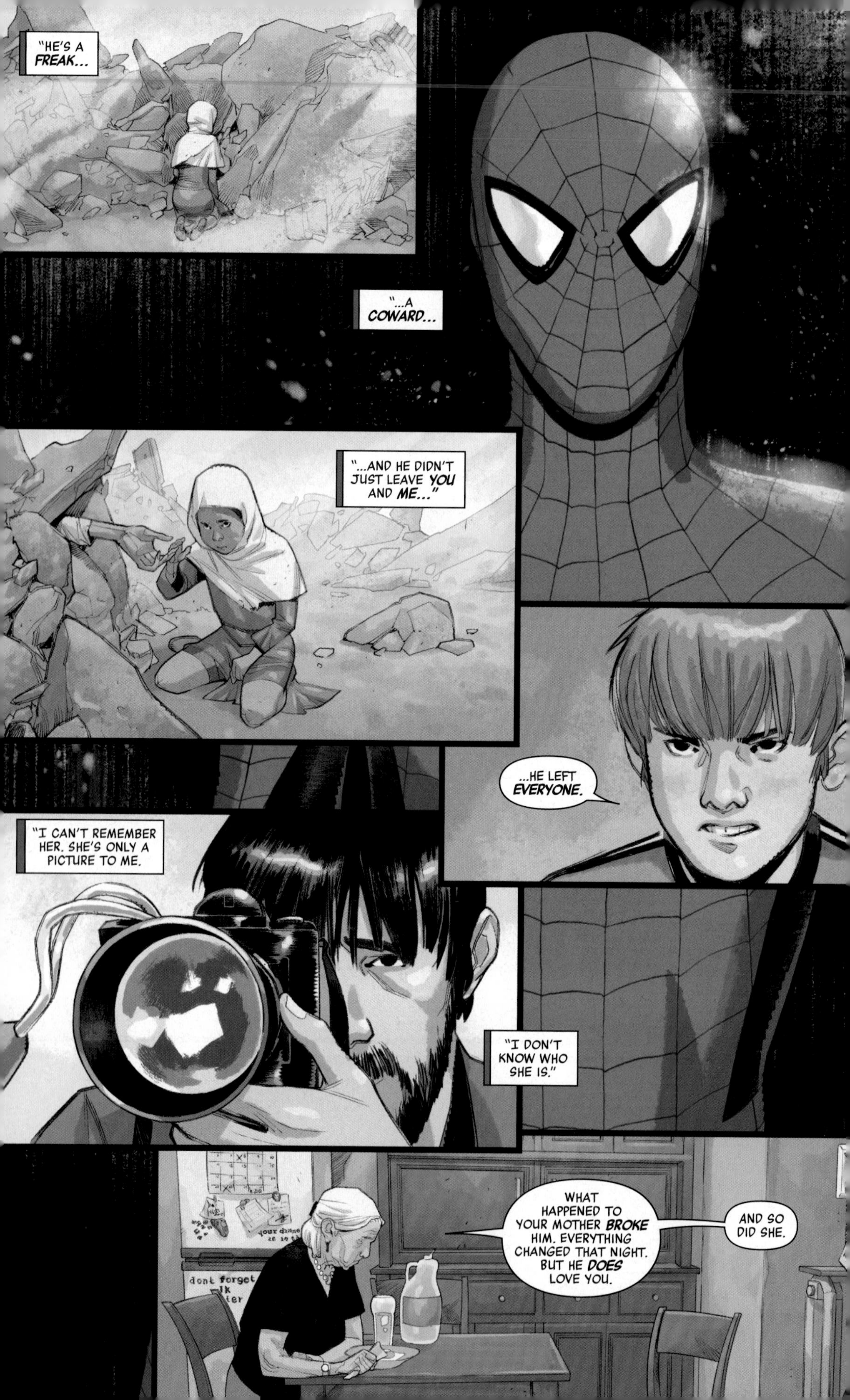
"HE'S A FREAK...
"...A COWARD...
"...AND HE DIDN'T JUST LEAVE YOU AND ME..."
...HE LEFT EVERYONE.
"I CAN'T REMEMBER HER. SHE'S ONLY A PICTURE TO ME.
"I DON'T KNOW WHO SHE IS."
dont forget
WHAT HAPPENED TO YOUR MOTHER BROKE HIM. EVERYTHING CHANGED THAT NIGHT. BUT HE DOES LOVE YOU.
AND SO DID SHE.

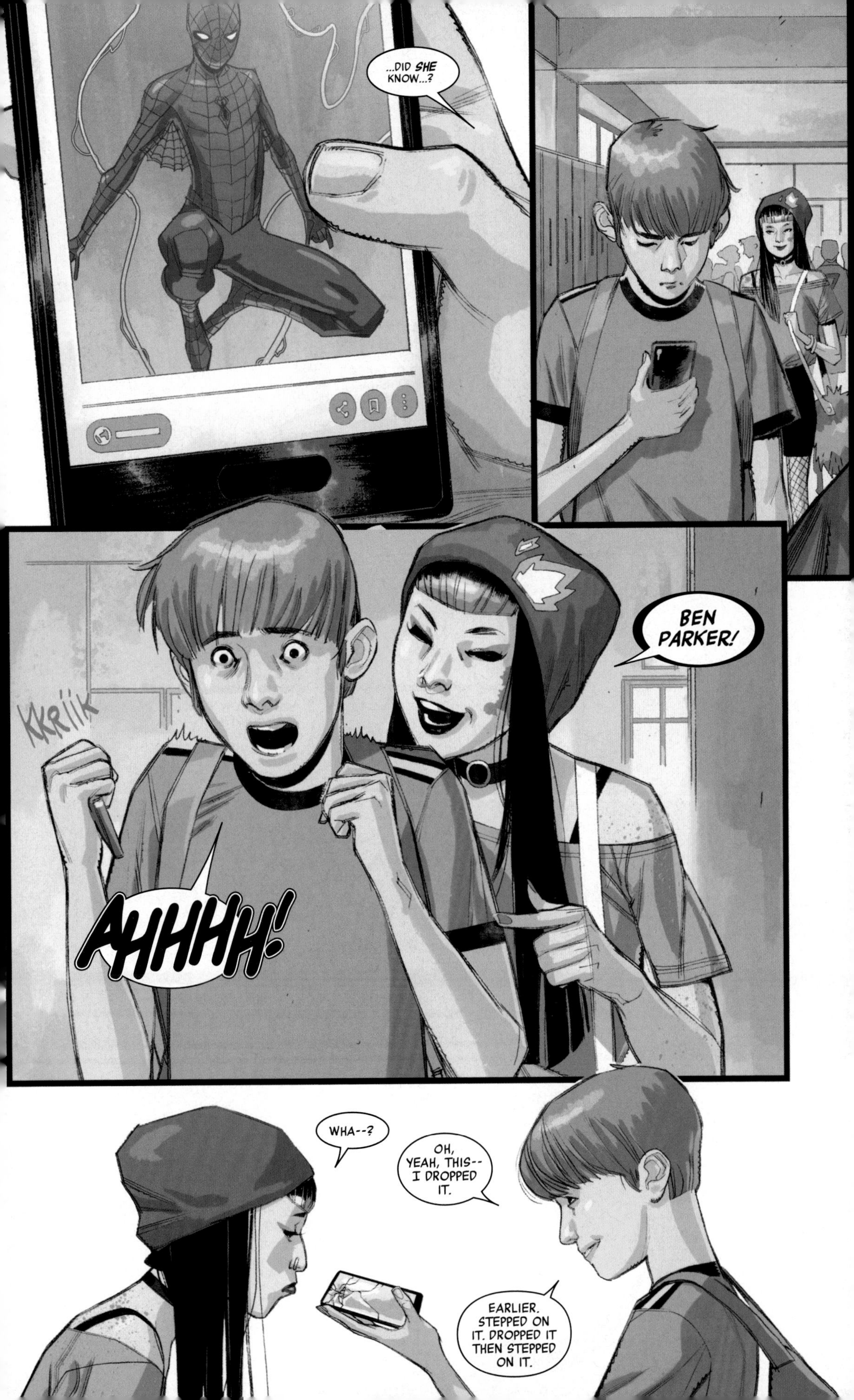
...DID SHE KNOW...?
BEN PARKER!
KKRIIK
AHHHH!
WHA--?
OH, YEAH, THIS-- I DROPPED IT.
EARLIER. STEPPED ON IT. DROPPED IT THEN STEPPED ON IT.

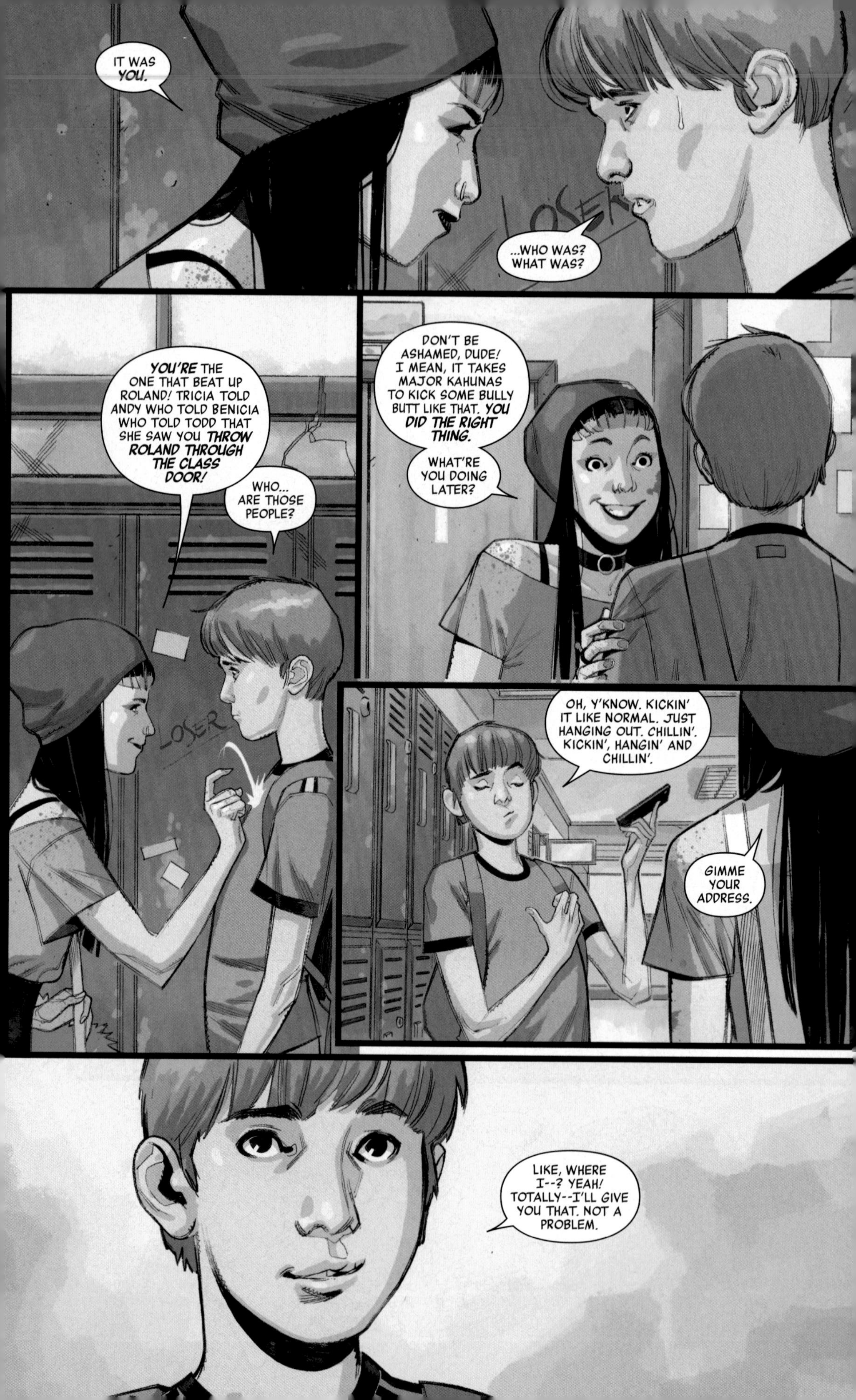
IT WAS YOU.
...WHO WAS? WHAT WAS?
YOU'RE THE ONE THAT BEAT UP ROLAND! TRICIA TOLD ANDY WHO TOLD BENICIA WHO TOLD TODD THAT SHE SAW YOU THROW ROLAND THROUGH THE CLASS DOOR!
WHO... ARE THOSE PEOPLE?
LOSER
DON'T BE ASHAMED, DUDE! I MEAN, IT TAKES MAJOR KAHUNAS TO KICK SOME BULLY BUTT LIKE THAT. YOU DID THE RIGHT THING.
WHAT'RE YOU DOING LATER?
OH, Y'KNOW. KICKIN' IT LIKE NORMAL. JUST HANGING OUT. CHILLIN'. KICKIN', HANGIN' AND CHILLIN'.
GIMME YOUR ADDRESS.
LIKE, WHERE I--? YEAH! TOTALLY--I'LL GIVE YOU THAT. NOT A PROBLEM.

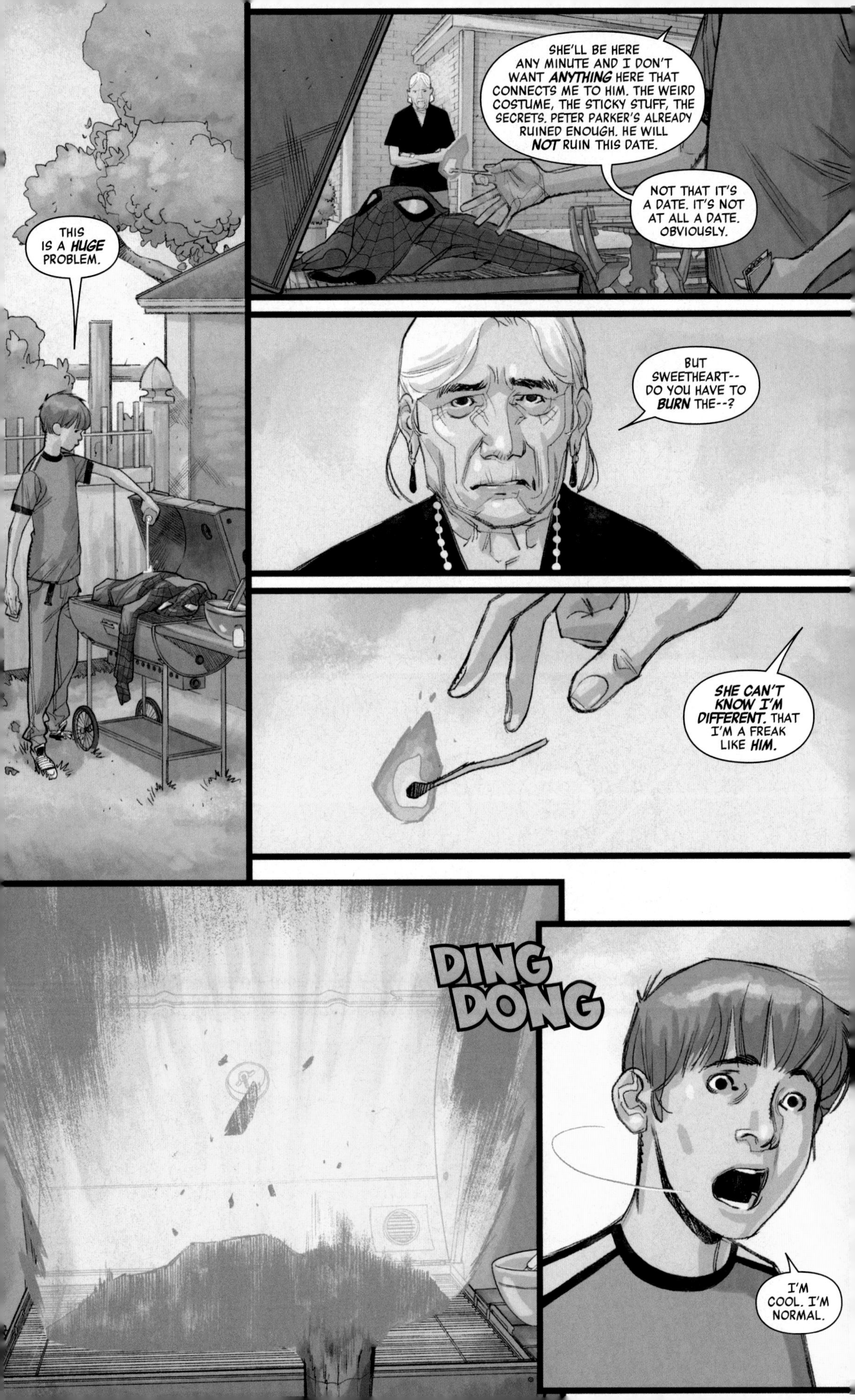
THIS IS A *HUGE* PROBLEM.
SHE'LL BE HERE ANY MINUTE AND I DON'T WANT *ANYTHING* HERE THAT CONNECTS ME TO HIM. THE WEIRD COSTUME, THE STICKY STUFF, THE SECRETS. PETER PARKER'S ALREADY RUINED ENOUGH. HE WILL *NOT* RUIN THIS DATE.
NOT THAT IT'S A DATE. IT'S NOT AT ALL A DATE. OBVIOUSLY.
BUT SWEETHEART-- DO YOU HAVE TO *BURN* THE--?
SHE CAN'T KNOW I'M DIFFERENT. THAT I'M A FREAK LIKE *HIM.*
DING DONG
I'M COOL. I'M NORMAL.

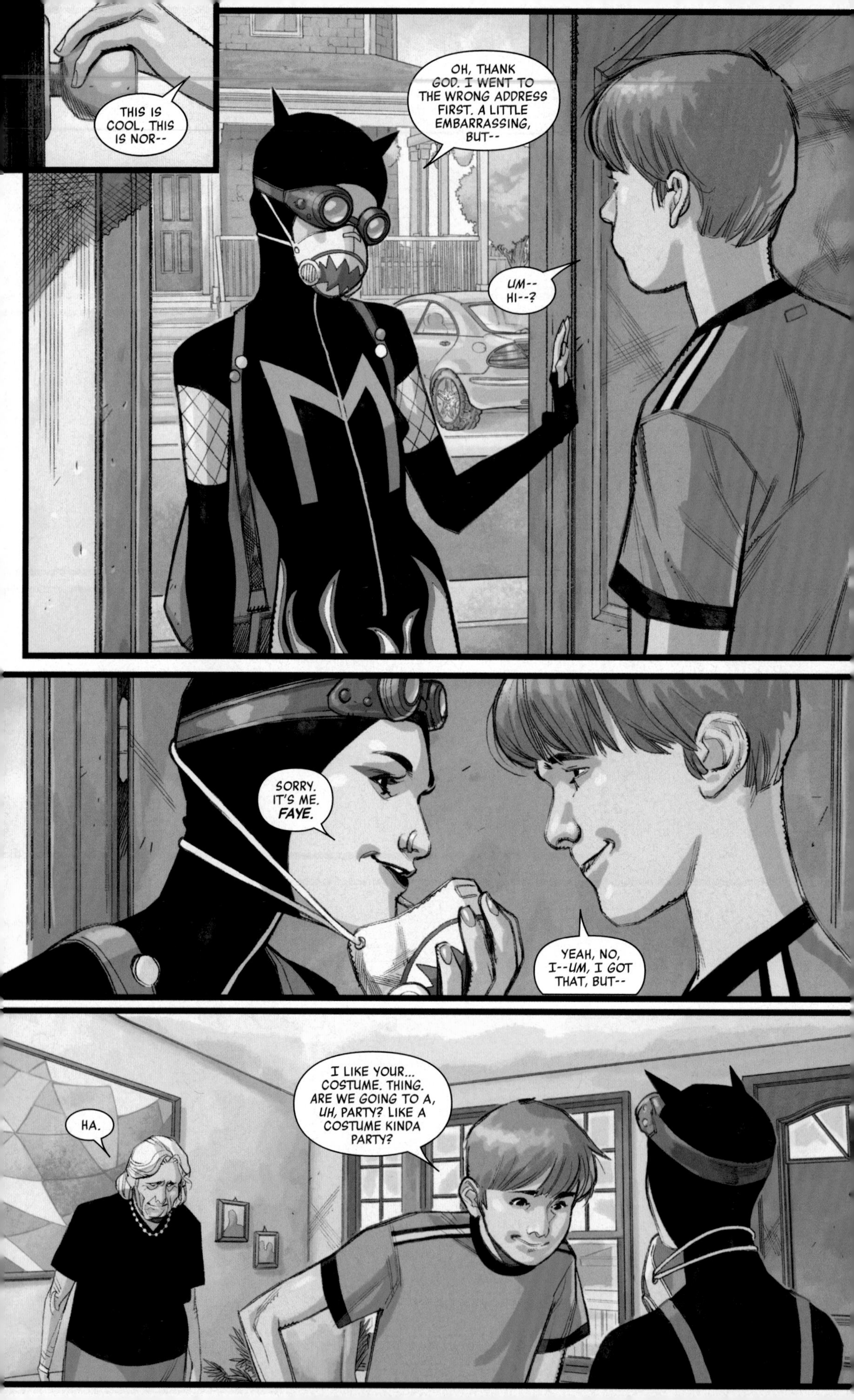

THIS IS COOL, THIS IS NOR--
OH, THANK GOD. I WENT TO THE WRONG ADDRESS FIRST. A LITTLE EMBARRASSING, BUT--
UM-- HI--?
SORRY. IT'S ME. FAYE.
YEAH, NO, I--UM, I GOT THAT, BUT--
I LIKE YOUR... COSTUME. THING. ARE WE GOING TO A, UH, PARTY? LIKE A COSTUME KINDA PARTY?
HA.

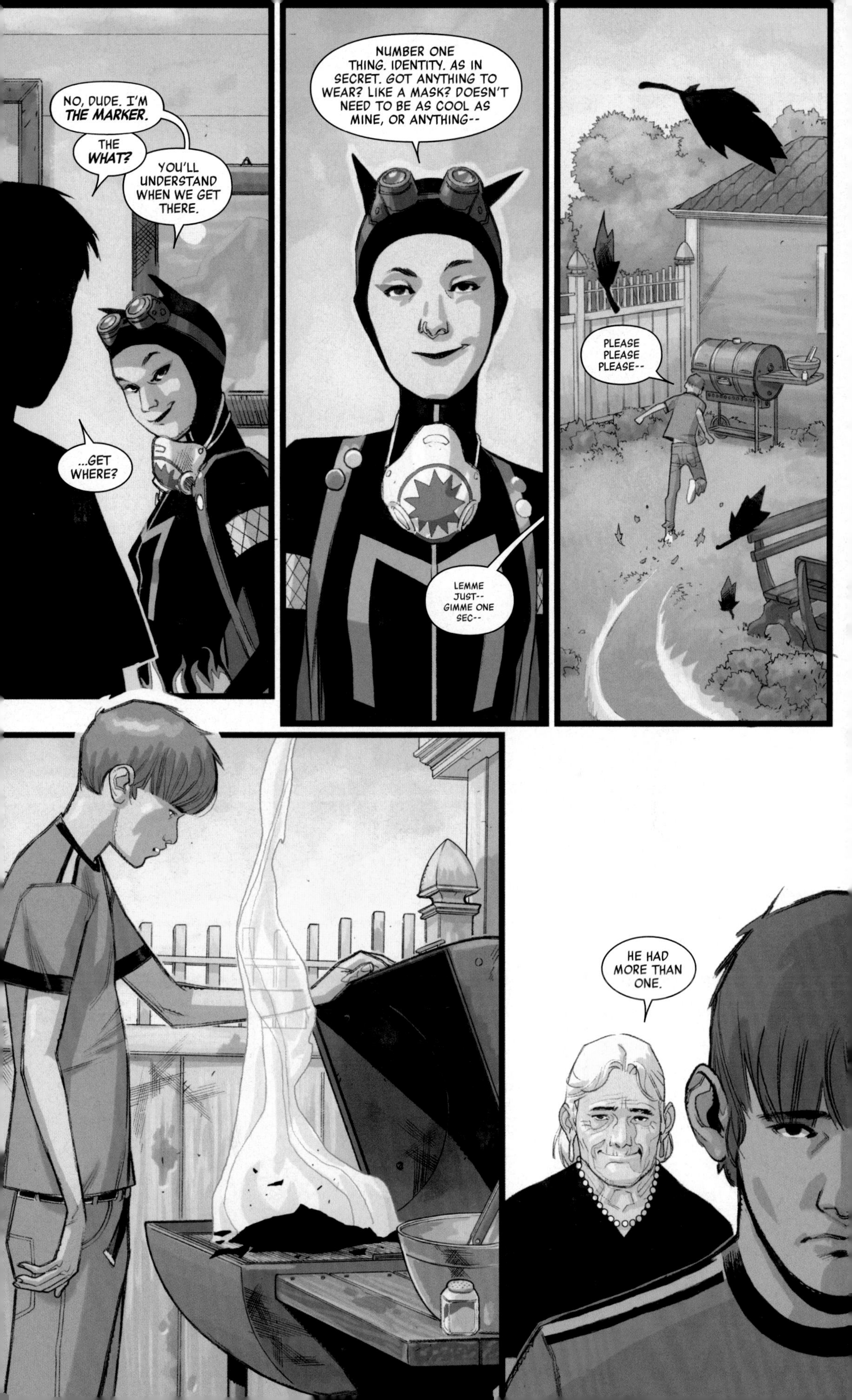
NO, DUDE. I'M THE MARKER.
THE WHAT?
YOU'LL UNDERSTAND WHEN WE GET THERE.
...GET WHERE?
NUMBER ONE THING. IDENTITY. AS IN SECRET. GOT ANYTHING TO WEAR? LIKE A MASK? DOESN'T NEED TO BE AS COOL AS MINE, OR ANYTHING--
LEMME JUST-- GIMME ONE SEC--
PLEASE PLEASE PLEASE--
HE HAD MORE THAN ONE.

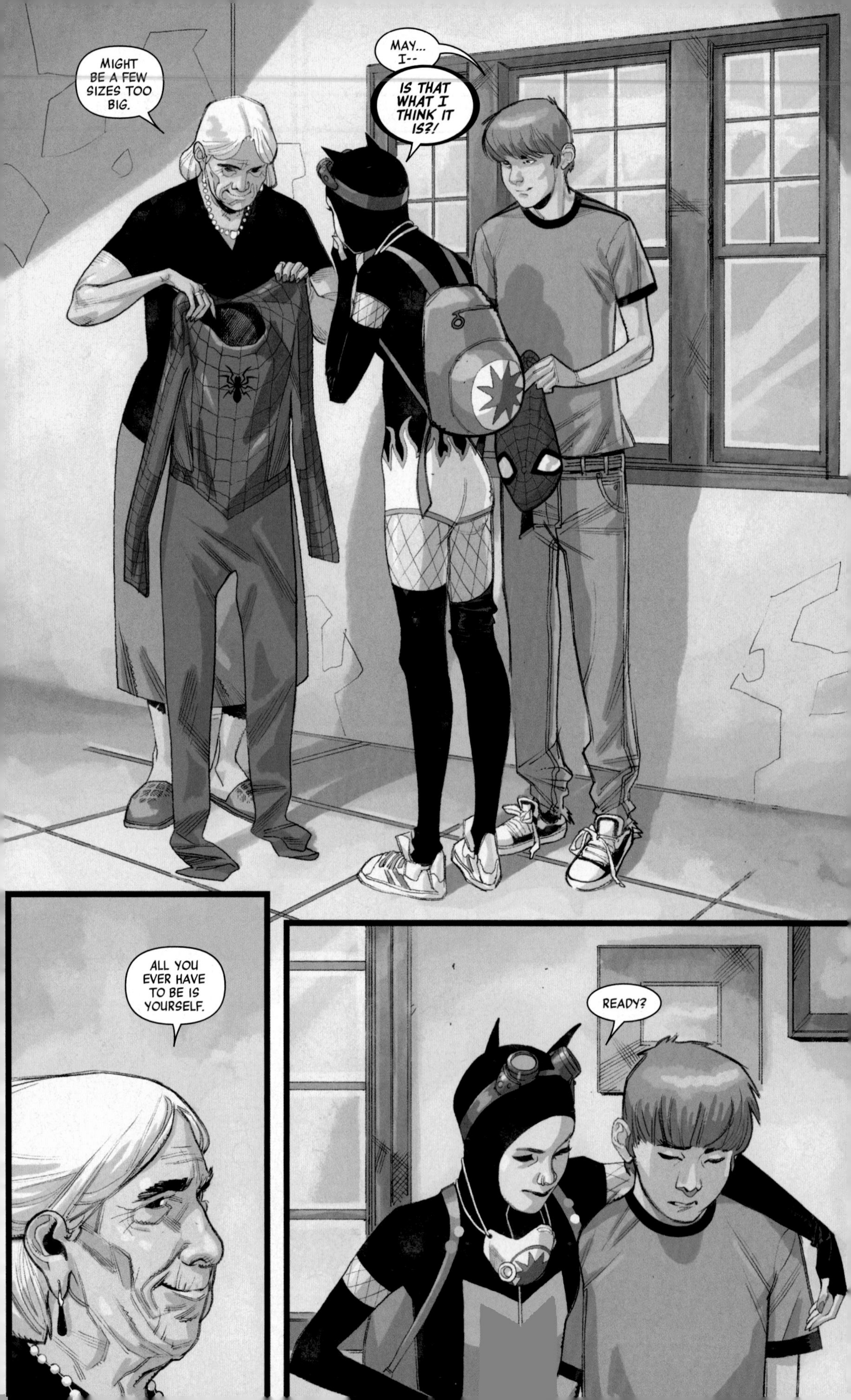
MIGHT BE A FEW SIZES TOO BIG.
MAY... I--
IS THAT WHAT I THINK IT IS?!
ALL YOU EVER HAVE TO BE IS YOURSELF.
READY?

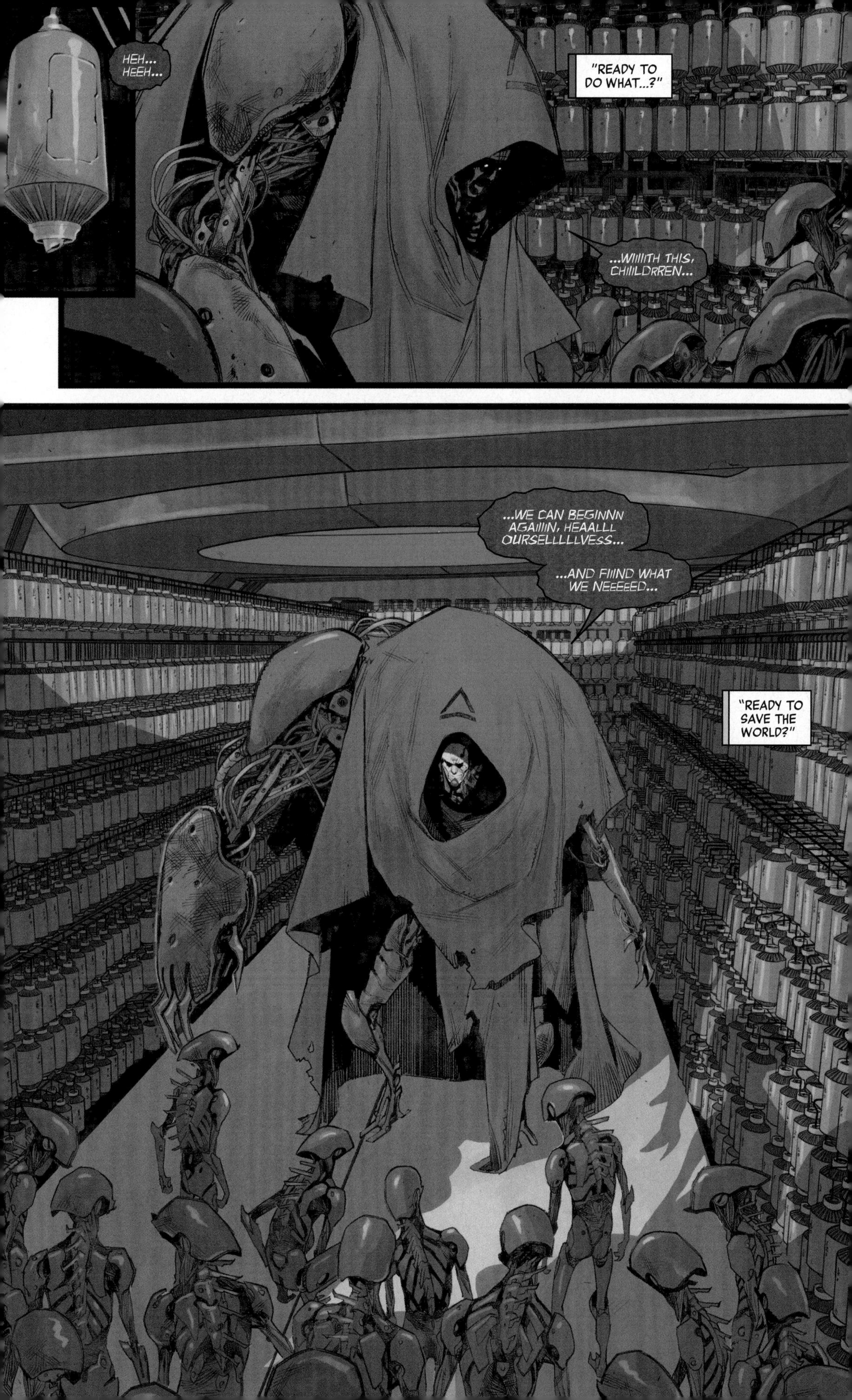
HEH... HEEH...
"READY TO DO WHAT...?"
...WIIIITH THIS, CHIIILDRREN...
...WE CAN BEGINNN AGAIIIN, HEAALLL OURSELLLLLVESS...
...AND FIIIND WHAT WE NEEEEED...
"READY TO SAVE THE WORLD?"

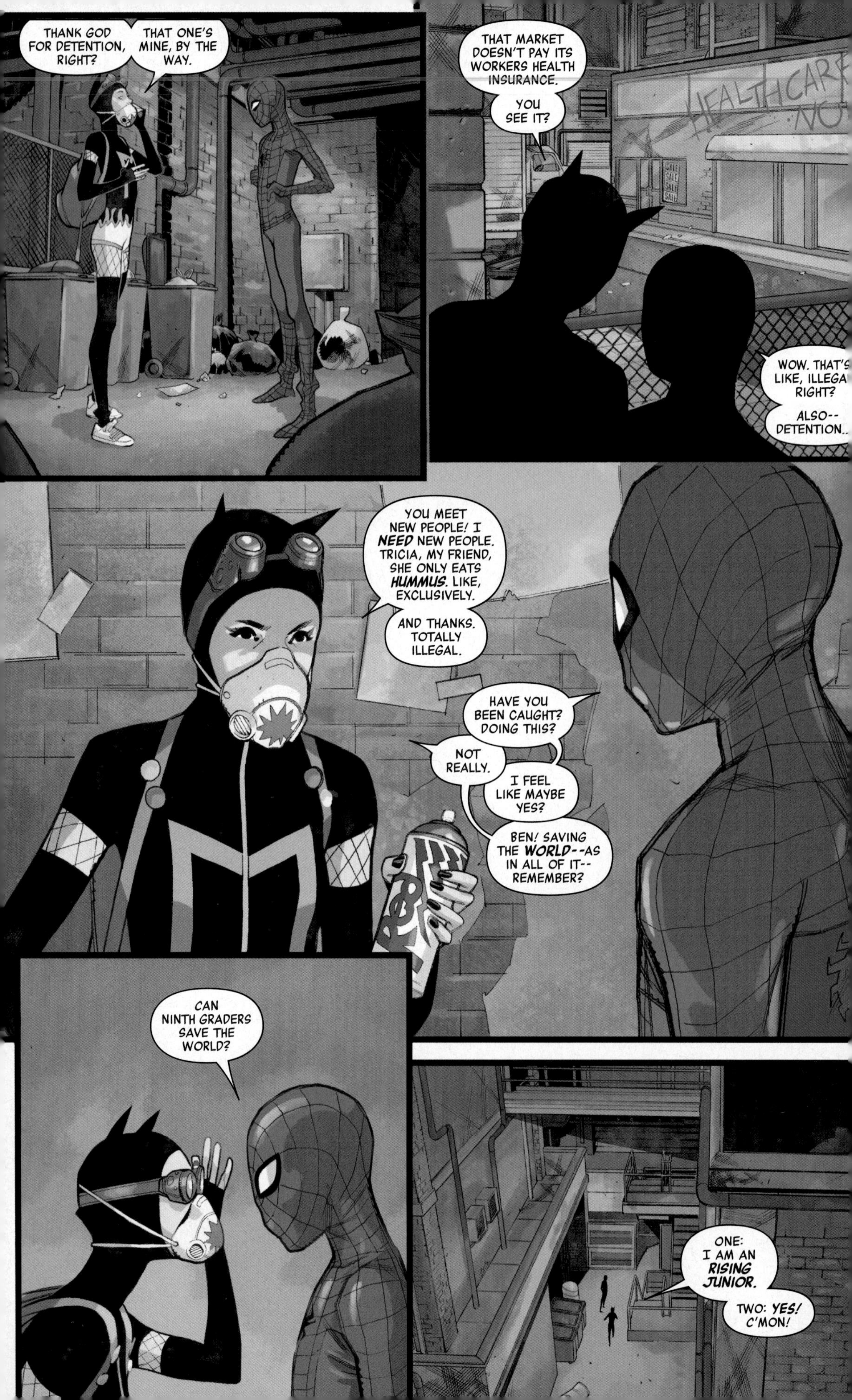
THANK GOD FOR DETENTION, RIGHT?
THAT ONE'S MINE, BY THE WAY.
THAT MARKET DOESN'T PAY ITS WORKERS HEALTH INSURANCE.
YOU SEE IT?
HEALTHCARE NO
SALE SALE SALE SALE
WOW. THAT'S LIKE, ILLEGA RIGHT?
ALSO-- DETENTION..
YOU MEET NEW PEOPLE! I NEED NEW PEOPLE. TRICIA, MY FRIEND, SHE ONLY EATS HUMMUS. LIKE, EXCLUSIVELY.
AND THANKS. TOTALLY ILLEGAL.
HAVE YOU BEEN CAUGHT? DOING THIS?
NOT REALLY.
I FEEL LIKE MAYBE YES?
BEN! SAVING THE WORLD--AS IN ALL OF IT-- REMEMBER?
CAN NINTH GRADERS SAVE THE WORLD?
ONE: I AM AN RISING JUNIOR.
TWO: YES! C'MON!

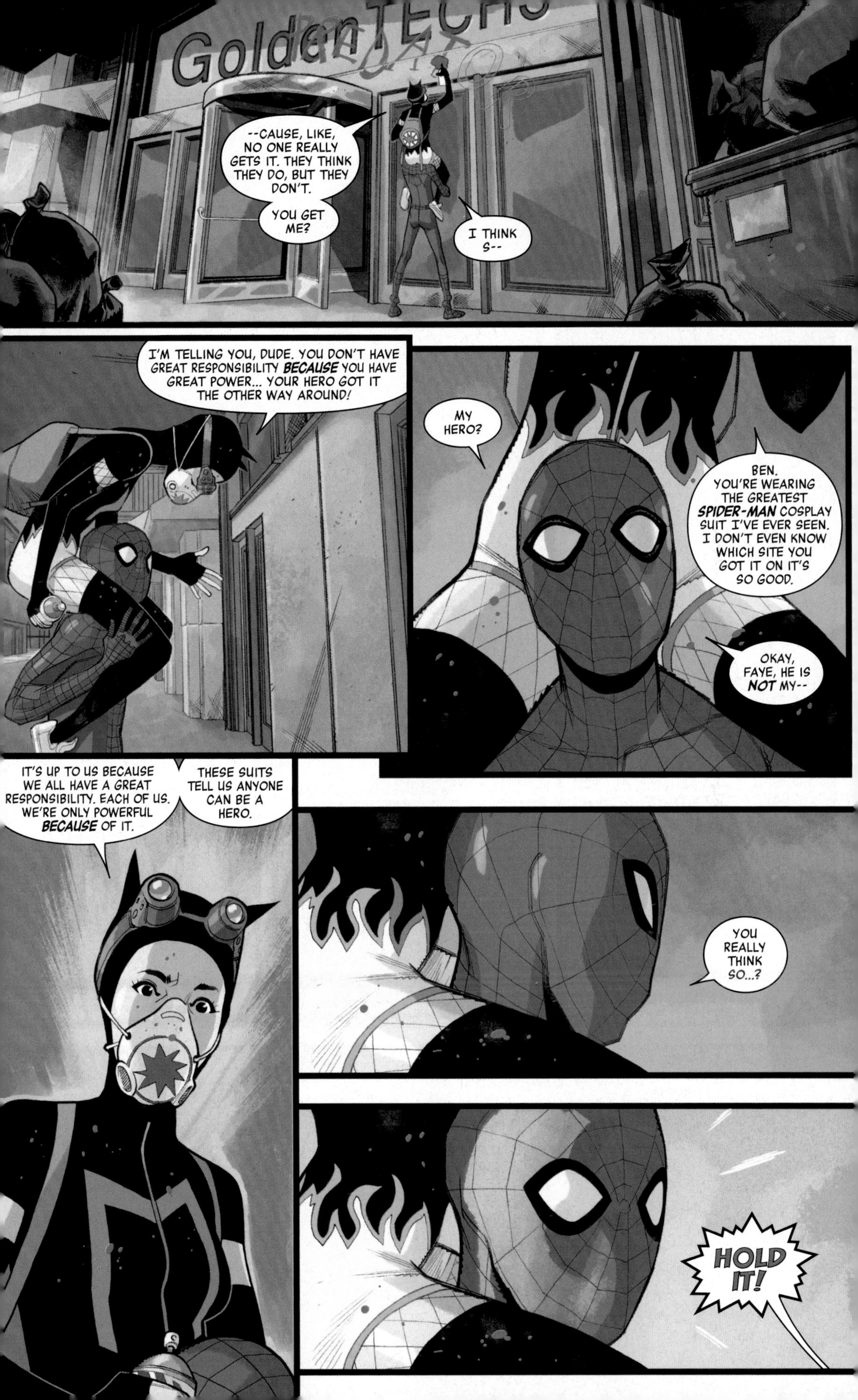
Golden
--CAUSE, LIKE, NO ONE REALLY GETS IT. THEY THINK THEY DO, BUT THEY DON'T.
YOU GET ME?
I THINK S--
I'M TELLING YOU, DUDE. YOU DON'T HAVE GREAT RESPONSIBILITY *BECAUSE* YOU HAVE GREAT POWER... YOUR HERO GOT IT THE OTHER WAY AROUND!
MY HERO?
BEN. YOU'RE WEARING THE GREATEST *SPIDER-MAN* COSPLAY SUIT I'VE EVER SEEN. I DON'T EVEN KNOW WHICH SITE YOU GOT IT ON IT'S SO GOOD.
OKAY, FAYE, HE IS *NOT* MY--
IT'S UP TO US BECAUSE WE ALL HAVE A GREAT RESPONSIBILITY. EACH OF US. WE'RE ONLY POWERFUL *BECAUSE* OF IT.
THESE SUITS TELL US ANYONE CAN BE A HERO.
YOU REALLY THINK SO...?
HOLD IT!

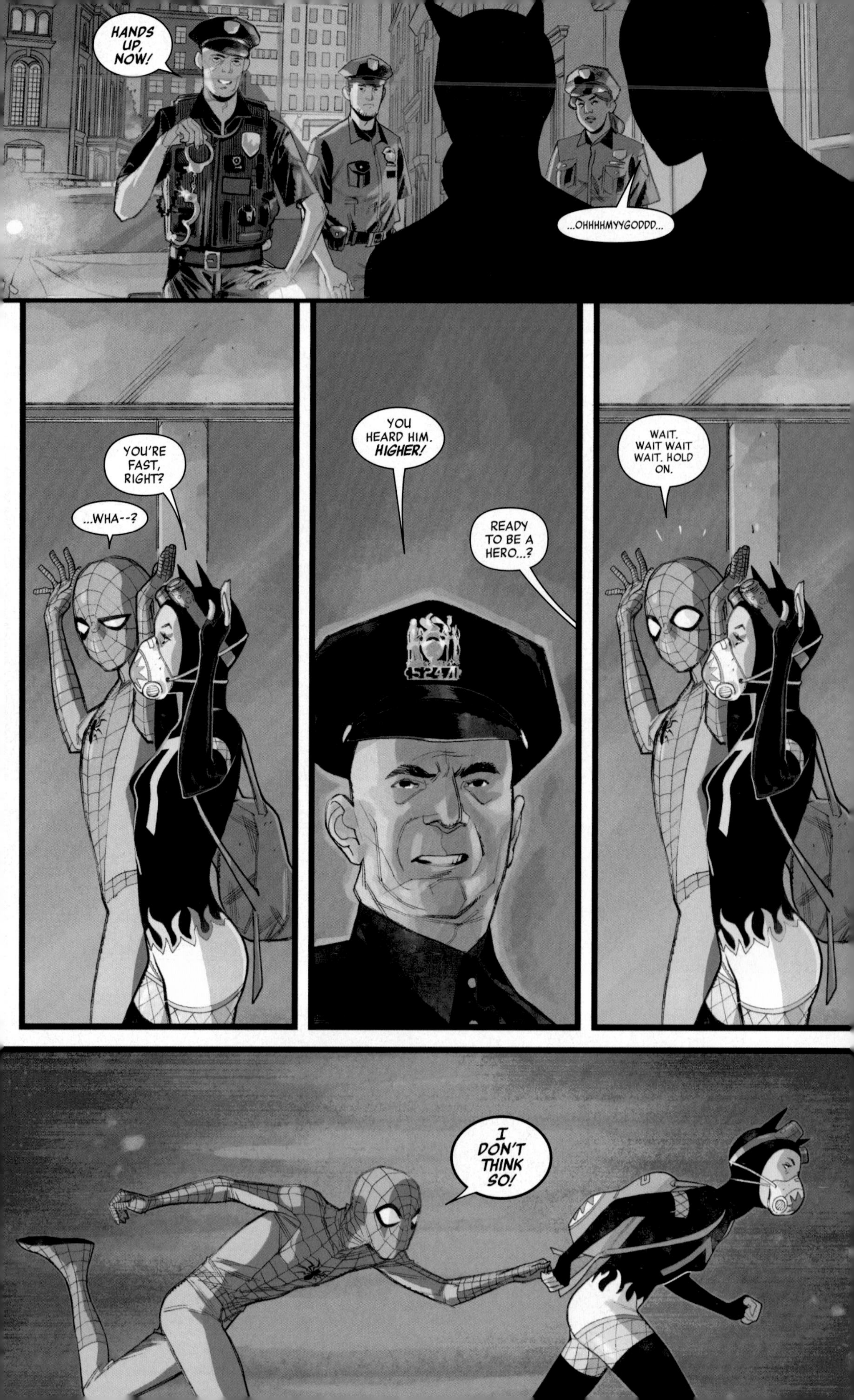
HANDS UP, NOW!
...OHHHHMYYGODDD...
...WHA--?
YOU'RE FAST, RIGHT?
YOU HEARD HIM. HIGHER!
READY TO BE A HERO...?
WAIT. WAIT WAIT WAIT. HOLD ON.
I DON'T THINK SO!

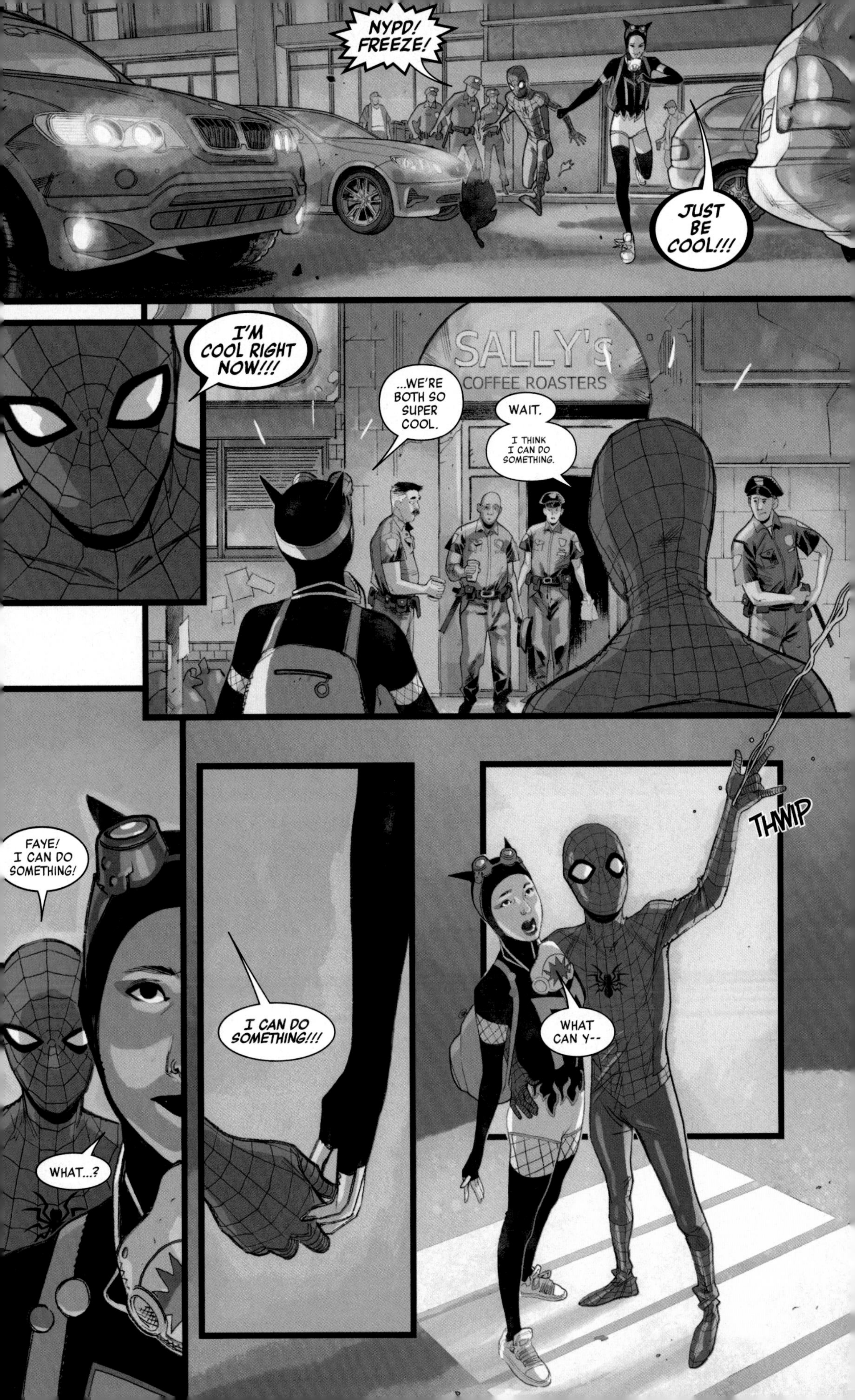

NYPD! FREEZE!
JUST BE COOL!!!
I'M COOL RIGHT NOW!!!
SALLY'S
COFFEE ROASTERS
...WE'RE BOTH SO SUPER COOL.
WAIT.
I THINK I CAN DO SOMETHING.
FAYE! I CAN DO SOMETHING!
WHAT...?
I CAN DO SOMETHING!!!
THWIP
WHAT CAN Y--

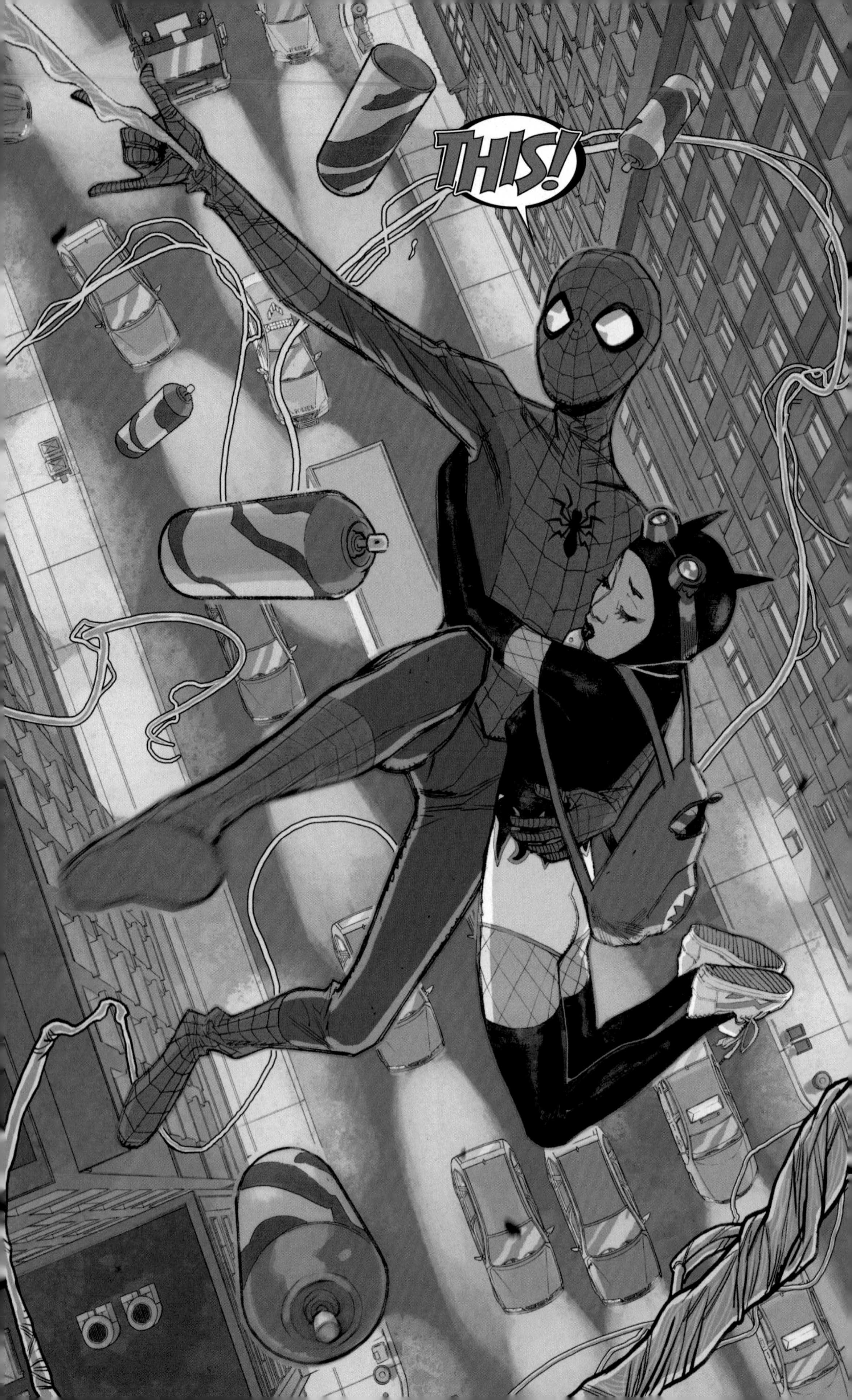
THIS!

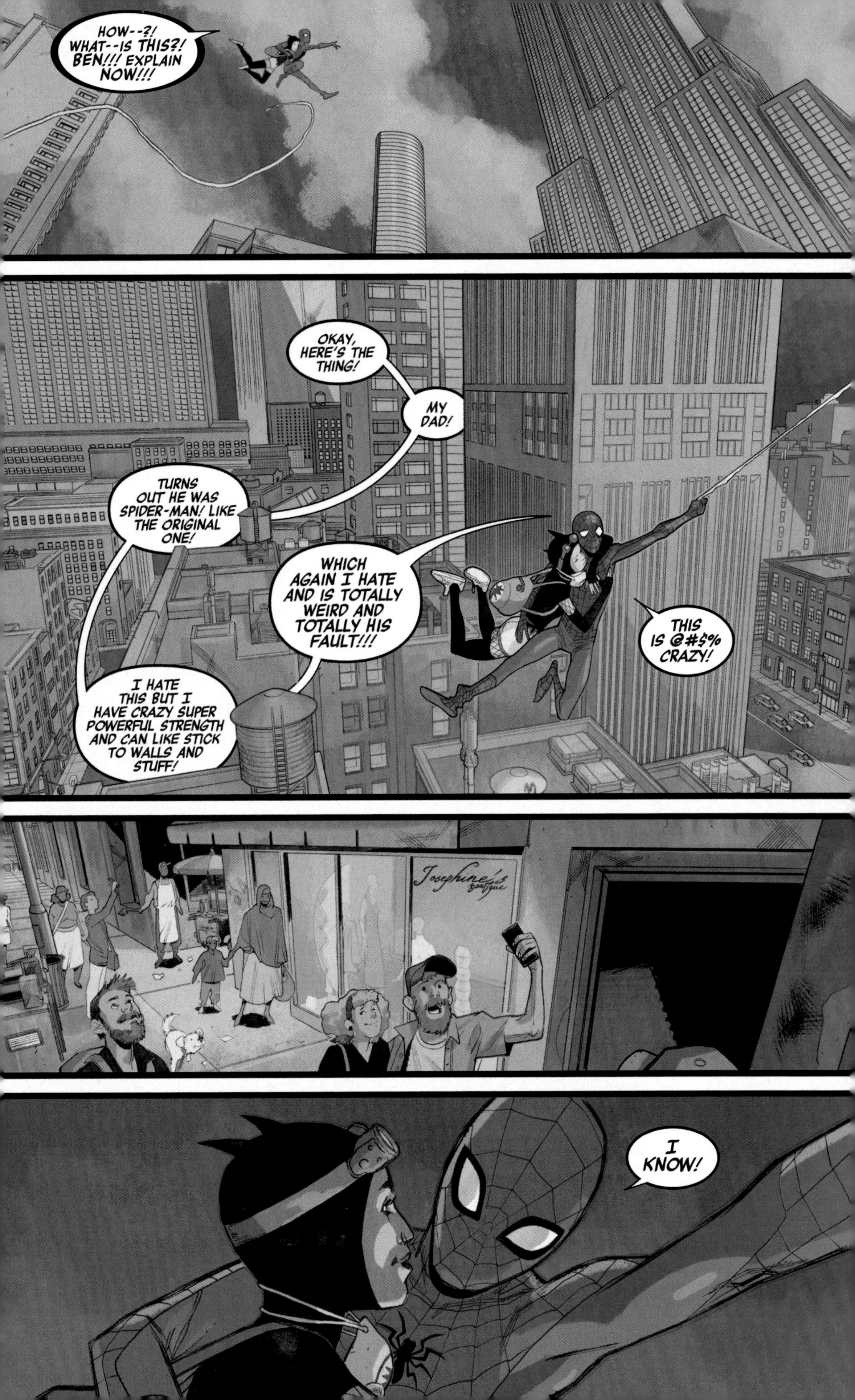
HOW--?! WHAT--IS THIS?! BEN!!! EXPLAIN NOW!!!
OKAY, HERE'S THE THING!
MY DAD!
TURNS OUT HE WAS SPIDER-MAN! LIKE THE ORIGINAL ONE!
I HATE THIS BUT I HAVE CRAZY SUPER POWERFUL STRENGTH AND CAN LIKE STICK TO WALLS AND STUFF!
WHICH AGAIN I HATE AND IS TOTALLY WEIRD AND TOTALLY HIS FAULT!!!
THIS IS @#$% CRAZY!
Josephine's Boutique
I KNOW!

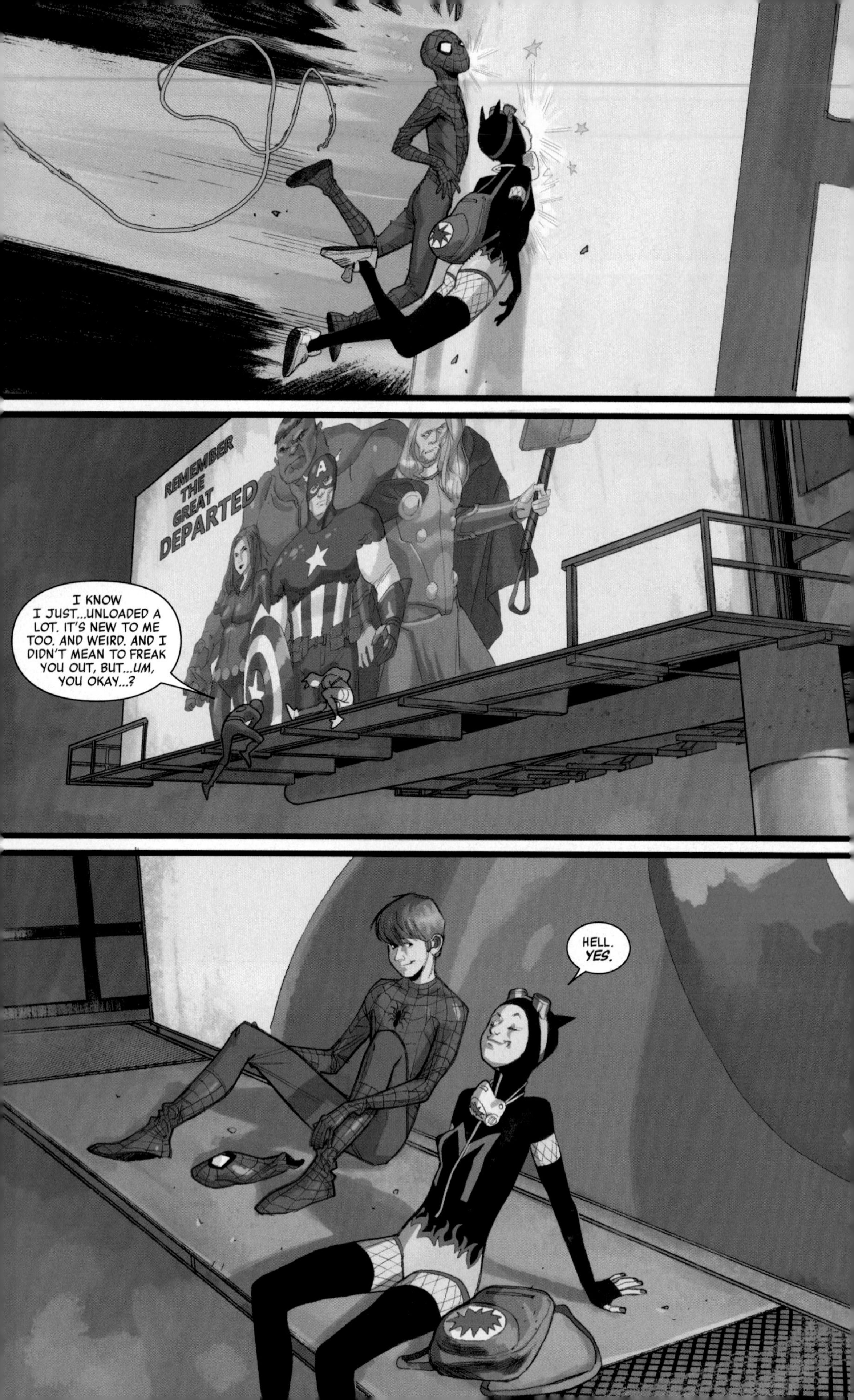
REMEMBER THE GREAT DEPARTED
I KNOW I JUST...UNLOADED A LOT. IT'S NEW TO ME TOO. AND WEIRD. AND I DIDN'T MEAN TO FREAK YOU OUT, BUT...UM, YOU OKAY...?
HELL. YES.

...WHAT IS THI--

HEH...

...I KNEEEW... IT-T-T...WOUUULDD COMMMME BAACK... EV-EN-TUALLLLY...

MY CHIIIILDREN...TOOO HEEAAALLL, TO UNLOCKKK...

PRESS PASS

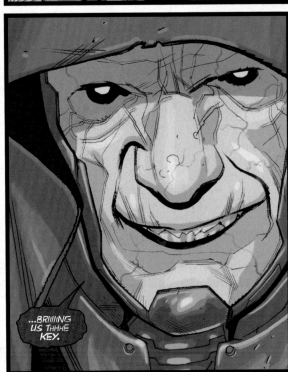

...BRIIIING US THHHE KEY.

...THE ONLY SURVIVING MEMBER, TONY STARK, HAS DECLINED TO COMMENT.

IT HAS BEEN TWELVE YEARS SINCE SPIDER-MAN VANISHED, SINCE HIS BATTLE WITH THE ELUSIVE CADAVEROUS, AND WE CAN STILL ONLY SPECULATE AS TO WHERE THIS HERO HAS BEEN...

...BENNY... NO...

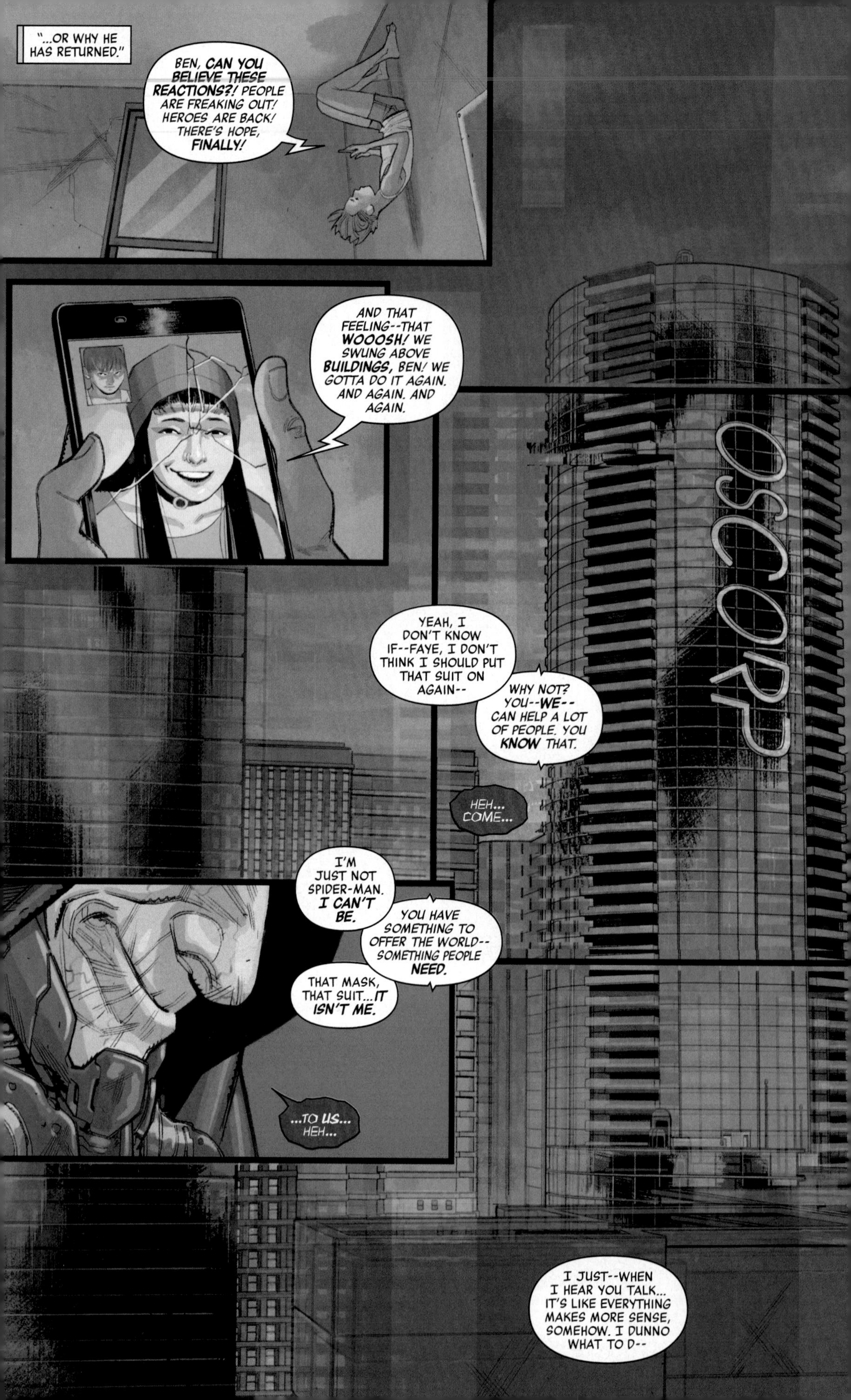

"...OR WHY HE HAS RETURNED."
BEN, CAN YOU BELIEVE THESE REACTIONS?! PEOPLE ARE FREAKING OUT! HEROES ARE BACK! THERE'S HOPE, FINALLY!
AND THAT FEELING--THAT WOOOSH! WE SWUNG ABOVE BUILDINGS, BEN! WE GOTTA DO IT AGAIN. AND AGAIN. AND AGAIN.
OSCORP
YEAH, I DON'T KNOW IF--FAYE, I DON'T THINK I SHOULD PUT THAT SUIT ON AGAIN--
WHY NOT? YOU--WE--CAN HELP A LOT OF PEOPLE. YOU KNOW THAT.
HEH... COME...
I'M JUST NOT SPIDER-MAN. I CAN'T BE.
YOU HAVE SOMETHING TO OFFER THE WORLD--SOMETHING PEOPLE NEED.
THAT MASK, THAT SUIT...IT ISN'T ME.
...TO US... HEH...
I JUST--WHEN I HEAR YOU TALK... IT'S LIKE EVERYTHING MAKES MORE SENSE, SOMEHOW. I DUNNO WHAT TO D--

BREAKING NEWS
OSCORP HEADQUA
BREAKING NEWS TREMENDOUS EXPLOSION AT OSCORP HE
--OH MY GOD--DID YOU GET THAT ALERT?
...I THINK SO...
...WHAT DO I--
YOU KNOW.
THIS ISN'T SOME GAME.
WE AREN'T JUST PLAYING DRESS UP.

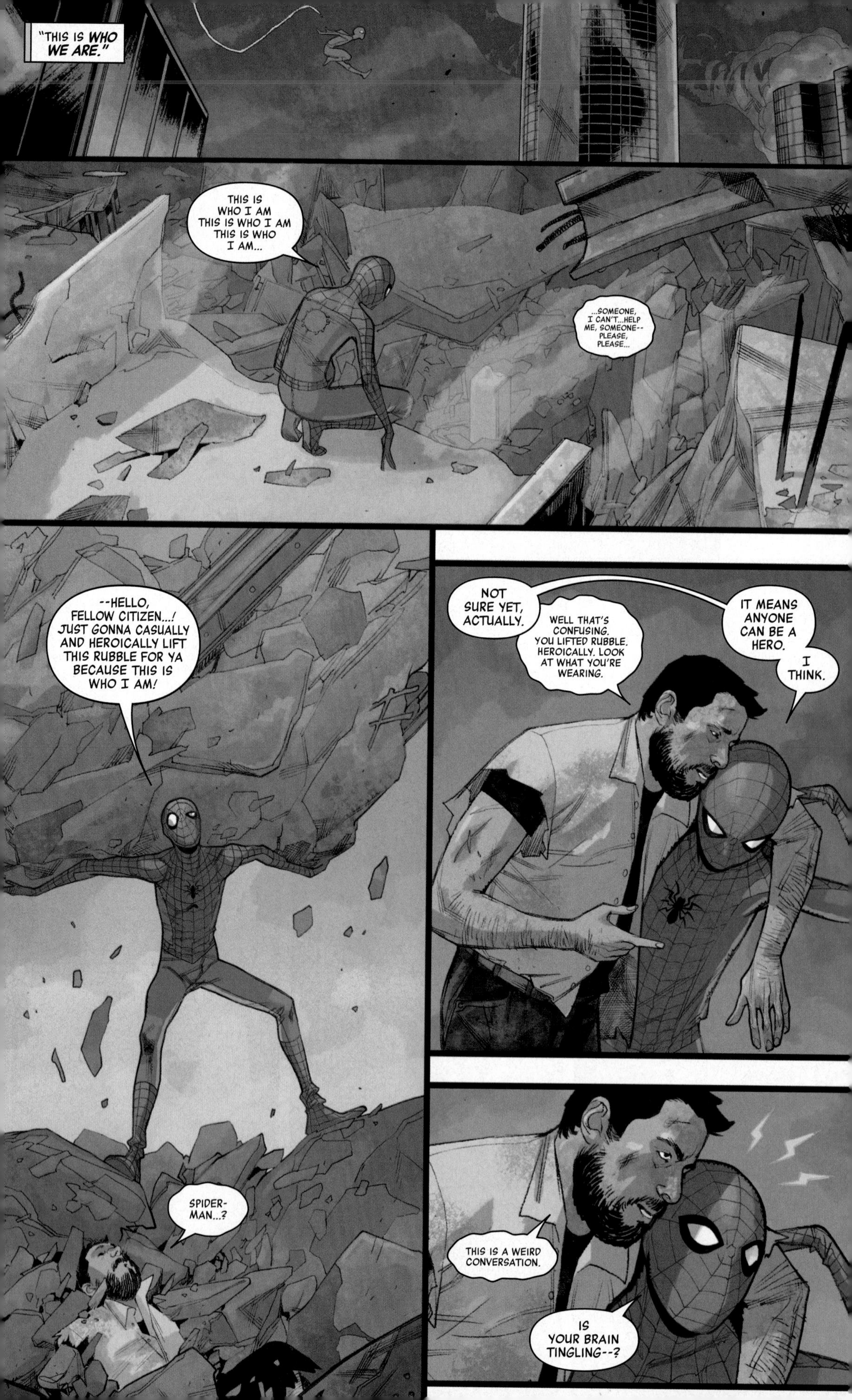
"THIS IS WHO WE ARE."
THIS IS WHO I AM THIS IS WHO I AM THIS IS WHO I AM...
...SOMEONE, I CAN'T...HELP ME, SOMEONE-- PLEASE, PLEASE...
--HELLO, FELLOW CITIZEN...! JUST GONNA CASUALLY AND HEROICALLY LIFT THIS RUBBLE FOR YA BECAUSE THIS IS WHO I AM!
SPIDER-MAN...?
WELL THAT'S CONFUSING. YOU LIFTED RUBBLE. HEROICALLY. LOOK AT WHAT YOU'RE WEARING.
NOT SURE YET, ACTUALLY.
IT MEANS ANYONE CAN BE A HERO.
I THINK.
THIS IS A WEIRD CONVERSATION.
IS YOUR BRAIN TINGLING--?

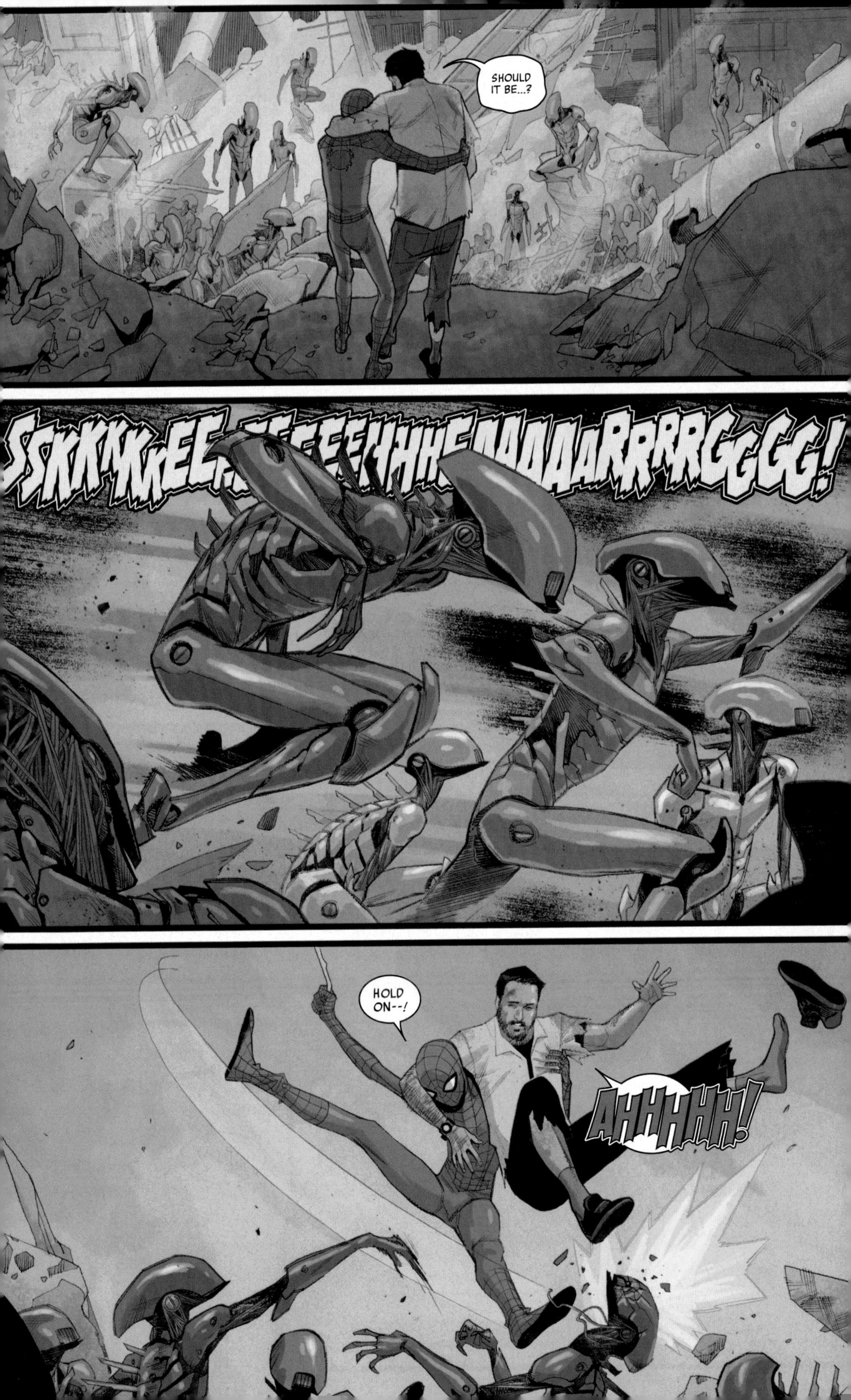

SHOULD IT BE...?
SSKKKKKEE...EEEEEHHHEAAAAARRRRGGGG!
HOLD ON--!
AHHHHH!

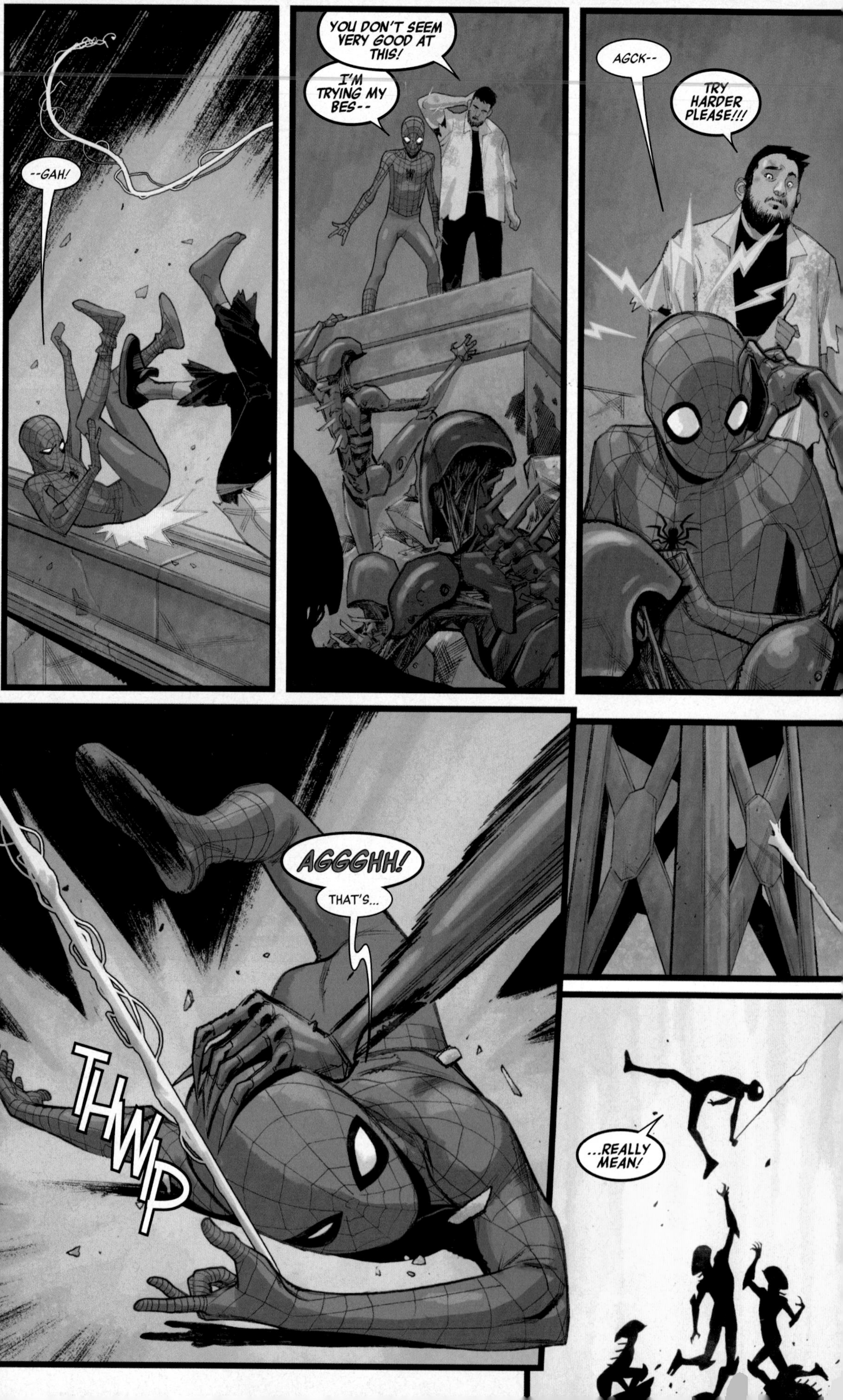

--GAH!
YOU DON'T SEEM VERY GOOD AT THIS!
I'M TRYING MY BES--
AGCK--
TRY HARDER PLEASE!!!
AGGGHH!
THAT'S...
THWIP
...REALLY MEAN!

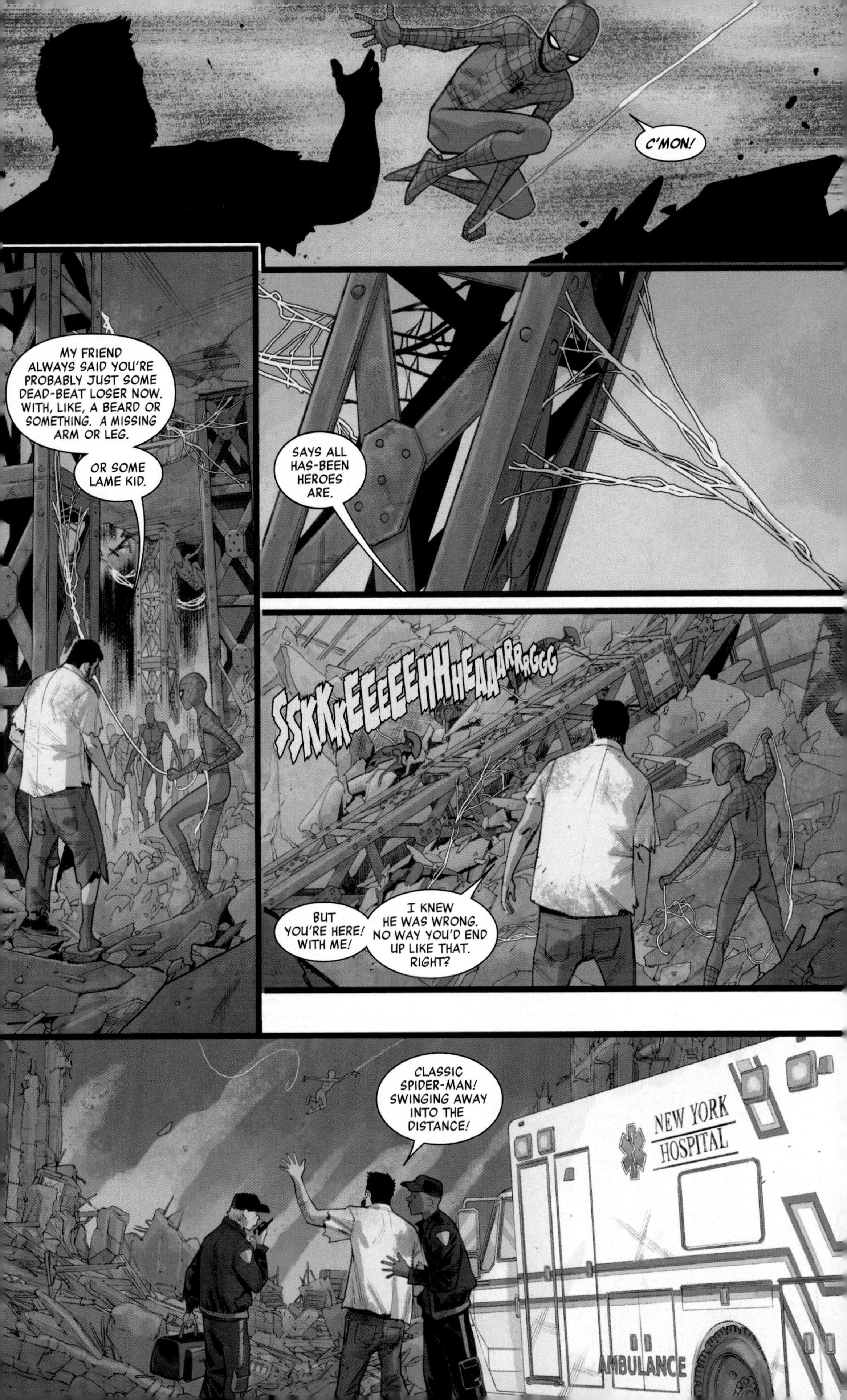
C'MON!
MY FRIEND ALWAYS SAID YOU'RE PROBABLY JUST SOME DEAD-BEAT LOSER NOW. WITH, LIKE, A BEARD OR SOMETHING. A MISSING ARM OR LEG.
OR SOME LAME KID.
SAYS ALL HAS-BEEN HEROES ARE.
SSKKKKEEEEEEHHHEAAARRRGGG
BUT YOU'RE HERE! WITH ME!
I KNEW HE WAS WRONG. NO WAY YOU'D END UP LIKE THAT. RIGHT?
CLASSIC SPIDER-MAN! SWINGING AWAY INTO THE DISTANCE!
NEW YORK HOSPITAL
AMBULANCE

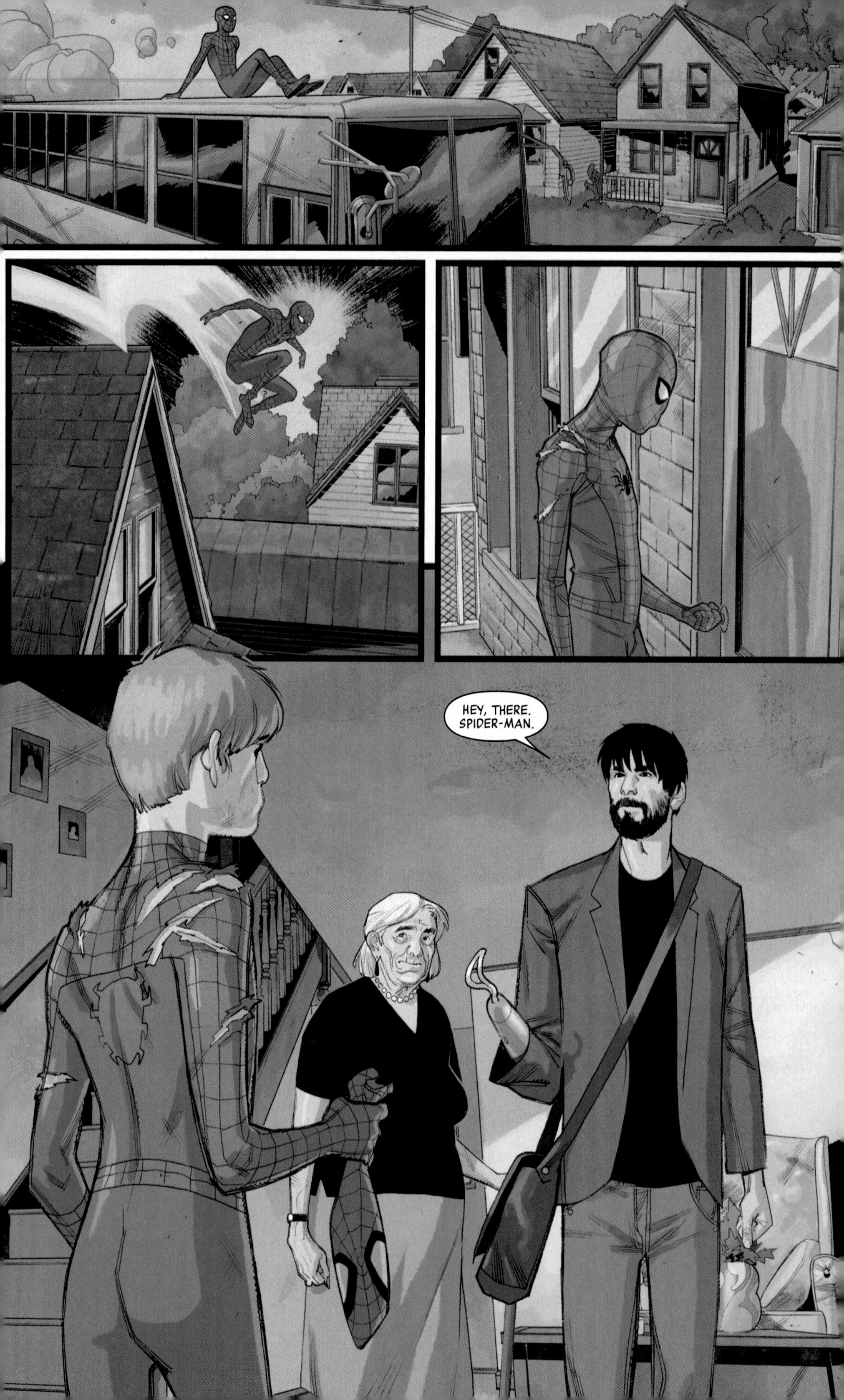
HEY, THERE. SPIDER-MAN.

3

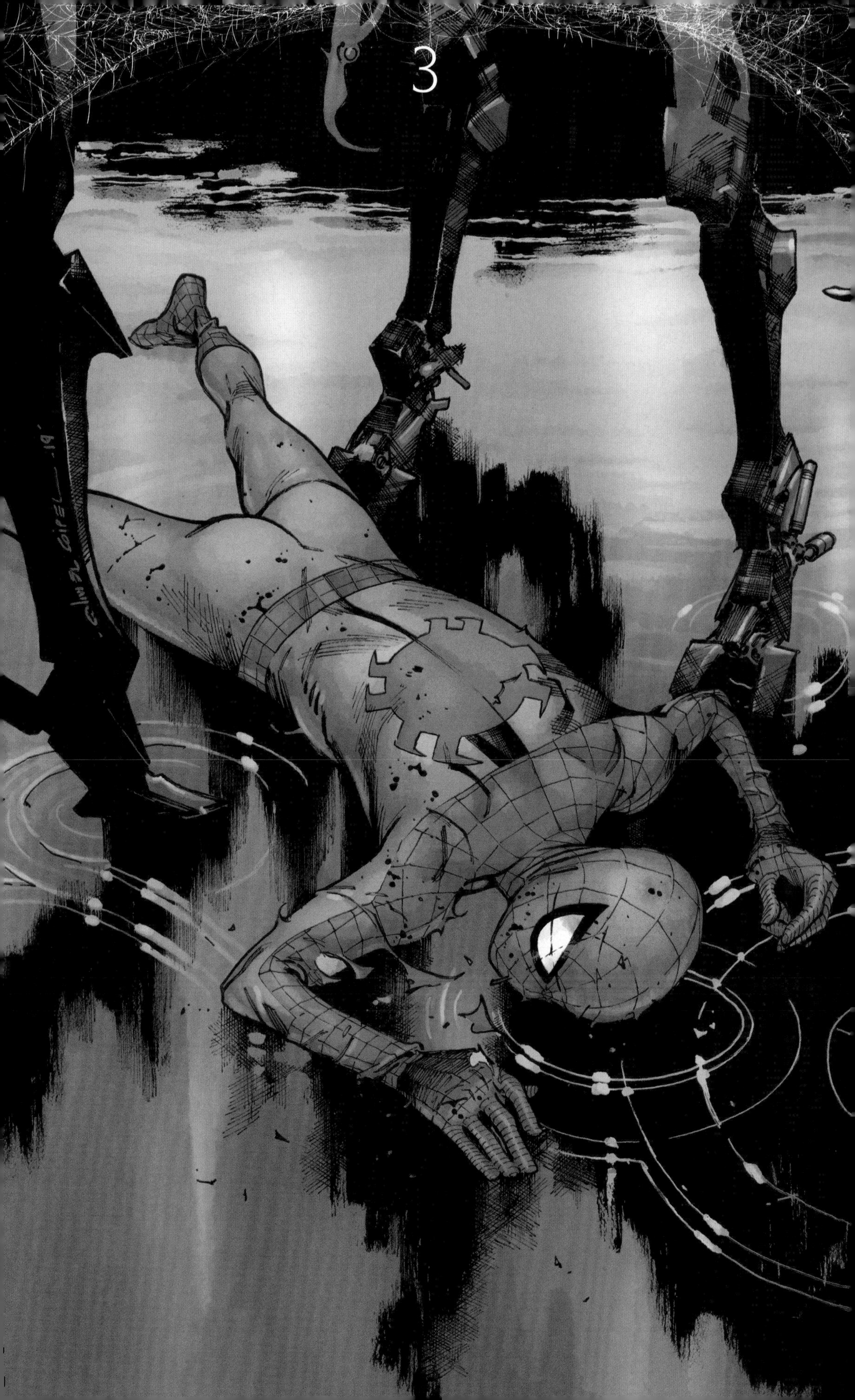

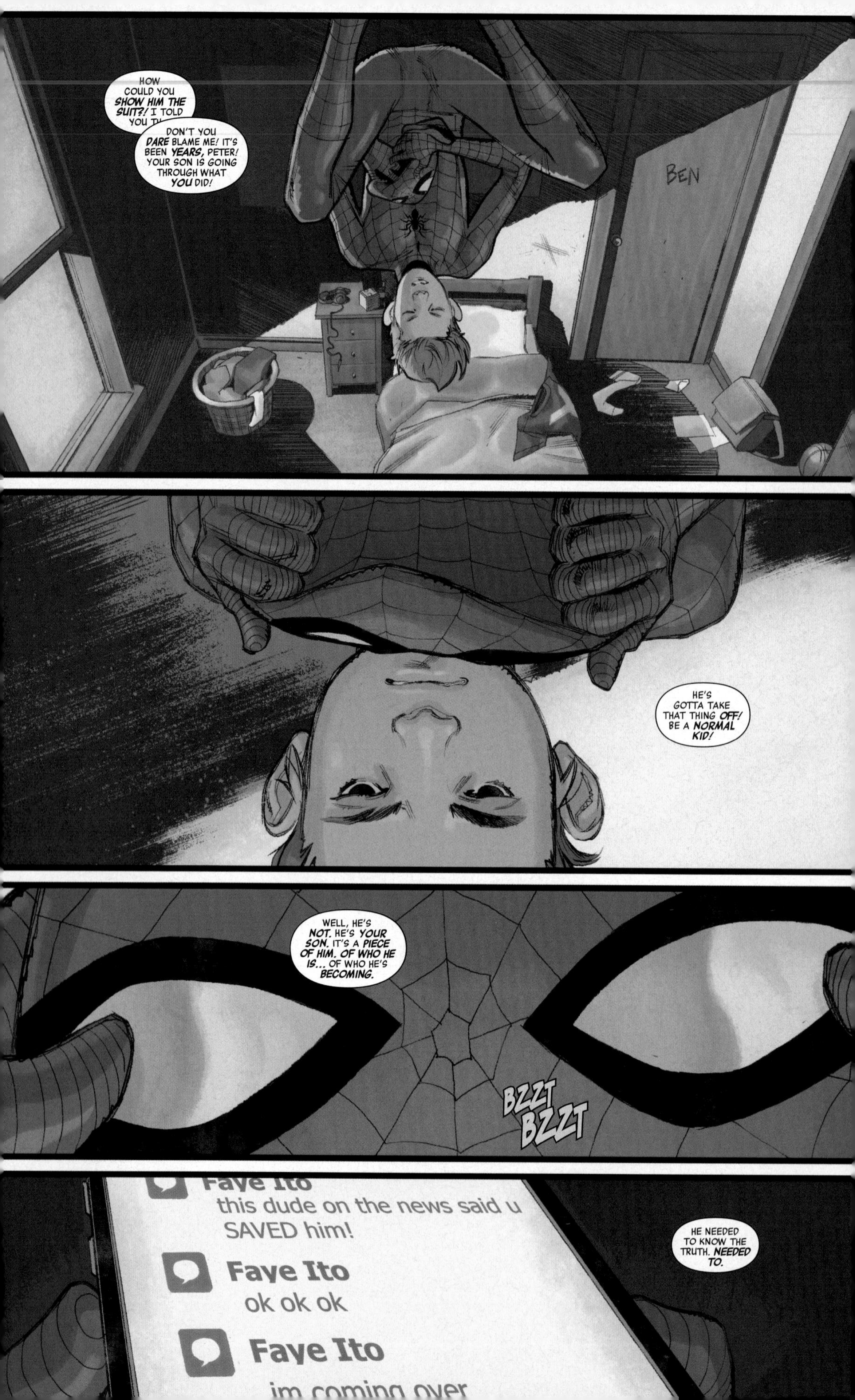
HOW COULD YOU SHOW HIM THE SUIT?! I TOLD YOU TH--
DON'T YOU DARE BLAME ME! IT'S BEEN YEARS, PETER! YOUR SON IS GOING THROUGH WHAT YOU DID!
BEN
HE'S GOTTA TAKE THAT THING OFF! BE A NORMAL KID!
WELL, HE'S NOT. HE'S YOUR SON. IT'S A PIECE OF HIM. OF WHO HE IS... OF WHO HE'S BECOMING.
BZZT BZZT
Faye Ito
this dude on the news said u SAVED him!
Faye Ito
ok ok ok
Faye Ito
im coming over
HE NEEDED TO KNOW THE TRUTH. NEEDED TO.

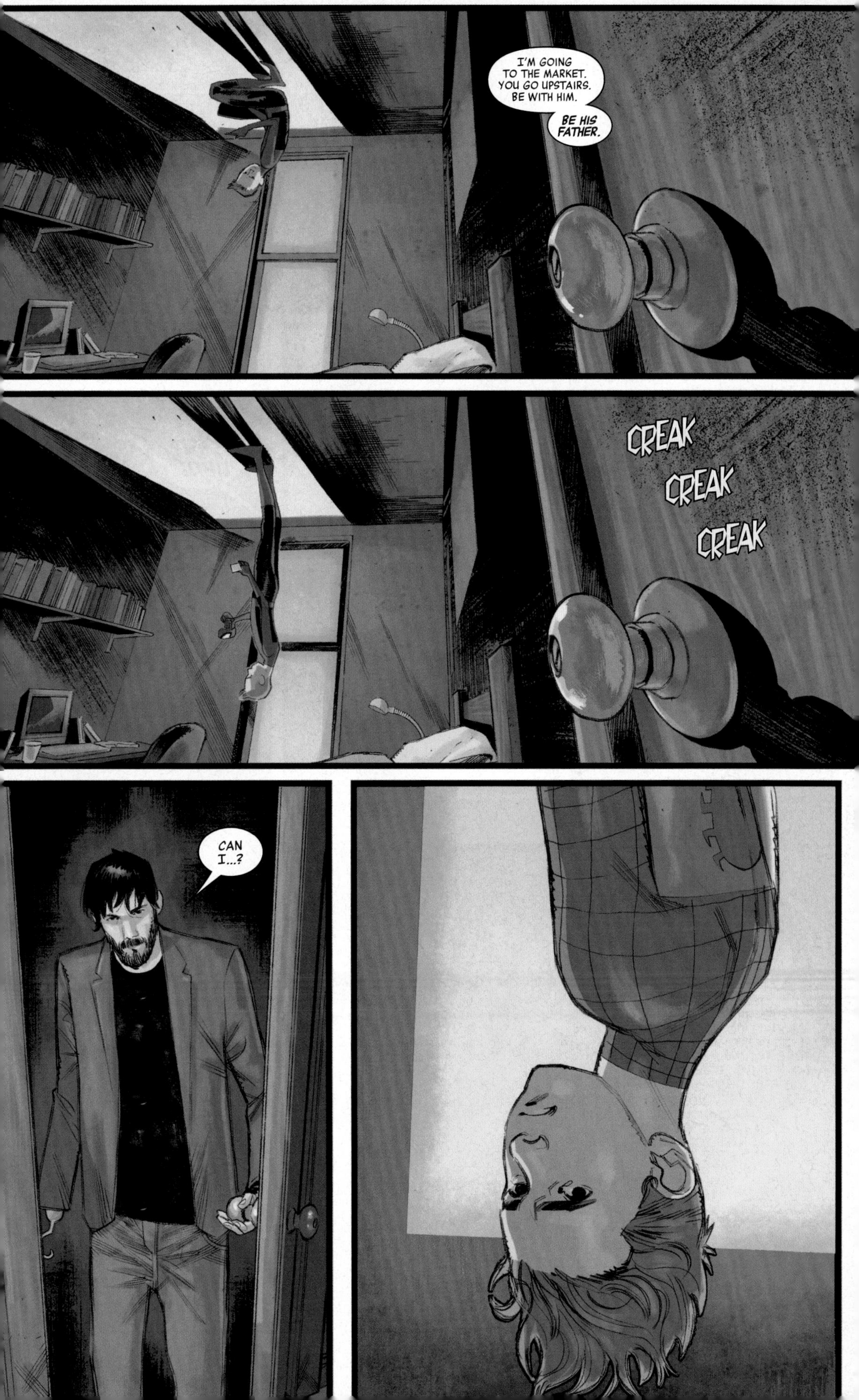
I'M GOING TO THE MARKET. YOU GO UPSTAIRS. BE WITH HIM.
BE HIS FATHER.
CREAK
CREAK
CREAK
CAN I...?

...THIN WALLS, HUH?

I WANNA SAY I DON'T KNOW HOW CONFUSED YOU ARE... BUT I KNOW EXACTLY.

BEN...YOU CAN'T DO THIS. BEING... IT...DEMANDS EVERY PIECE OF YOURSELF. AND THEN IT DEMANDS MORE. I DON'T WANT THIS FOR YOU--YOUR MOTHER WOULDN'T WANT IT FOR--

DON'T TALK ABOUT HER.

IT'S NOT WHAT YOU THINK. YOU HAVE TO PUSH IT AWAY. ALL OF IT. I CAN'T PROTECT YOU FROM--

SHUT UP!!!

PROTECT ME?! YOU DON'T EVEN CARE ABOUT ME!

PLEASE, PLEASE, WHEN I'M AWAY, IT'S ALWAYS FOR YOU. I KNOW IT'S HARD TO--

IT'S NOT EVEN UP TO YOU WHAT I DO, OKAY? YOU DON'T HAVE TO COME AROUND ME... YOU DON'T HAVE TO SEE ME IF IT BOTHERS YOU...

NO...I DON'T KNOW HOW TO SAY IT BUT PLEASE LISTEN, BENNY...PLEASE, I NEED YOU TO PLEASE LISTEN AND STOP THIS. STOP! I NEED YOU TO PLEASE--PLEASE JUST TAKE THAT THING OFF AND LISTEN TO--

I WAS AFRAID OF ME! I THOUGHT I WAS A MONSTER AND YOU WEREN'T EVEN HERE!!!

GET AWAY FROM ME!!!...

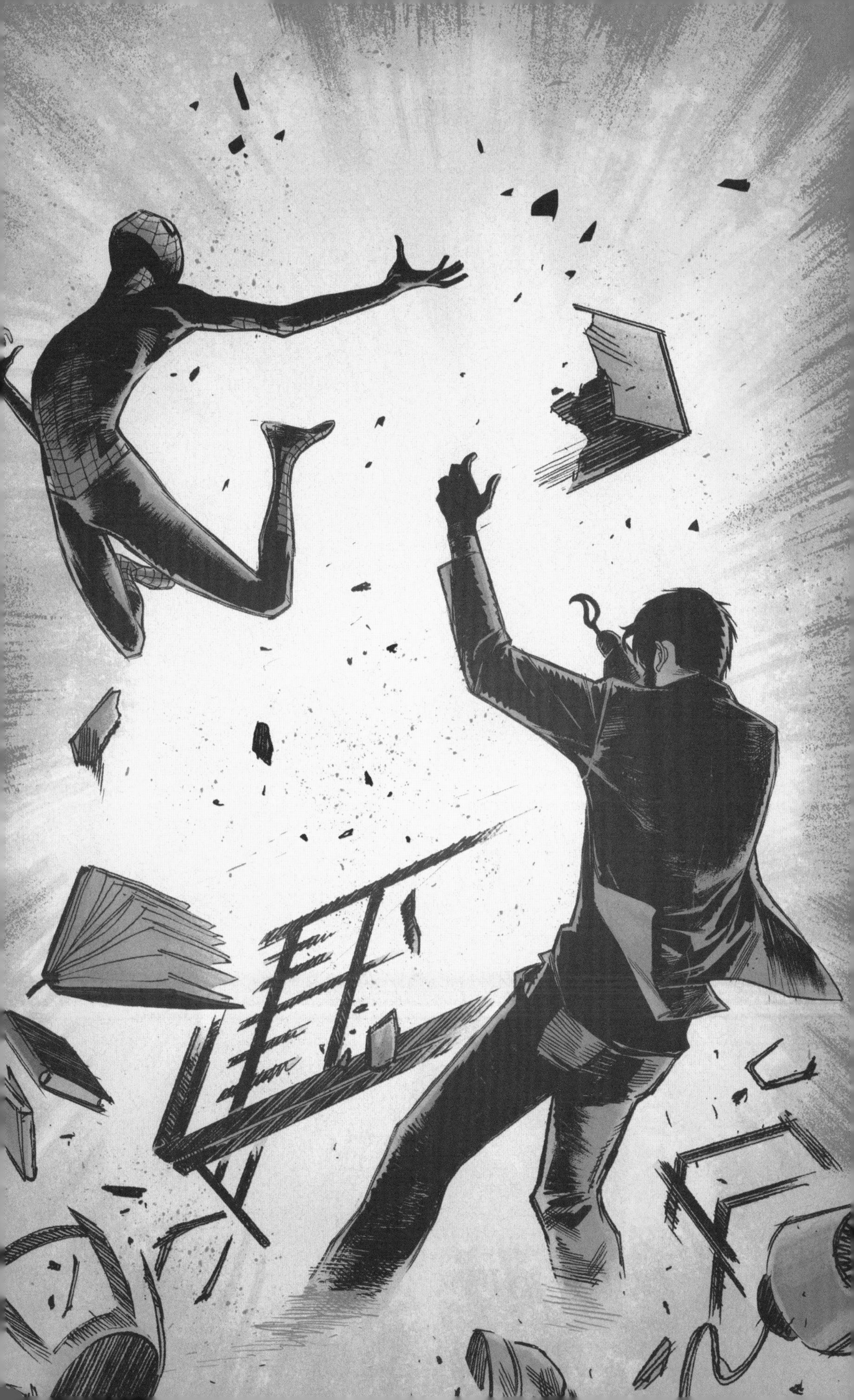

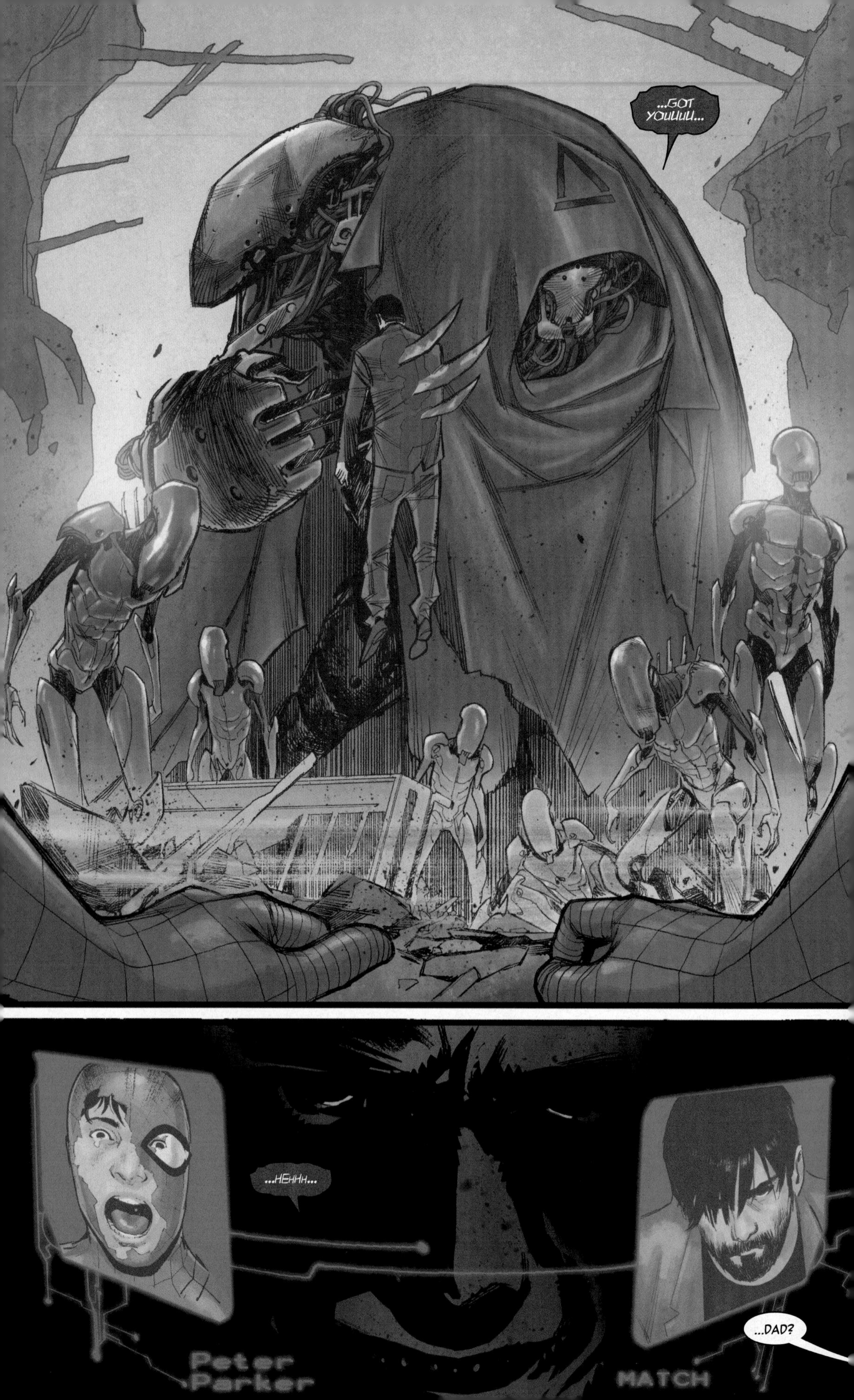
...GOT YOUUUU...
...HEHHH...
Peter Parker
MATCH
...DAD?

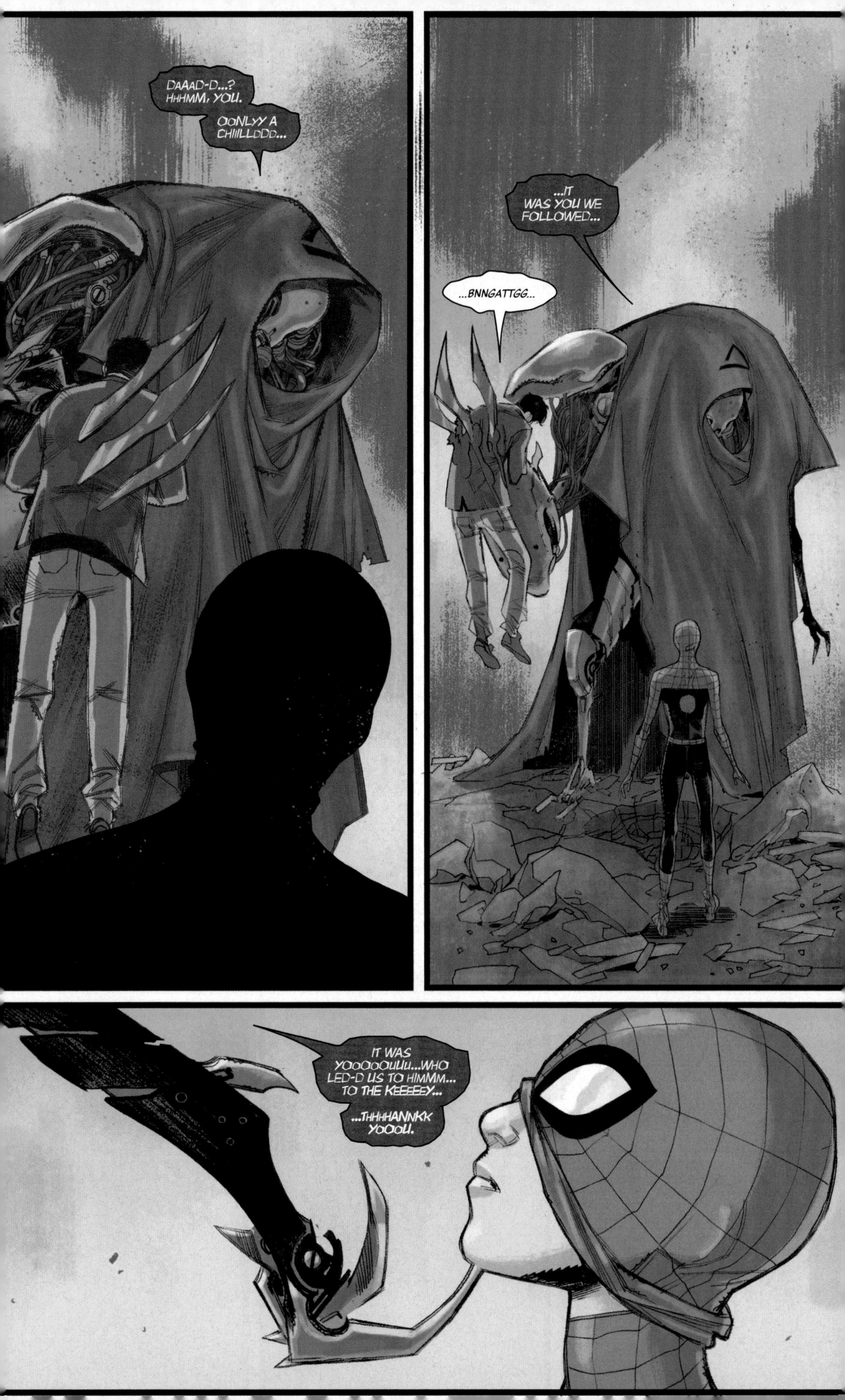
DAAAD-D...? HHHMM, YOU.
OONLYY A CHIIILLDDD...
...IT WAS YOU WE FOLLOWED...
...BNNGATTGG...
IT WAS YOOOOOUUU...WHO LED-D US TO HIMMM... TO THE KEEEEEY...
...THHHHANNKK YOOOU.

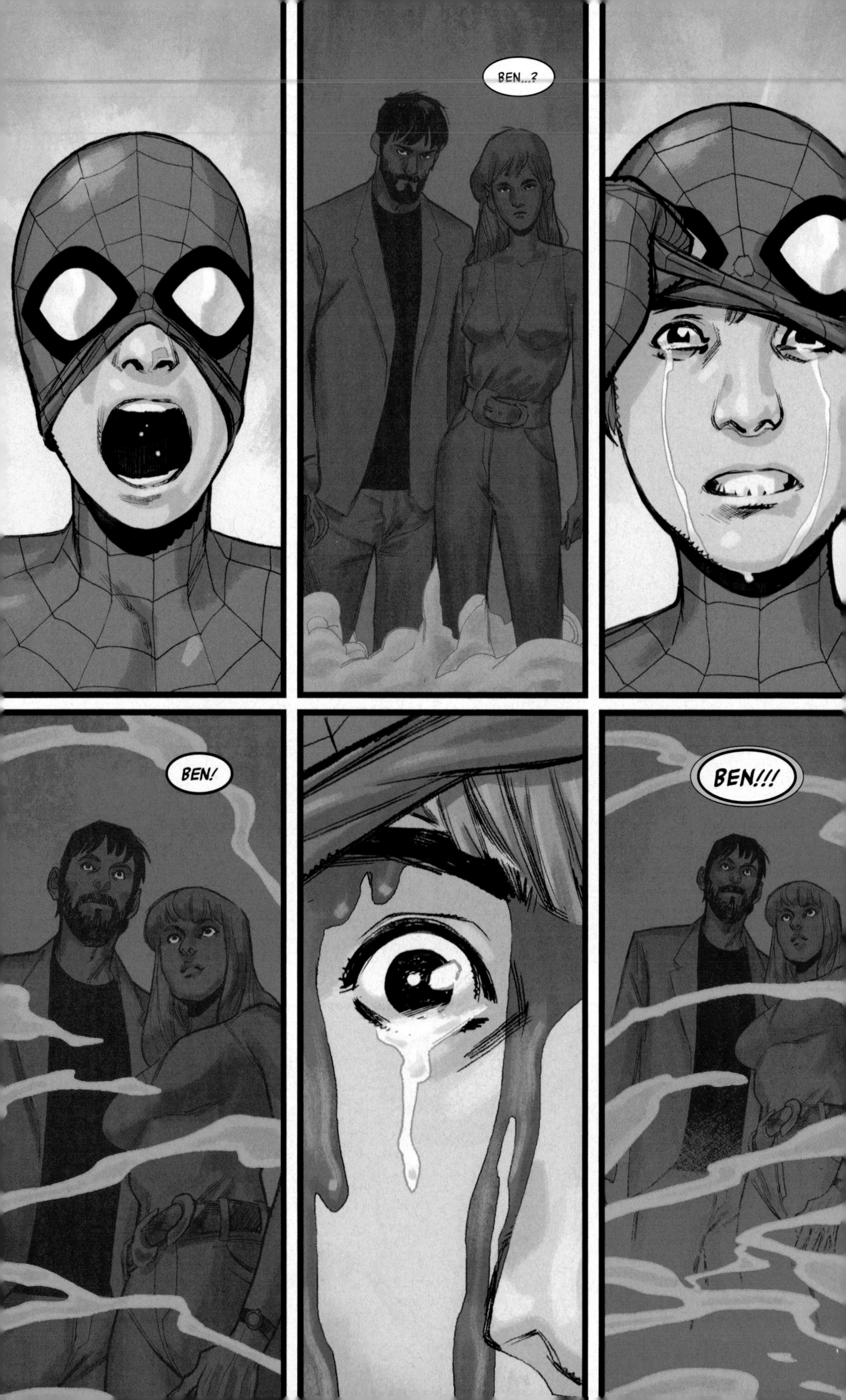
BEN...?
BEN!
BEN!!!

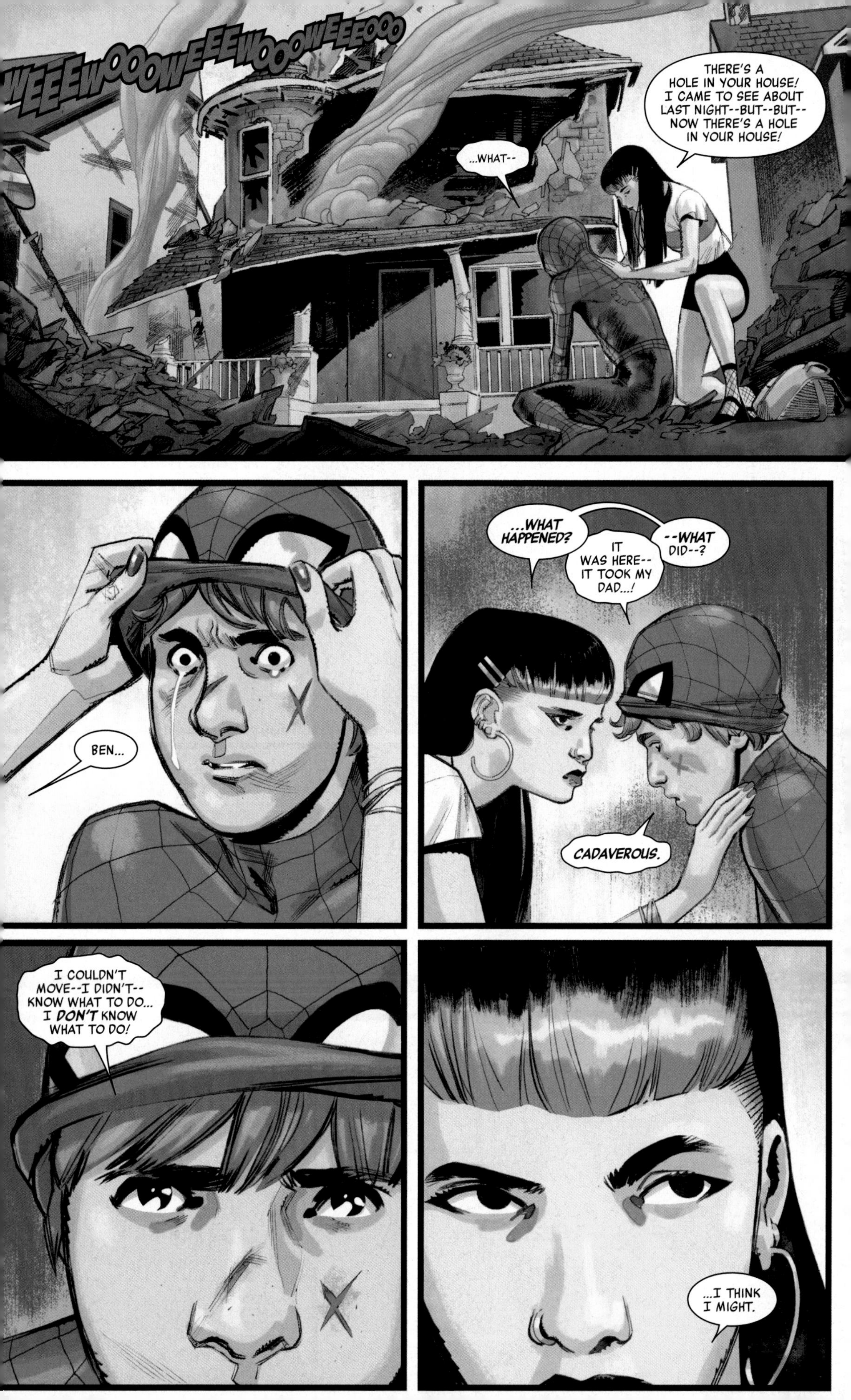
WEEEWOOOOWEEEWOOOWEEEOOO
...WHAT--
THERE'S A HOLE IN YOUR HOUSE! I CAME TO SEE ABOUT LAST NIGHT--BUT--BUT-- NOW THERE'S A HOLE IN YOUR HOUSE!
BEN...
...WHAT HAPPENED?
--WHAT DID--?
IT WAS HERE-- IT TOOK MY DAD...!
CADAVEROUS.
I COULDN'T MOVE--I DIDN'T-- KNOW WHAT TO DO... I DON'T KNOW WHAT TO DO!
...I THINK I MIGHT.

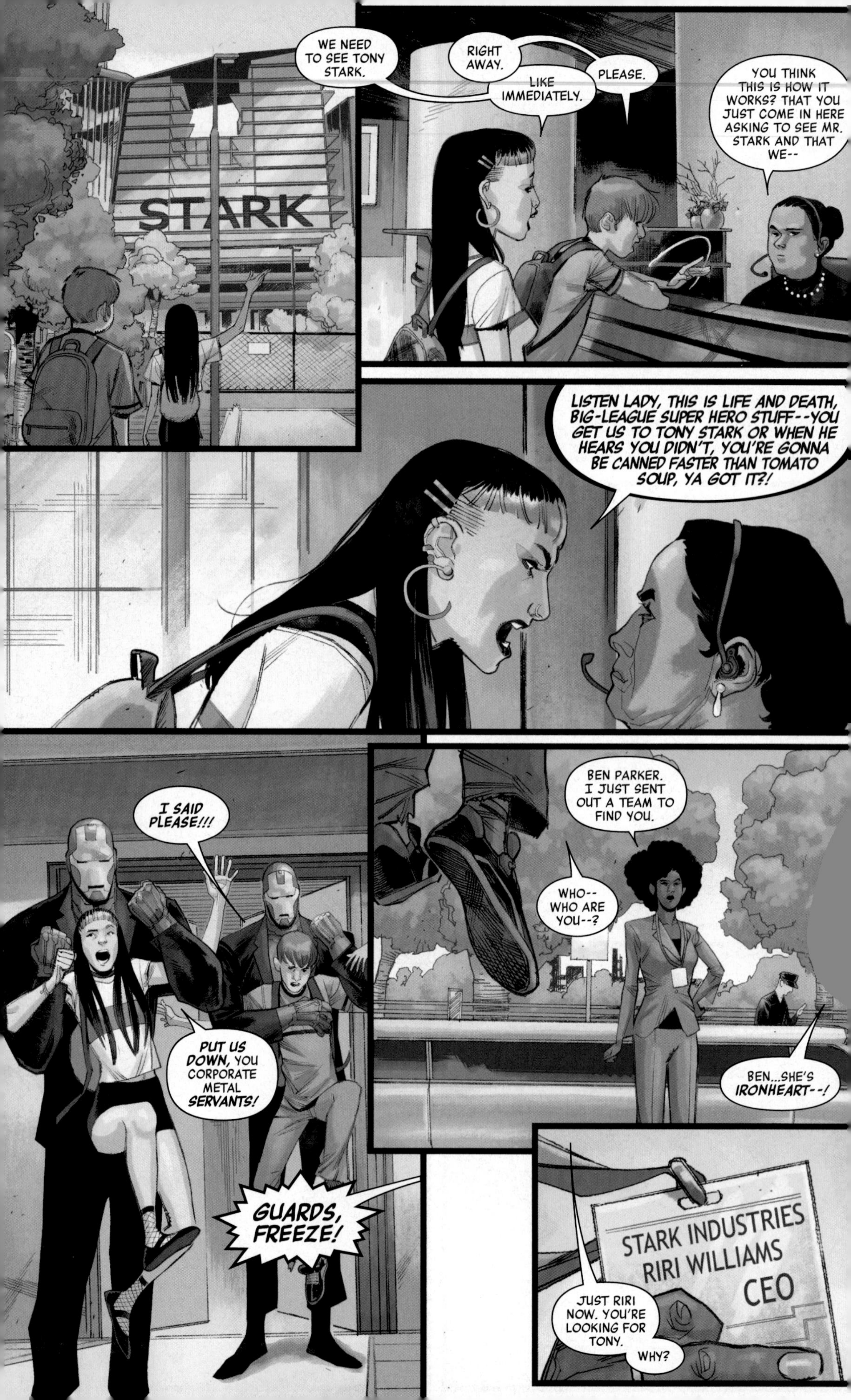
STARK
WE NEED TO SEE TONY STARK.
RIGHT AWAY.
LIKE IMMEDIATELY.
PLEASE.
YOU THINK THIS IS HOW IT WORKS? THAT YOU JUST COME IN HERE ASKING TO SEE MR. STARK AND THAT WE--
LISTEN LADY, THIS IS LIFE AND DEATH, BIG-LEAGUE SUPER HERO STUFF--YOU GET US TO TONY STARK OR WHEN HE HEARS YOU DIDN'T, YOU'RE GONNA BE CANNED FASTER THAN TOMATO SOUP, YA GOT IT?!
I SAID PLEASE!!!
PUT US DOWN, YOU CORPORATE METAL SERVANTS!
GUARDS, FREEZE!
BEN PARKER. I JUST SENT OUT A TEAM TO FIND YOU.
WHO-- WHO ARE YOU--?
BEN...SHE'S IRONHEART--!
STARK INDUSTRIES
RIRI WILLIAMS
CEO
JUST RIRI NOW. YOU'RE LOOKING FOR TONY.
WHY?

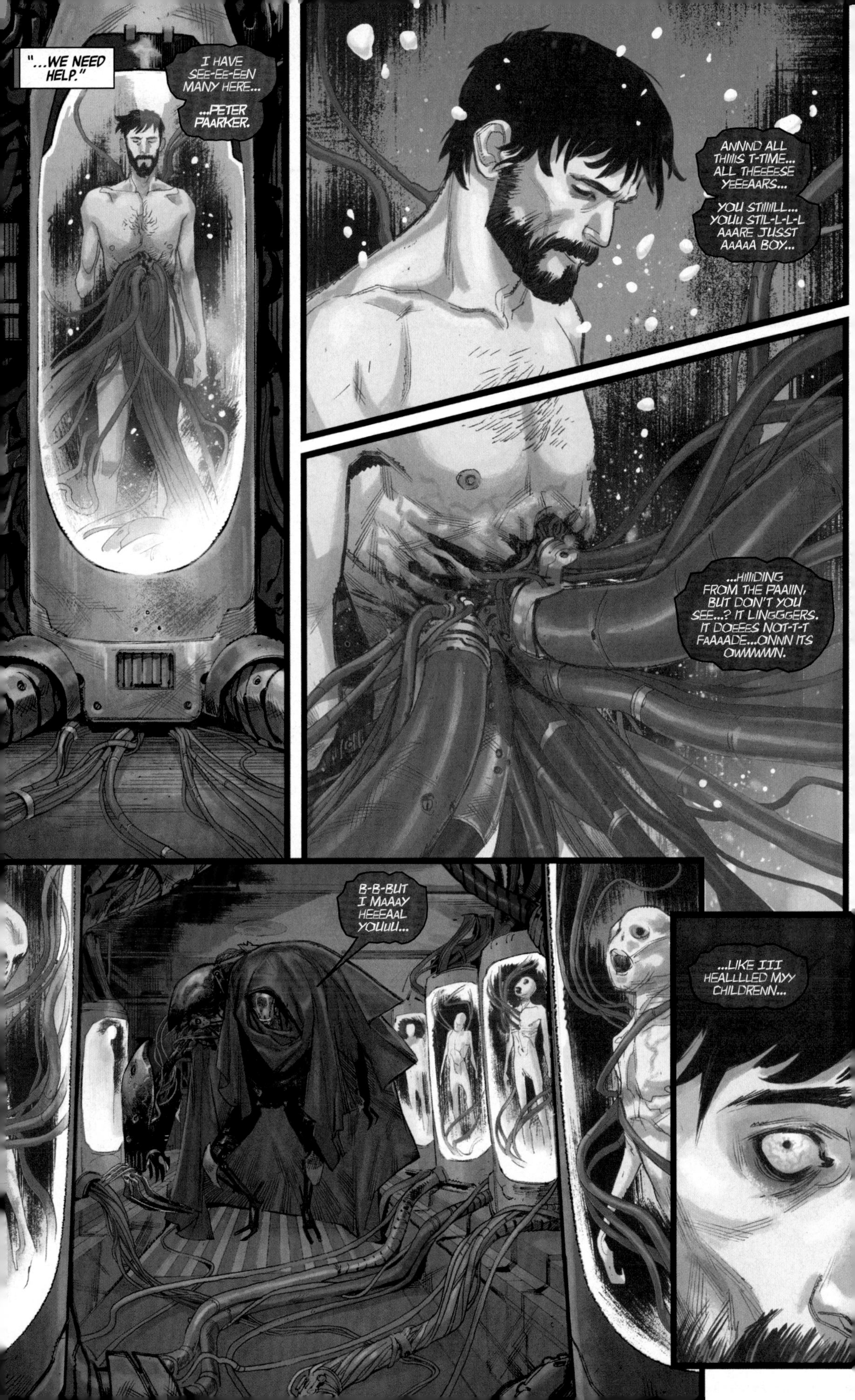
"...WE NEED HELP."
I HAVE SEE-EE-EEN MANY HERE...
...PETER PAARKER.
ANNND ALL THIIIS T-TIME... ALL THEEEESE YEEEAARS...
YOU STIIIILL... YOUU STIL-L-L-L AAARE JUSST AAAAA BOY...
...HIIIDING FROM THE PAAIIN, BUT DON'T YOU SEE...? IT LINGGGERS. IT DOEEES NOT-T-T FAAAADE...ONNN ITS OWWWWN.
B-B-BUT I MAAAY HEEEAAL YOUUU...
...LIKE III HEALLLLED MYY CHILDRENN...

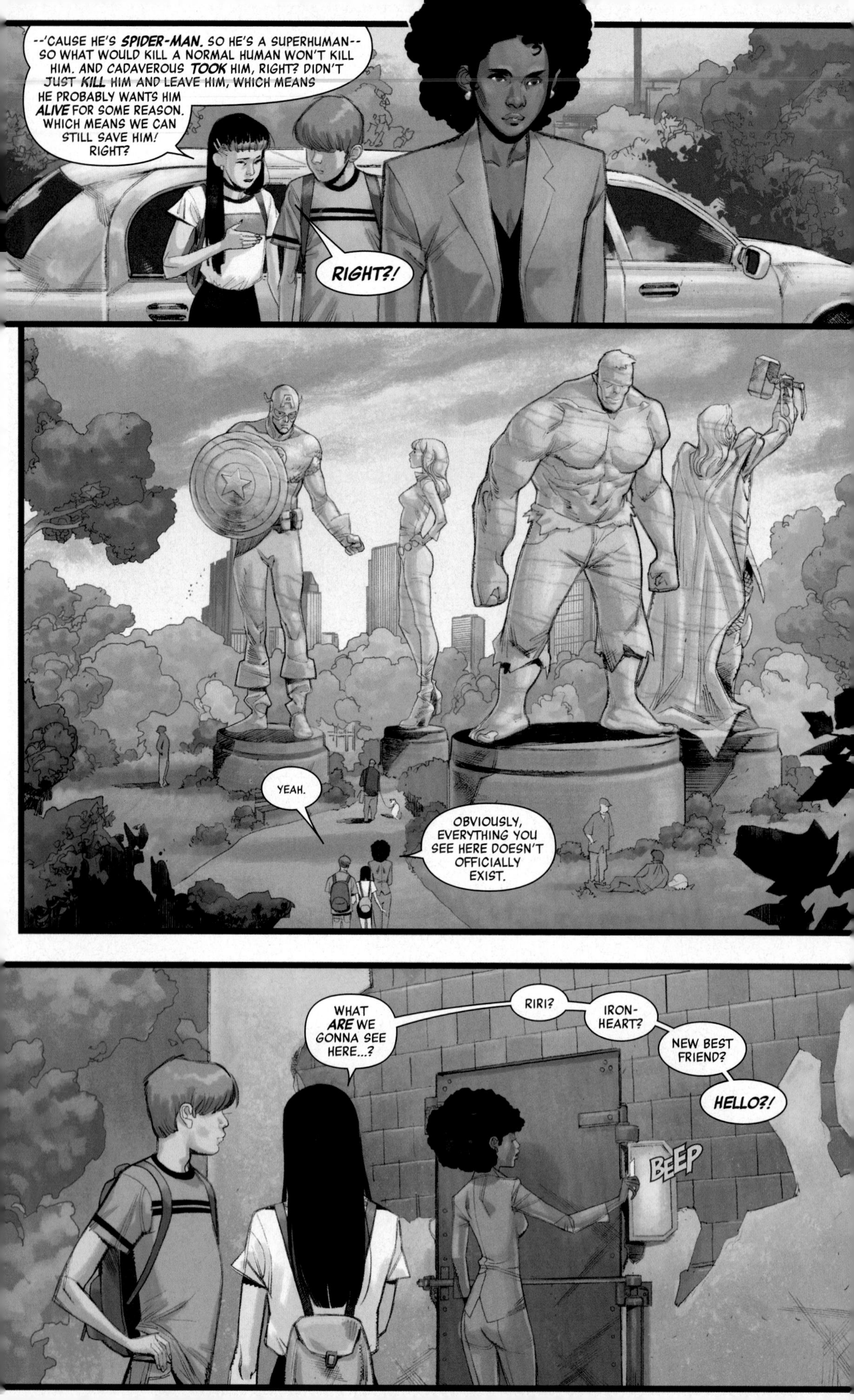
--'CAUSE HE'S SPIDER-MAN. SO HE'S A SUPERHUMAN-- SO WHAT WOULD KILL A NORMAL HUMAN WON'T KILL HIM. AND CADAVEROUS TOOK HIM, RIGHT? DIDN'T JUST KILL HIM AND LEAVE HIM, WHICH MEANS HE PROBABLY WANTS HIM ALIVE FOR SOME REASON. WHICH MEANS WE CAN STILL SAVE HIM! RIGHT?
RIGHT?!
YEAH.
OBVIOUSLY, EVERYTHING YOU SEE HERE DOESN'T OFFICIALLY EXIST.
WHAT ARE WE GONNA SEE HERE...?
RIRI?
IRON-HEART?
NEW BEST FRIEND?
HELLO?!
BEEP

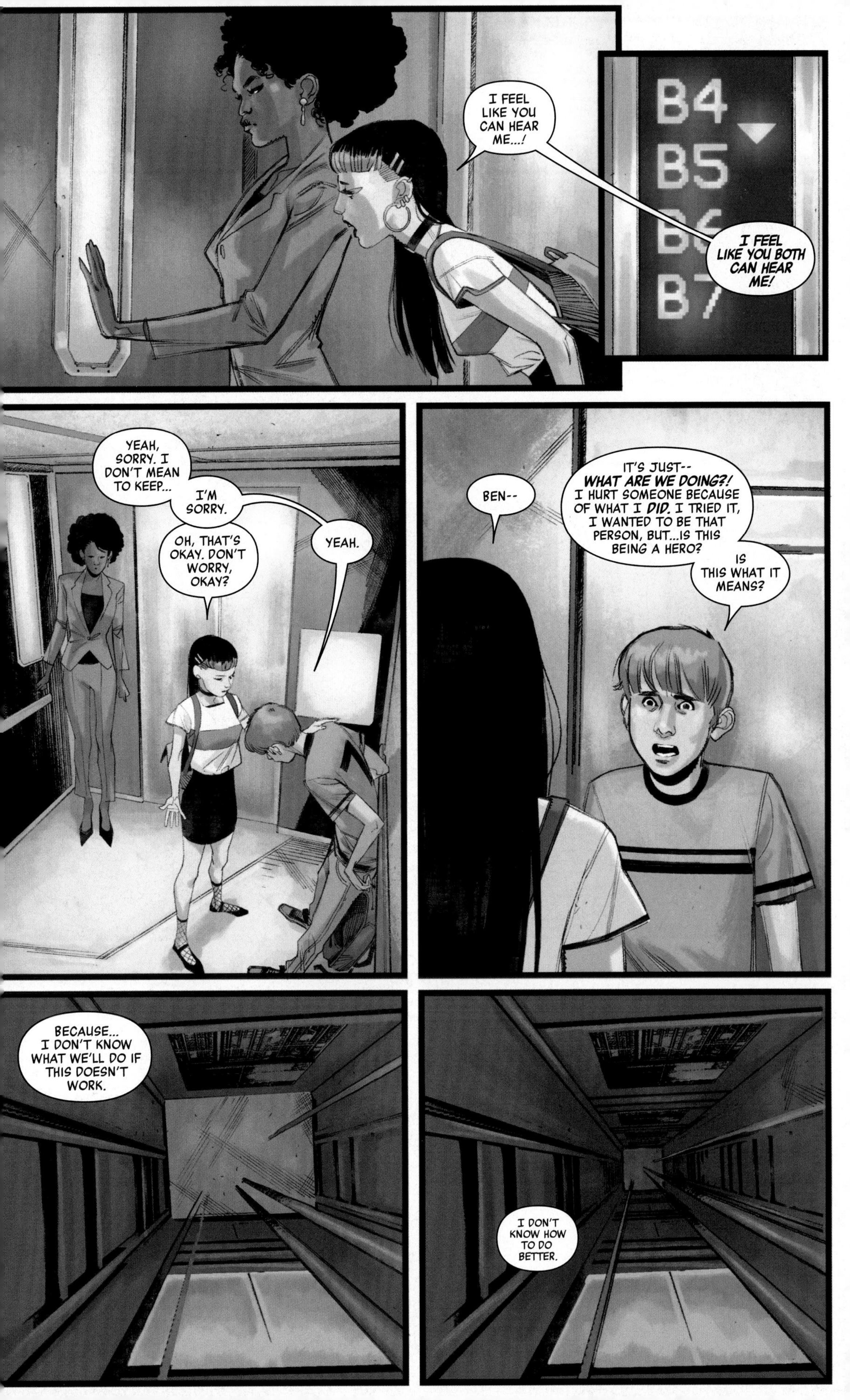
I FEEL LIKE YOU CAN HEAR ME...!
B4
B5
B7
I FEEL LIKE YOU BOTH CAN HEAR ME!
YEAH, SORRY. I DON'T MEAN TO KEEP...
I'M SORRY.
OH, THAT'S OKAY. DON'T WORRY, OKAY?
YEAH.
BEN--
IT'S JUST-- WHAT ARE WE DOING?! I HURT SOMEONE BECAUSE OF WHAT I DID. I TRIED IT, I WANTED TO BE THAT PERSON, BUT...IS THIS BEING A HERO?
IS THIS WHAT IT MEANS?
BECAUSE... I DON'T KNOW WHAT WE'LL DO IF THIS DOESN'T WORK.
I DON'T KNOW HOW TO DO BETTER.

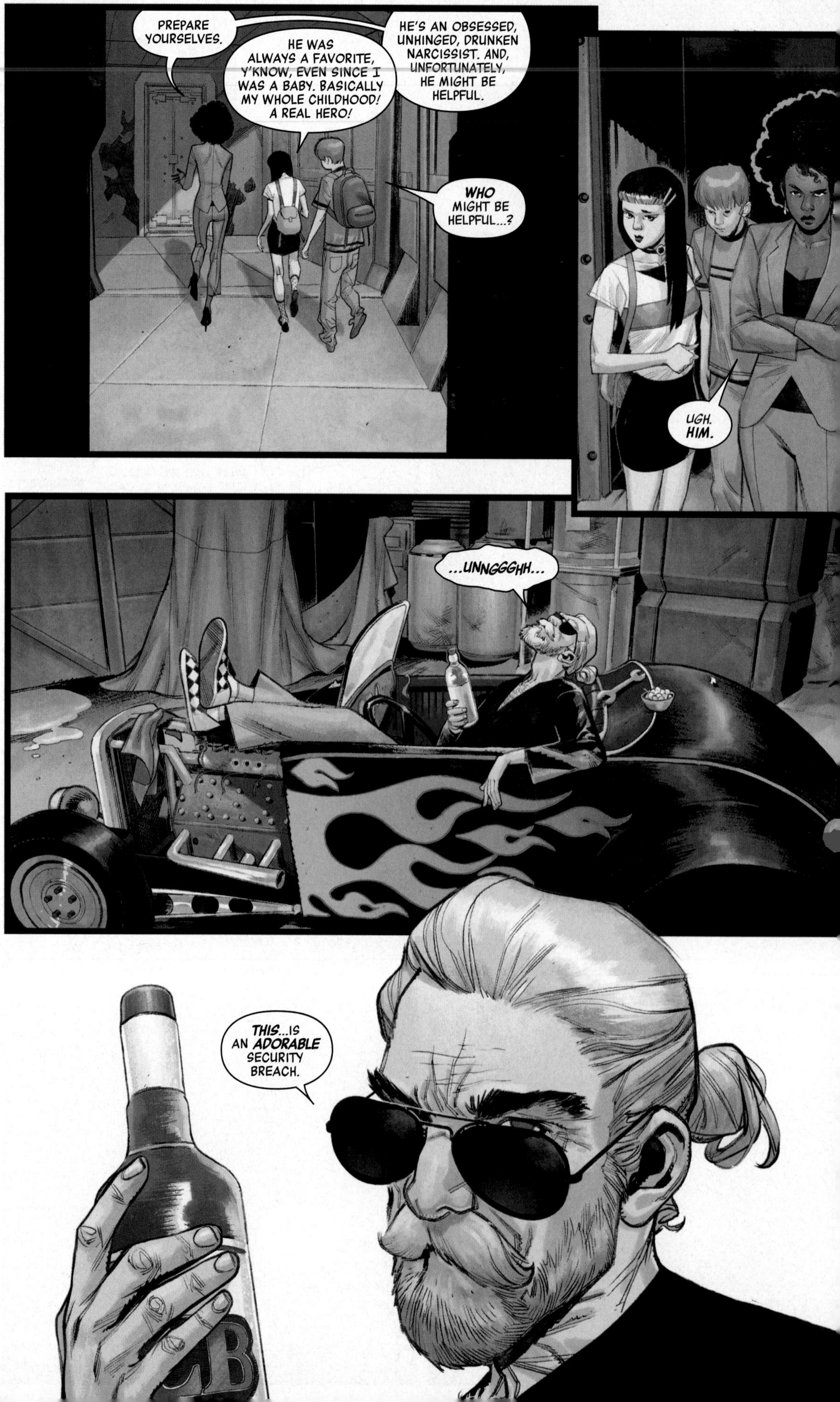
PREPARE YOURSELVES.
HE'S AN OBSESSED, UNHINGED, DRUNKEN NARCISSIST. AND, UNFORTUNATELY, HE MIGHT BE HELPFUL.
HE WAS ALWAYS A FAVORITE, Y'KNOW, EVEN SINCE I WAS A BABY. BASICALLY MY WHOLE CHILDHOOD! A REAL HERO!
WHO MIGHT BE HELPFUL...?
UGH. HIM.
...UNNGGGHH...
THIS...IS AN ADORABLE SECURITY BREACH.

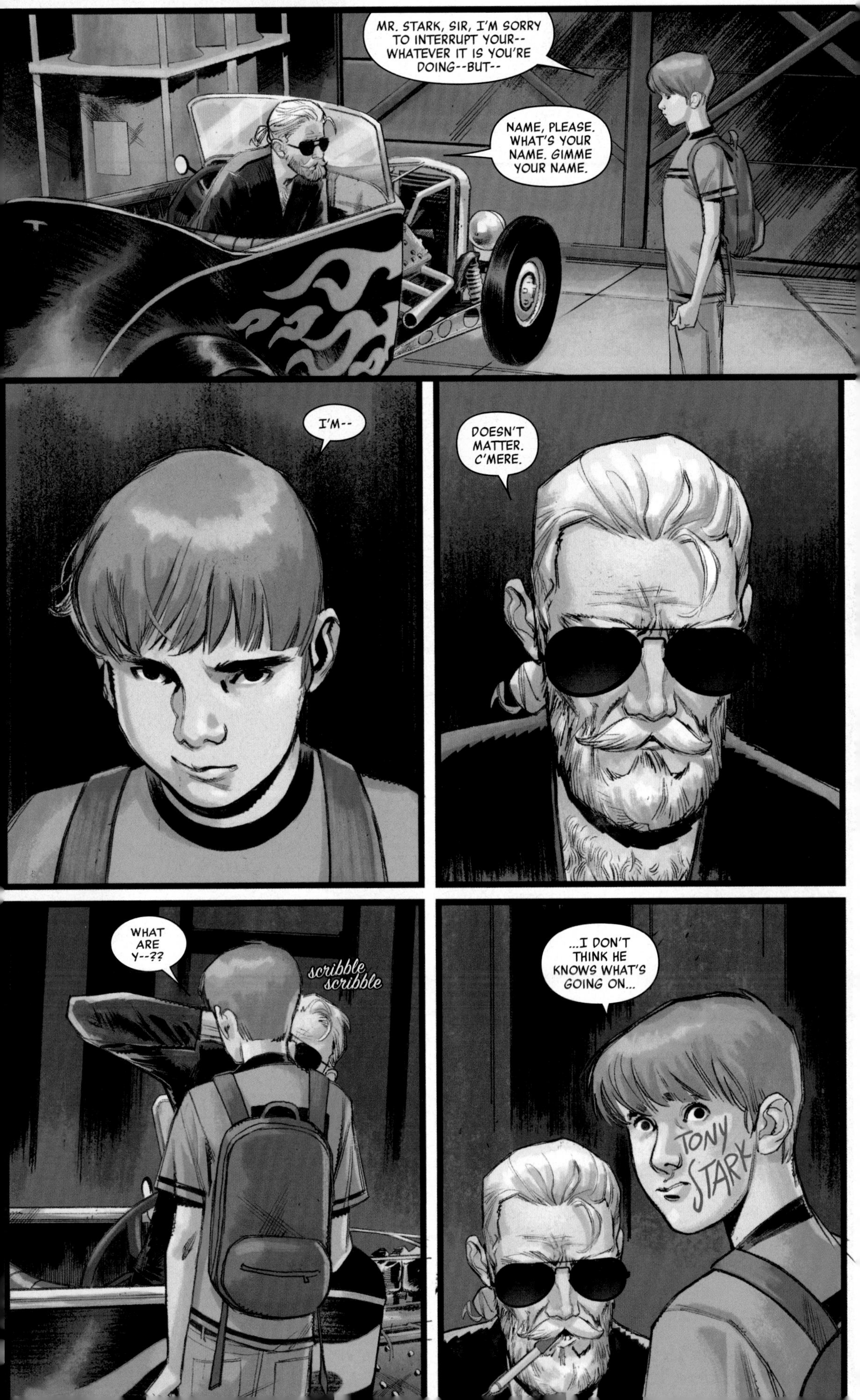
MR. STARK, SIR, I'M SORRY TO INTERRUPT YOUR-- WHATEVER IT IS YOU'RE DOING--BUT--
NAME, PLEASE. WHAT'S YOUR NAME. GIMME YOUR NAME.
I'M--
DOESN'T MATTER. C'MERE.
WHAT ARE Y--??
scribble scribble
...I DON'T THINK HE KNOWS WHAT'S GOING ON...
TONY STARK

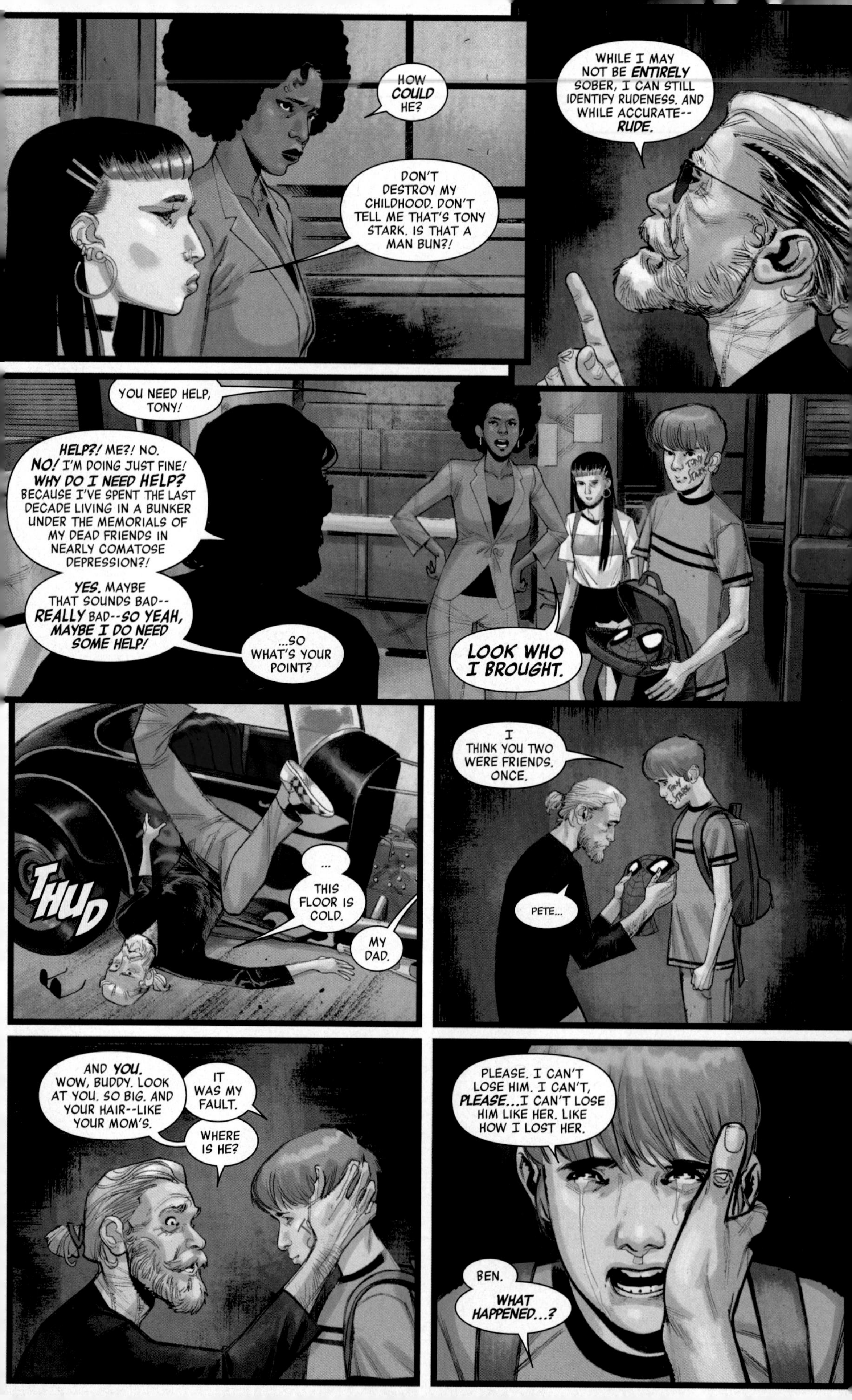

HOW COULD HE?
DON'T DESTROY MY CHILDHOOD. DON'T TELL ME THAT'S TONY STARK. IS THAT A MAN BUN?!
WHILE I MAY NOT BE ENTIRELY SOBER, I CAN STILL IDENTIFY RUDENESS. AND WHILE ACCURATE--RUDE.
YOU NEED HELP, TONY!
HELP?! ME?! NO. NO! I'M DOING JUST FINE! WHY DO I NEED HELP? BECAUSE I'VE SPENT THE LAST DECADE LIVING IN A BUNKER UNDER THE MEMORIALS OF MY DEAD FRIENDS IN NEARLY COMATOSE DEPRESSION?!
YES. MAYBE THAT SOUNDS BAD--REALLY BAD--SO YEAH, MAYBE I DO NEED SOME HELP!
...SO WHAT'S YOUR POINT?
LOOK WHO I BROUGHT.
TONY STARK
THUD
...
THIS FLOOR IS COLD.
MY DAD.
I THINK YOU TWO WERE FRIENDS. ONCE.
TONY STARK
PETE...
AND YOU. WOW, BUDDY. LOOK AT YOU. SO BIG. AND YOUR HAIR--LIKE YOUR MOM'S.
IT WAS MY FAULT.
WHERE IS HE?
PLEASE. I CAN'T LOSE HIM. I CAN'T, PLEASE...I CAN'T LOSE HIM LIKE HER. LIKE HOW I LOST HER.
BEN.
WHAT HAPPENED...?

"CADAVEROUS."

"WHY DON'T YOU ALL FOLLOW ME DOWNSTAIRS...THERE'S SOMETHING YOU SHOULD SEE.

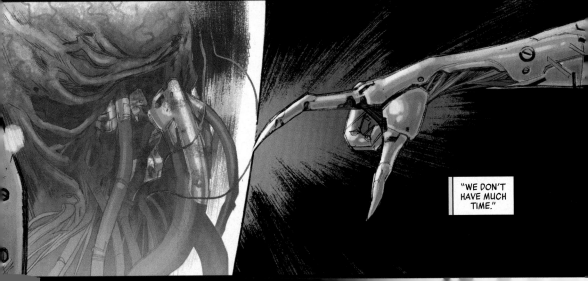

"WE DON'T HAVE MUCH TIME."

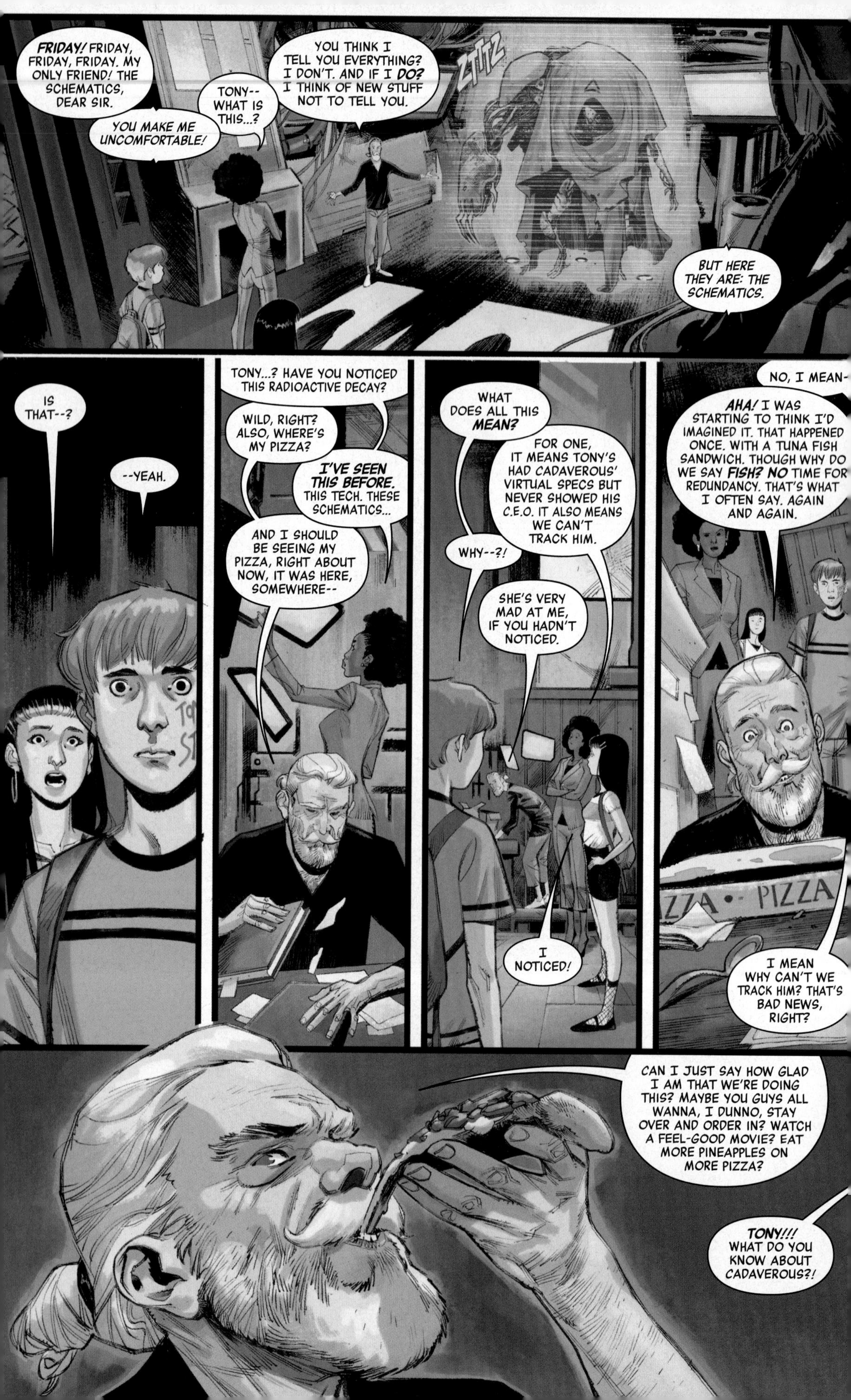
FRIDAY! FRIDAY, FRIDAY, FRIDAY. MY ONLY FRIEND! THE SCHEMATICS, DEAR SIR.
YOU MAKE ME UNCOMFORTABLE!
TONY-- WHAT IS THIS...?
YOU THINK I TELL YOU EVERYTHING? I DON'T. AND IF I DO? I THINK OF NEW STUFF NOT TO TELL YOU.
ZTTTZ
BUT HERE THEY ARE: THE SCHEMATICS.
IS THAT--?
--YEAH.
TONY...? HAVE YOU NOTICED THIS RADIOACTIVE DECAY?
WILD, RIGHT? ALSO, WHERE'S MY PIZZA?
I'VE SEEN THIS BEFORE. THIS TECH. THESE SCHEMATICS...
AND I SHOULD BE SEEING MY PIZZA, RIGHT ABOUT NOW, IT WAS HERE, SOMEWHERE--
WHAT DOES ALL THIS MEAN?
FOR ONE, IT MEANS TONY'S HAD CADAVEROUS' VIRTUAL SPECS BUT NEVER SHOWED HIS C.E.O. IT ALSO MEANS WE CAN'T TRACK HIM.
WHY--?!
SHE'S VERY MAD AT ME, IF YOU HADN'T NOTICED.
I NOTICED!
NO, I MEAN-
AHA! I WAS STARTING TO THINK I'D IMAGINED IT. THAT HAPPENED ONCE. WITH A TUNA FISH SANDWICH. THOUGH WHY DO WE SAY FISH? NO TIME FOR REDUNDANCY. THAT'S WHAT I OFTEN SAY. AGAIN AND AGAIN.
ZZA • PIZZA
I MEAN WHY CAN'T WE TRACK HIM? THAT'S BAD NEWS, RIGHT?
CAN I JUST SAY HOW GLAD I AM THAT WE'RE DOING THIS? MAYBE YOU GUYS ALL WANNA, I DUNNO, STAY OVER AND ORDER IN? WATCH A FEEL-GOOD MOVIE? EAT MORE PINEAPPLES ON MORE PIZZA?
TONY!!! WHAT DO YOU KNOW ABOUT CADAVEROUS?!

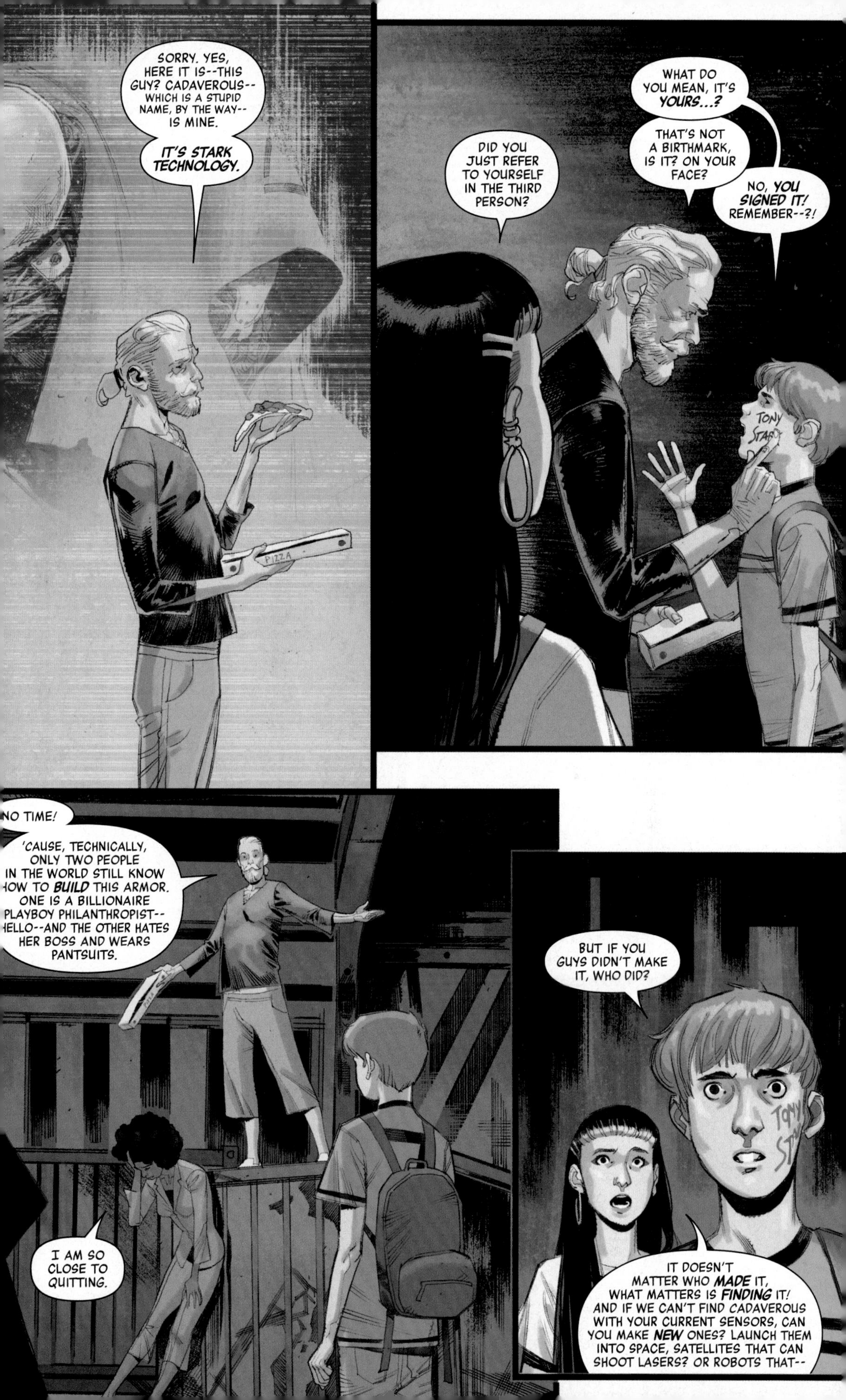

SORRY. YES, HERE IT IS--THIS GUY? CADAVEROUS--WHICH IS A STUPID NAME, BY THE WAY--IS MINE.
IT'S STARK TECHNOLOGY.
DID YOU JUST REFER TO YOURSELF IN THE THIRD PERSON?
WHAT DO YOU MEAN, IT'S YOURS...?
THAT'S NOT A BIRTHMARK, IS IT? ON YOUR FACE?
NO, YOU SIGNED IT! REMEMBER--?!
TONY STARK
PIZZA
NO TIME!
'CAUSE, TECHNICALLY, ONLY TWO PEOPLE IN THE WORLD STILL KNOW HOW TO BUILD THIS ARMOR. ONE IS A BILLIONAIRE PLAYBOY PHILANTHROPIST--HELLO--AND THE OTHER HATES HER BOSS AND WEARS PANTSUITS.
I AM SO CLOSE TO QUITTING.
BUT IF YOU GUYS DIDN'T MAKE IT, WHO DID?
IT DOESN'T MATTER WHO MADE IT, WHAT MATTERS IS FINDING IT! AND IF WE CAN'T FIND CADAVEROUS WITH YOUR CURRENT SENSORS, CAN YOU MAKE NEW ONES? LAUNCH THEM INTO SPACE, SATELLITES THAT CAN SHOOT LASERS? OR ROBOTS THAT--

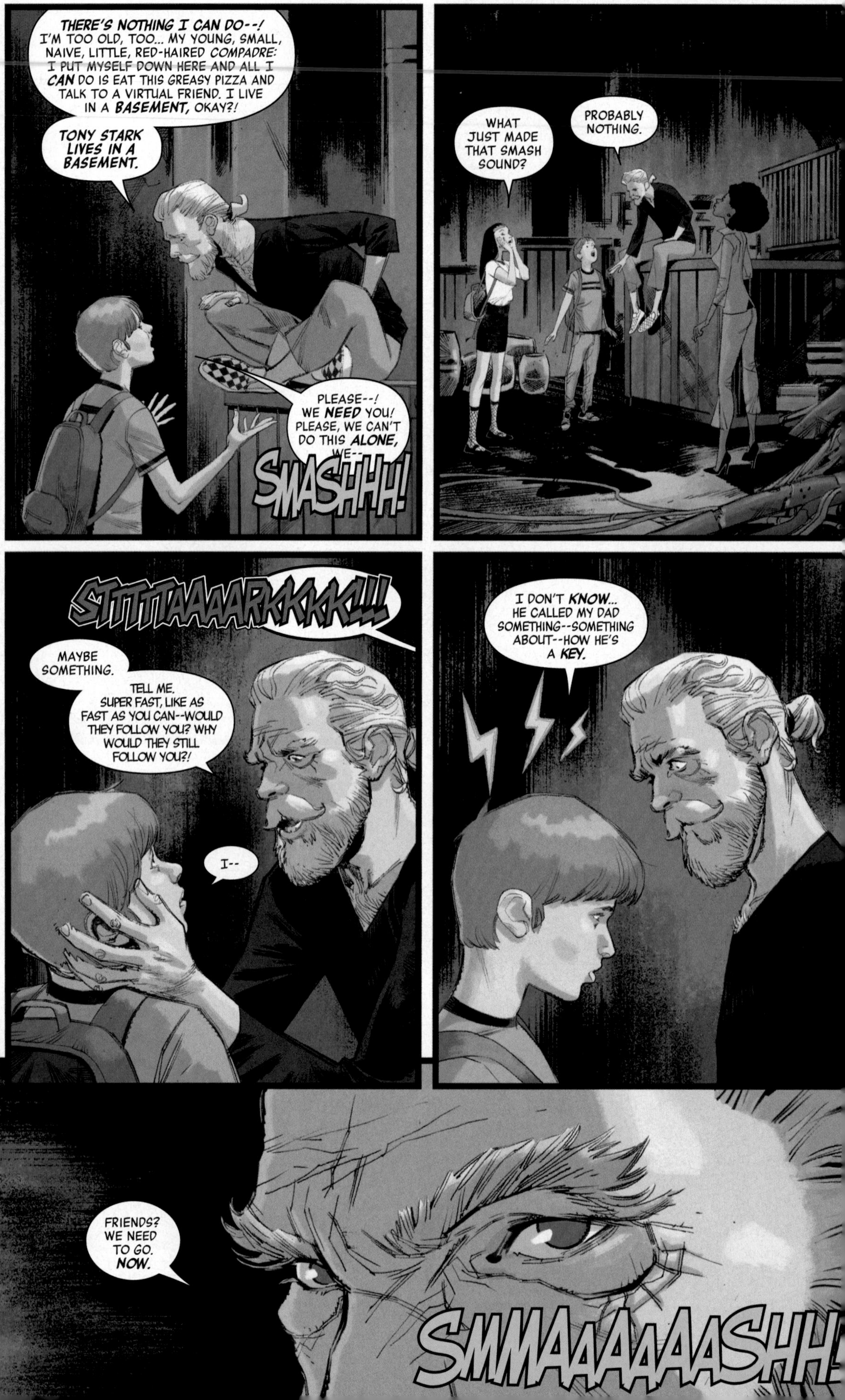
THERE'S NOTHING I CAN DO--! I'M TOO OLD, TOO... MY YOUNG, SMALL, NAIVE, LITTLE, RED-HAIRED COMPADRE: I PUT MYSELF DOWN HERE AND ALL I CAN DO IS EAT THIS GREASY PIZZA AND TALK TO A VIRTUAL FRIEND. I LIVE IN A BASEMENT, OKAY?!
TONY STARK LIVES IN A BASEMENT.
PLEASE--! WE NEED YOU! PLEASE, WE CAN'T DO THIS ALONE, WE--
SMASHHH!
WHAT JUST MADE THAT SMASH SOUND?
PROBABLY NOTHING.
STTTTTAAAARKKKK!!!!
MAYBE SOMETHING.
TELL ME. SUPER FAST, LIKE AS FAST AS YOU CAN--WOULD THEY FOLLOW YOU? WHY WOULD THEY STILL FOLLOW YOU?!
I--
I DON'T KNOW... HE CALLED MY DAD SOMETHING--SOMETHING ABOUT--HOW HE'S A KEY.
FRIENDS? WE NEED TO GO. NOW.
SMMAAAAAAASHH!

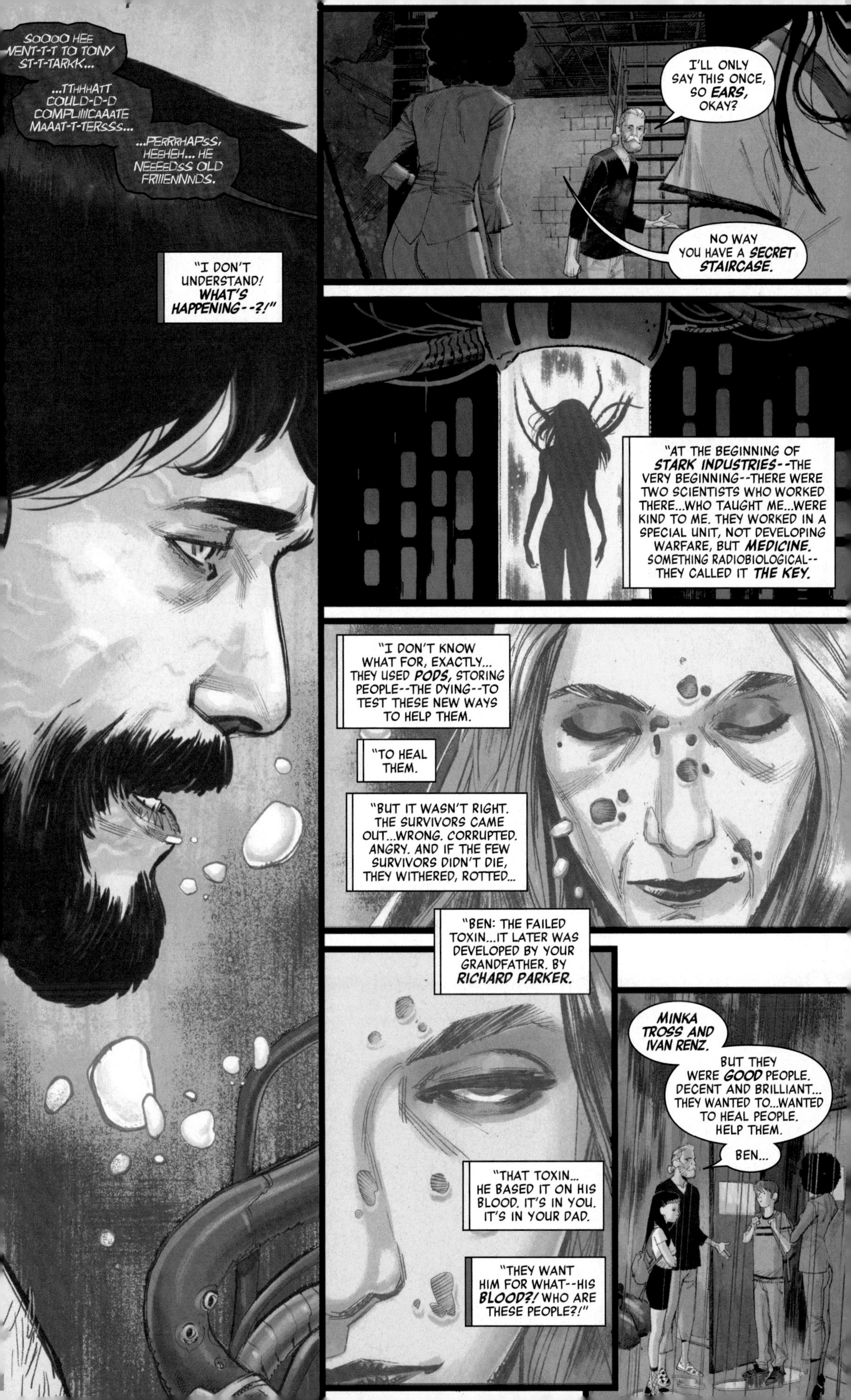
SOOOO HEE WENT-T-T TO TONY ST-T-TARKK...
...TTHHHATT COULD-D-D COMPLIIIICAAATE MAAAT-T-TERSSS...
...PERRRHAPSS, HEEHEH... HE NEEEEDSS OLD FRIIIENNNDS.
"I DON'T UNDERSTAND! WHAT'S HAPPENING--?!"
I'LL ONLY SAY THIS ONCE, SO EARS, OKAY?
NO WAY YOU HAVE A SECRET STAIRCASE.
"AT THE BEGINNING OF STARK INDUSTRIES--THE VERY BEGINNING--THERE WERE TWO SCIENTISTS WHO WORKED THERE...WHO TAUGHT ME...WERE KIND TO ME. THEY WORKED IN A SPECIAL UNIT, NOT DEVELOPING WARFARE, BUT MEDICINE. SOMETHING RADIOBIOLOGICAL--THEY CALLED IT THE KEY.
"I DON'T KNOW WHAT FOR, EXACTLY... THEY USED PODS, STORING PEOPLE--THE DYING--TO TEST THESE NEW WAYS TO HELP THEM.
"TO HEAL THEM.
"BUT IT WASN'T RIGHT. THE SURVIVORS CAME OUT...WRONG. CORRUPTED. ANGRY. AND IF THE FEW SURVIVORS DIDN'T DIE, THEY WITHERED, ROTTED...
"BEN: THE FAILED TOXIN...IT LATER WAS DEVELOPED BY YOUR GRANDFATHER. BY RICHARD PARKER.
MINKA TROSS AND IVAN RENZ.
BUT THEY WERE GOOD PEOPLE. DECENT AND BRILLIANT... THEY WANTED TO...WANTED TO HEAL PEOPLE. HELP THEM.
BEN...
"THAT TOXIN... HE BASED IT ON HIS BLOOD. IT'S IN YOU. IT'S IN YOUR DAD.
"THEY WANT HIM FOR WHAT--HIS BLOOD?! WHO ARE THESE PEOPLE?!"

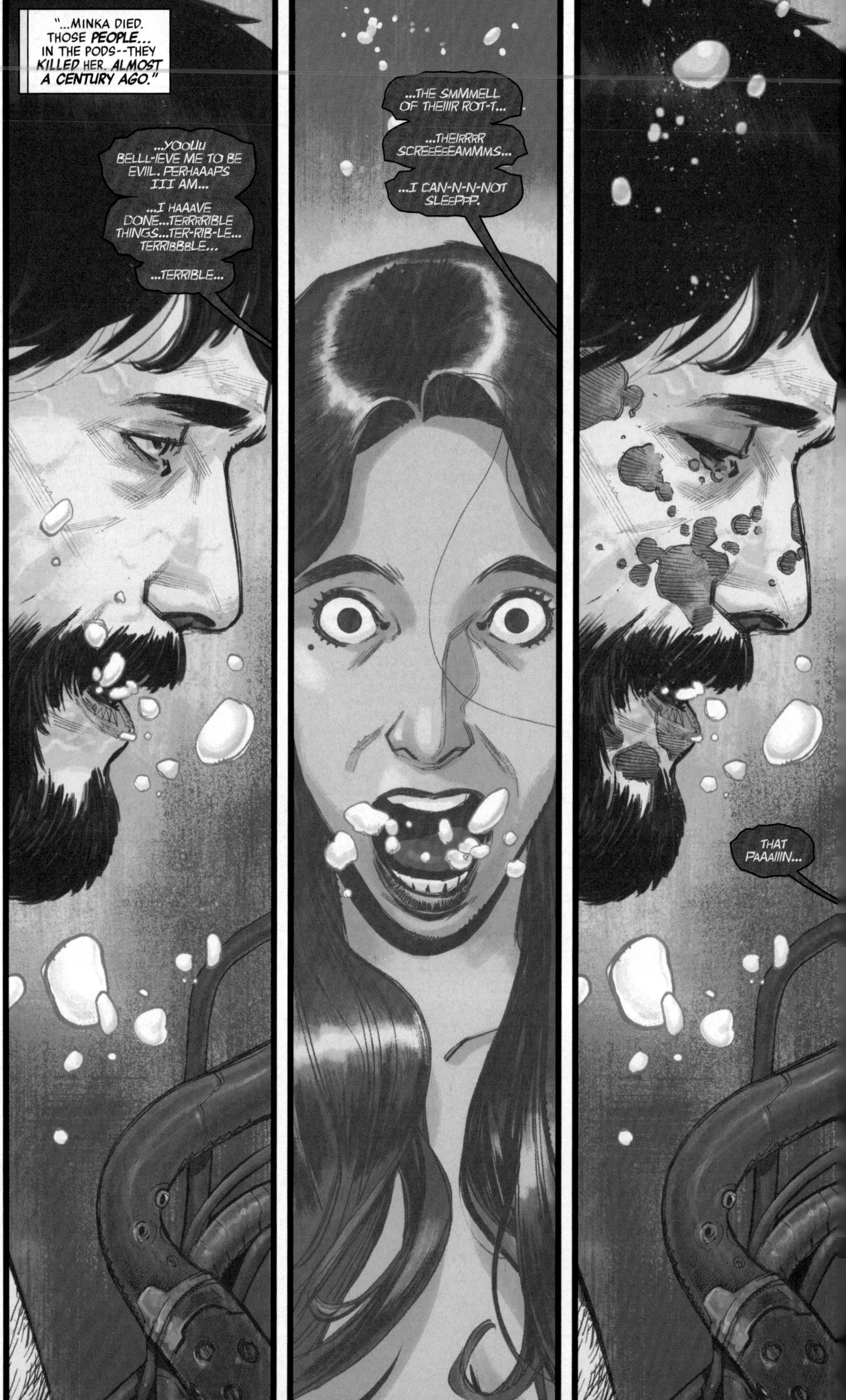
"...MINKA DIED. THOSE PEOPLE... IN THE PODS--THEY KILLED HER. ALMOST A CENTURY AGO."
...YOOUU BELLL-IEVE ME TO BE EVIIL. PERHAAAPS III AM...
...I HAAAVE DONE...TERRRRIBLE THINGS...TER-RIB-LE... TERRIBBBLE...
...TERRIBLE...
...THE SMMMELL OF THEIIIR ROT-T...
...THEIRRRR SCREEEEEAMMMS...
...I CAN-N-N-NOT SLEEPPP.
THAT PAAAIIIN...

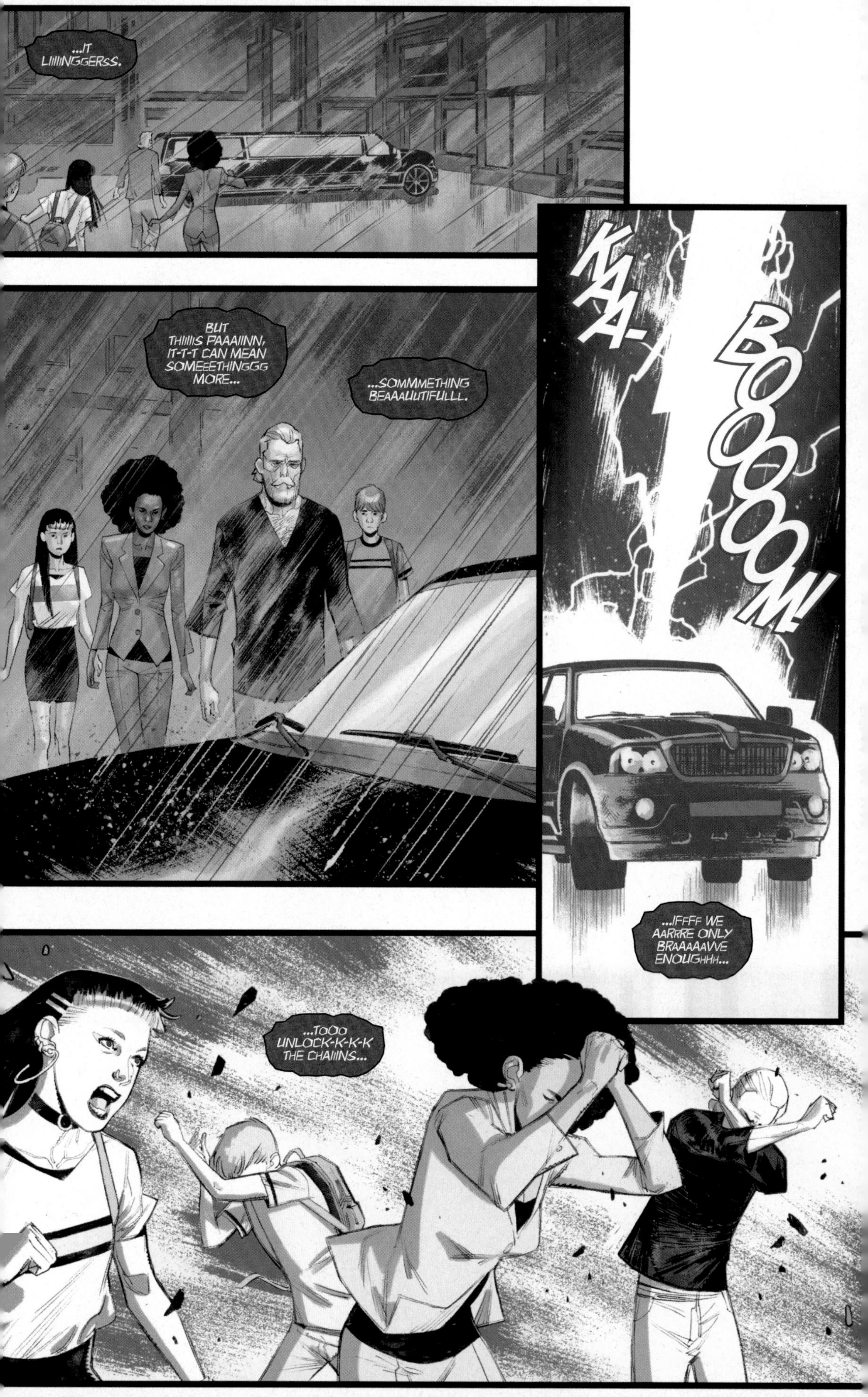
...IT LIIIIINGGERSS.
BUT THIIIIS PAAAIINN, IT-T-T CAN MEAN SOMEEETHINGGG MORE...
...SOMMMETHING BEAAAUUTIFULLL.
KAA-
BOOOOOM!
...IFFFF WE AARRRE ONLY BRAAAAAVVE ENOUGHHH...
...TOOO UNLOCK-K-K-K THE CHAIIINS...

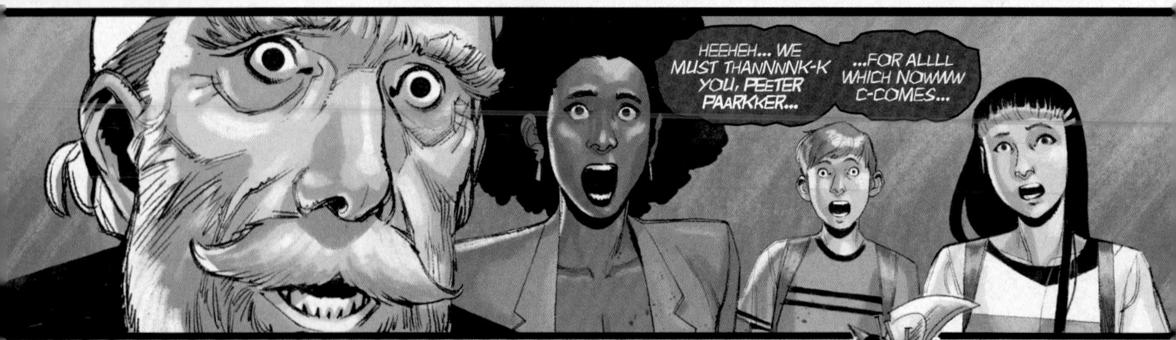
HEEHEH... WE MUST THANNNNK-K YOU, PEETER PAARKKER...
...FOR ALLLL WHICH NOWWW C-COMES...

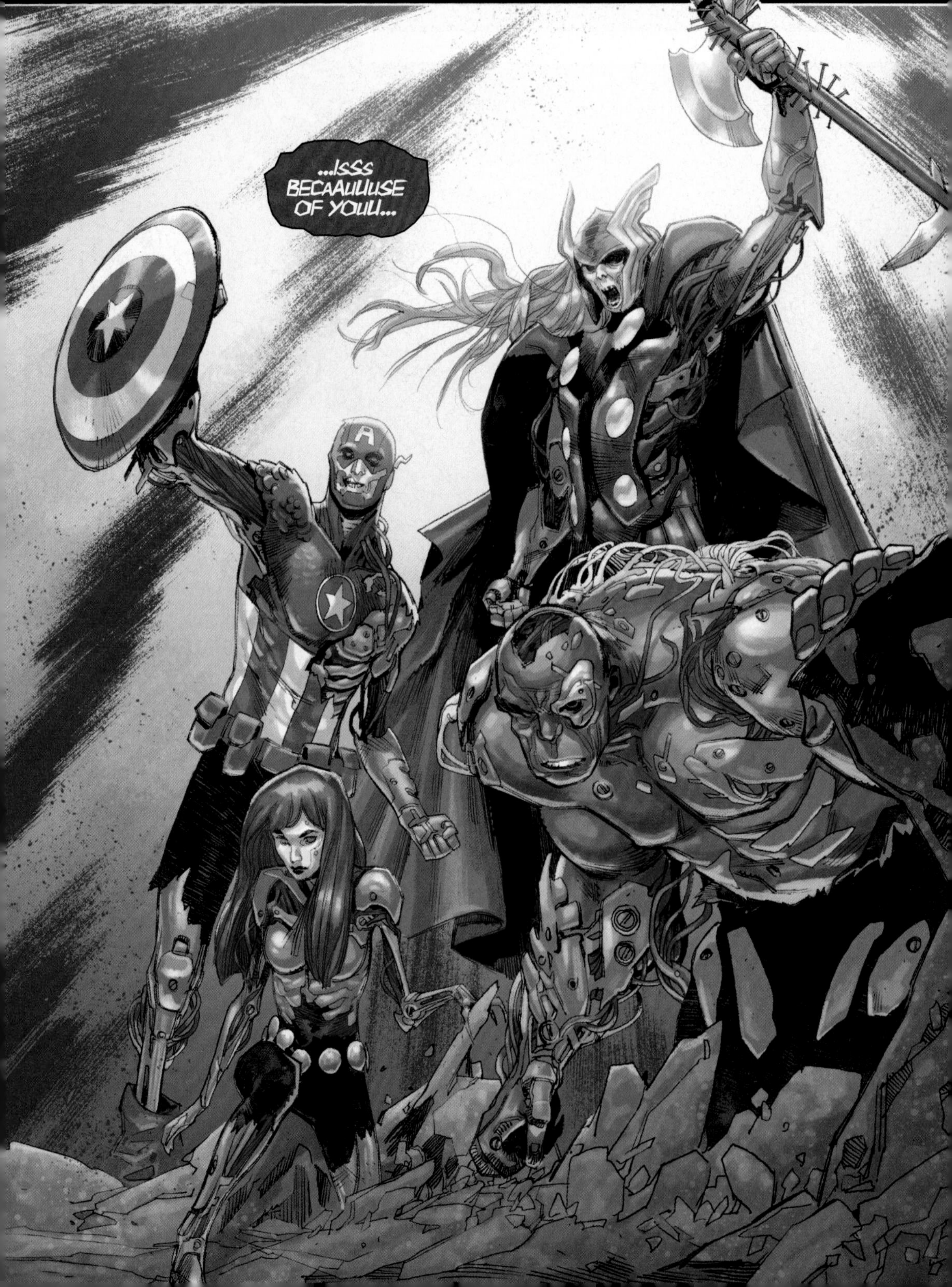
...ISSS BECAAUUUSE OF YOUU...

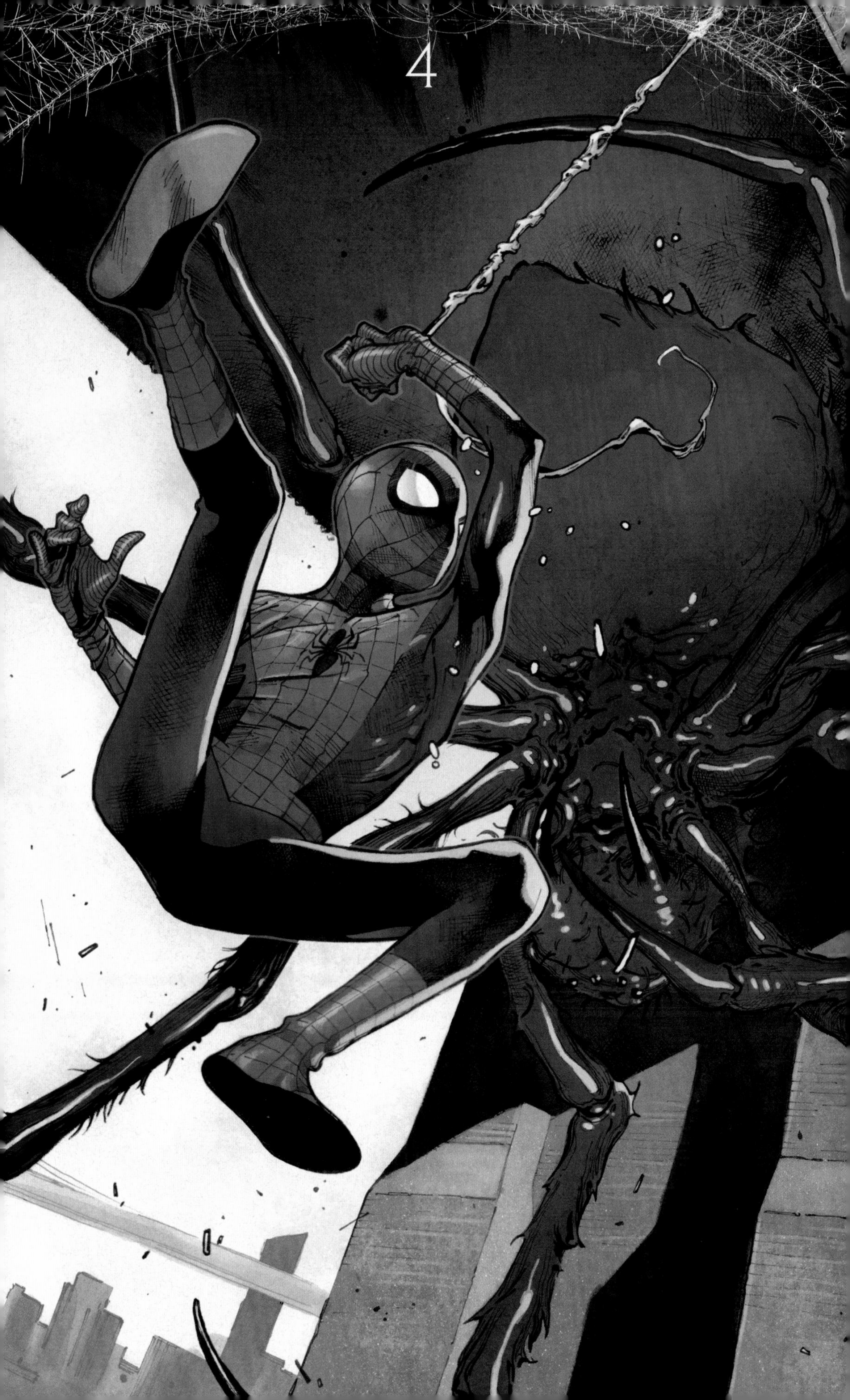
4

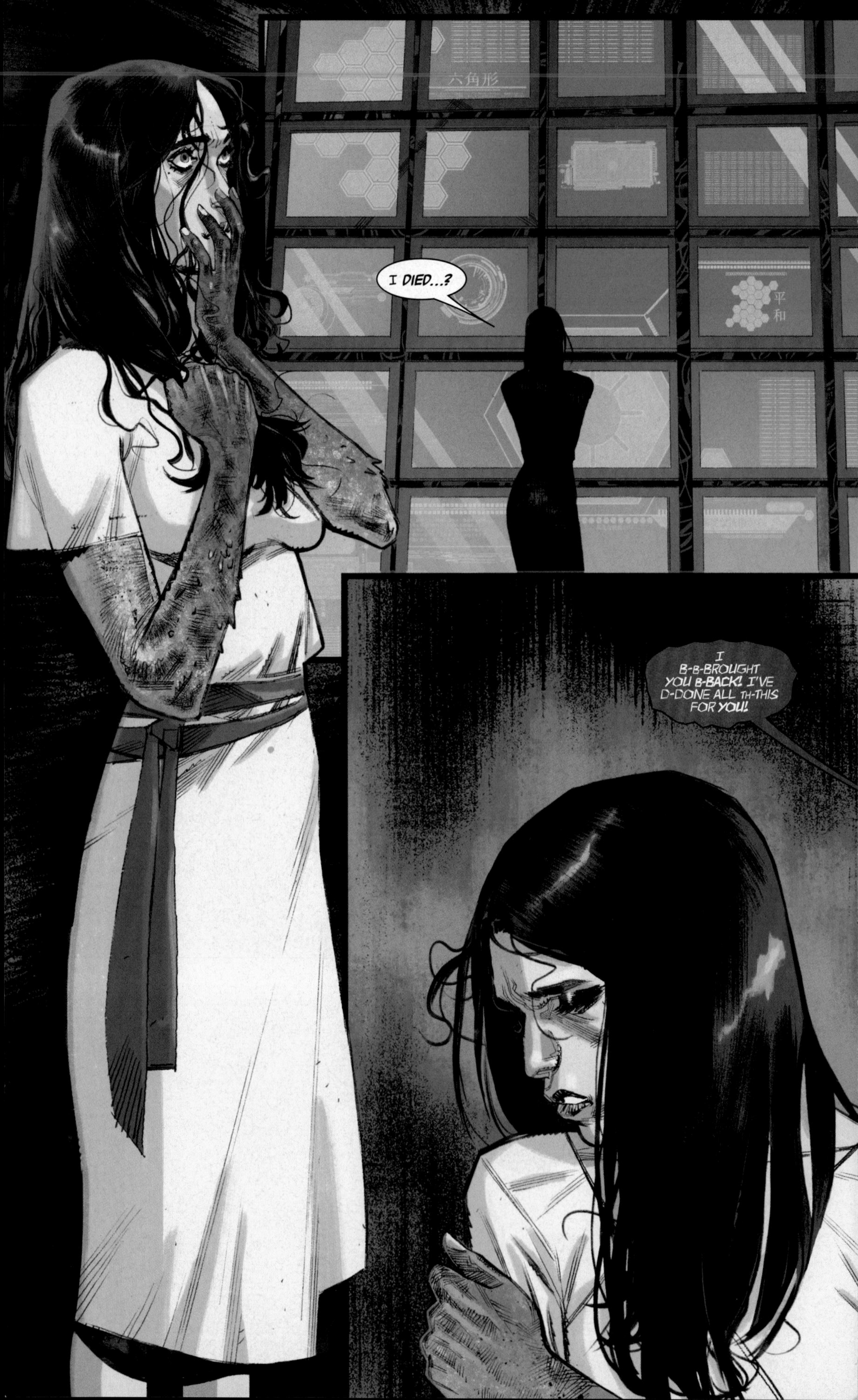
六角形
I DIED...?
平和
I B-B-BROUGHT YOU B-BACK! I'VE D-DONE ALL TH-THIS FOR YOU!

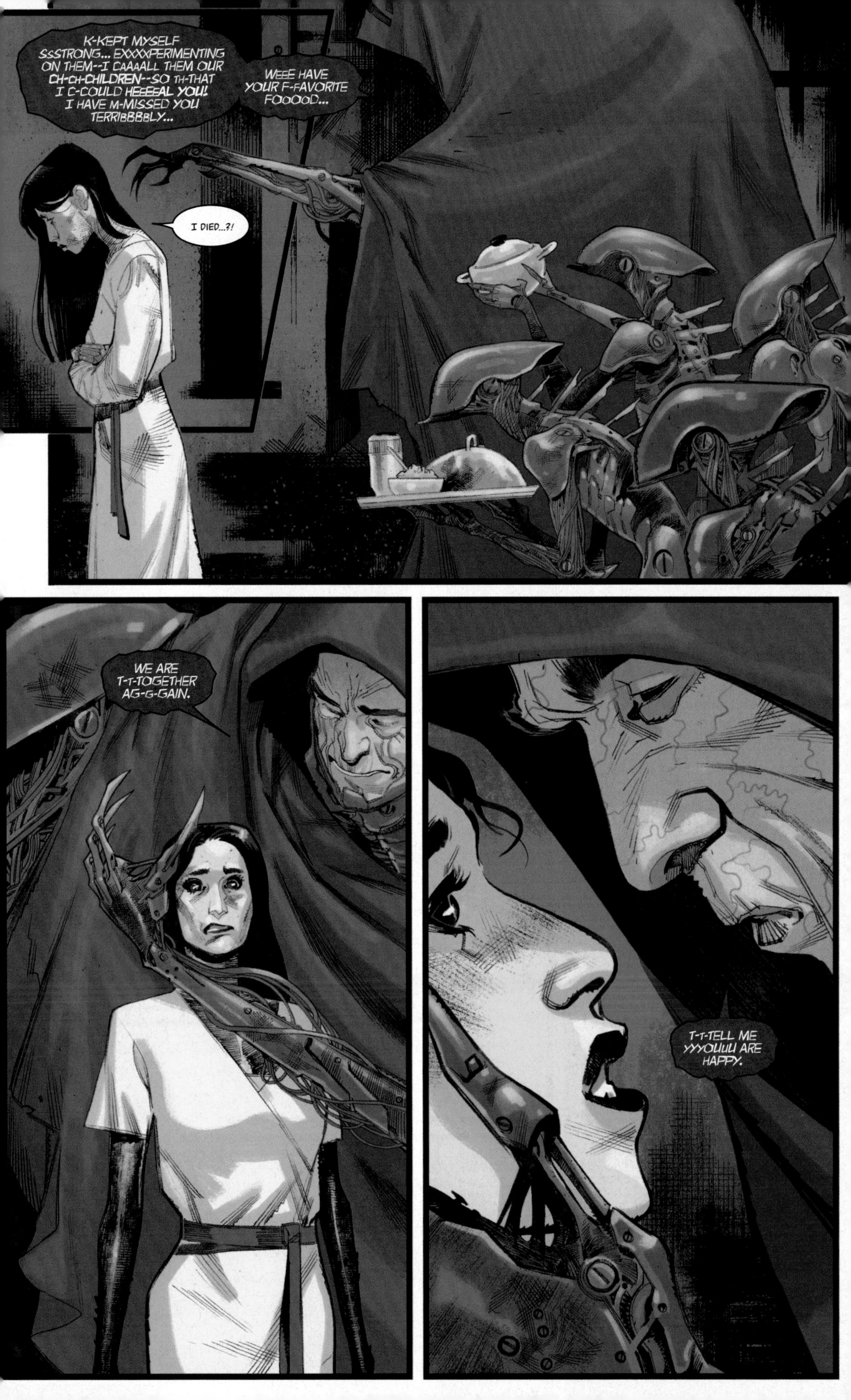
K-KEPT MYSELF SSSTRONG... EXXXXPERIMENTING ON THEM--I CAAAALL THEM OUR CH-CH-CHILDREN--SO TH-THAT I C-COULD HEEEEAL YOU! I HAVE M-MISSED YOU TERRIBBBBLY...
WEEE HAVE YOUR F-FAVORITE FOOOOOD...
I DIED...?!
WE ARE T-T-TOGETHER AG-G-GAIN.
T-T-TELL ME YYYOUUU ARE HAPPY.

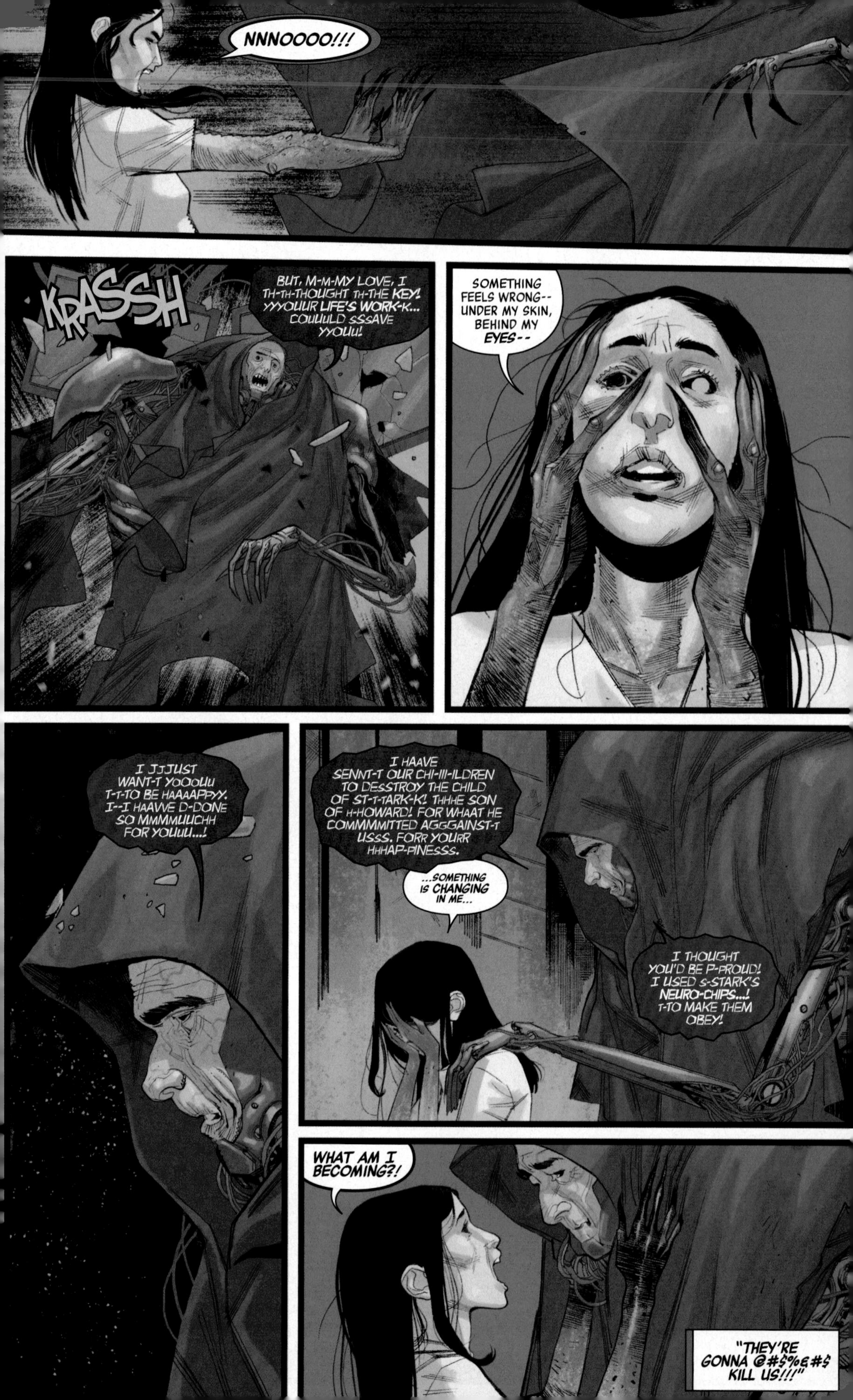
NNNOOOO!!!
KRASSH
BUT, M-M-MY LOVE, I TH-TH-THOUGHT TH-THE KEY! YYYOUUR LIFE'S WORK-K... COUUULD SSSAVE YYOUU!
SOMETHING FEELS WRONG-- UNDER MY SKIN, BEHIND MY EYES--
I JJJUST WANT-T YOOOUU T-T-TO BE HAAAAPPYY. I--I HAAVVE D-DONE SO MMMMUUCHH FOR YOUUU...!
I HAAVE SENNT-T OUR CHI-III-ILDREN TO DESSTROY THE CHILD OF ST-T-TARK-K! THHE SON OF H-HOWARD! FOR WHAAT HE COMMMMITTED AGGGAINST-T USSS. FORR YOURR HHHAP-PINESSS.
...SOMETHING IS CHANGING IN ME...
I THOUGHT YOU'D BE P-PROUD! I USED S-STARK'S NEURO-CHIPS...! T-TO MAKE THEM OBEY!
WHAT AM I BECOMING?!
"THEY'RE GONNA @#$%&#$ KILL US!!!"

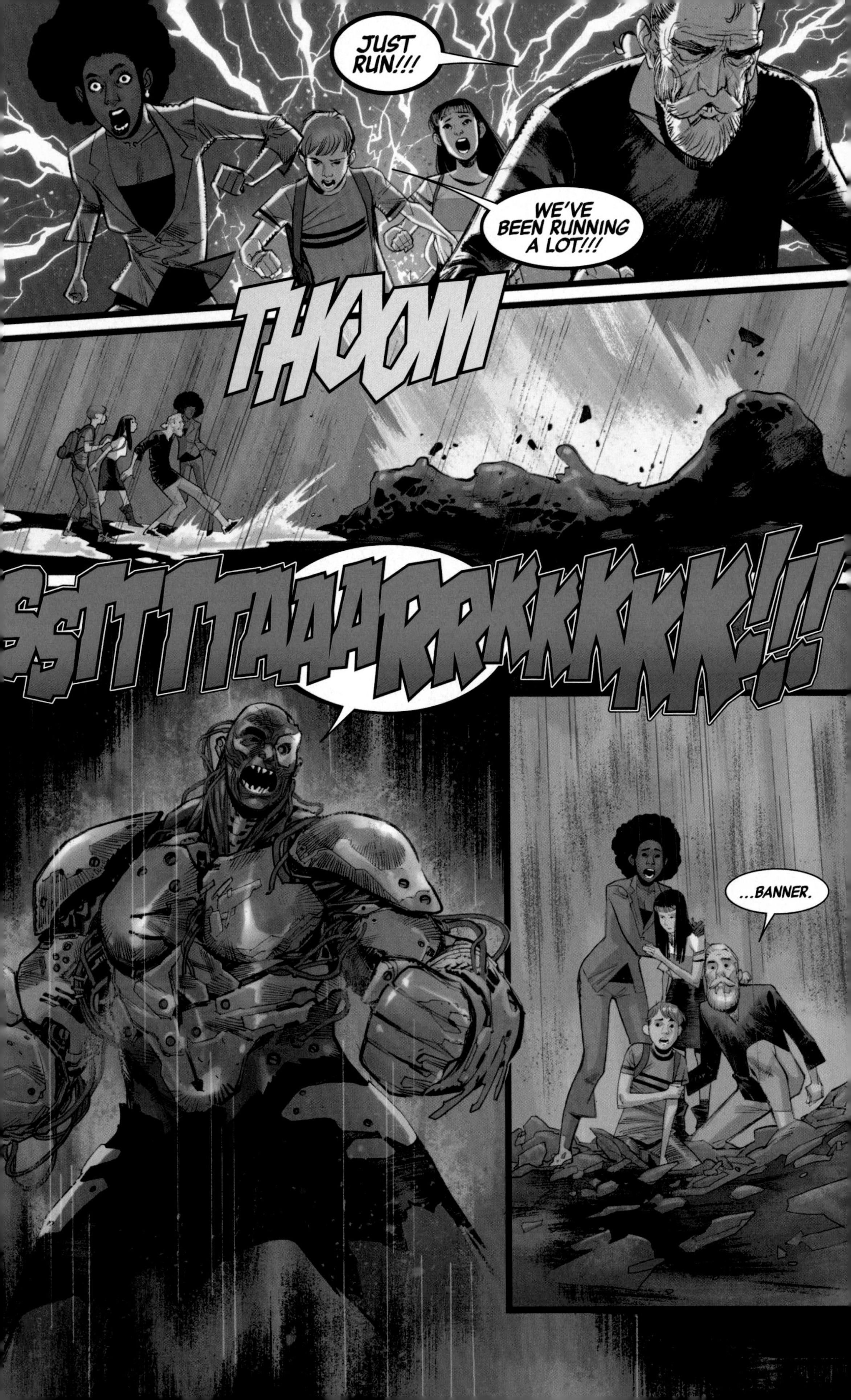
JUST RUN!!!
WE'VE BEEN RUNNING A LOT!!!
THOOM
SSTTTTAAARRRKKKKKKK!!!
...BANNER.

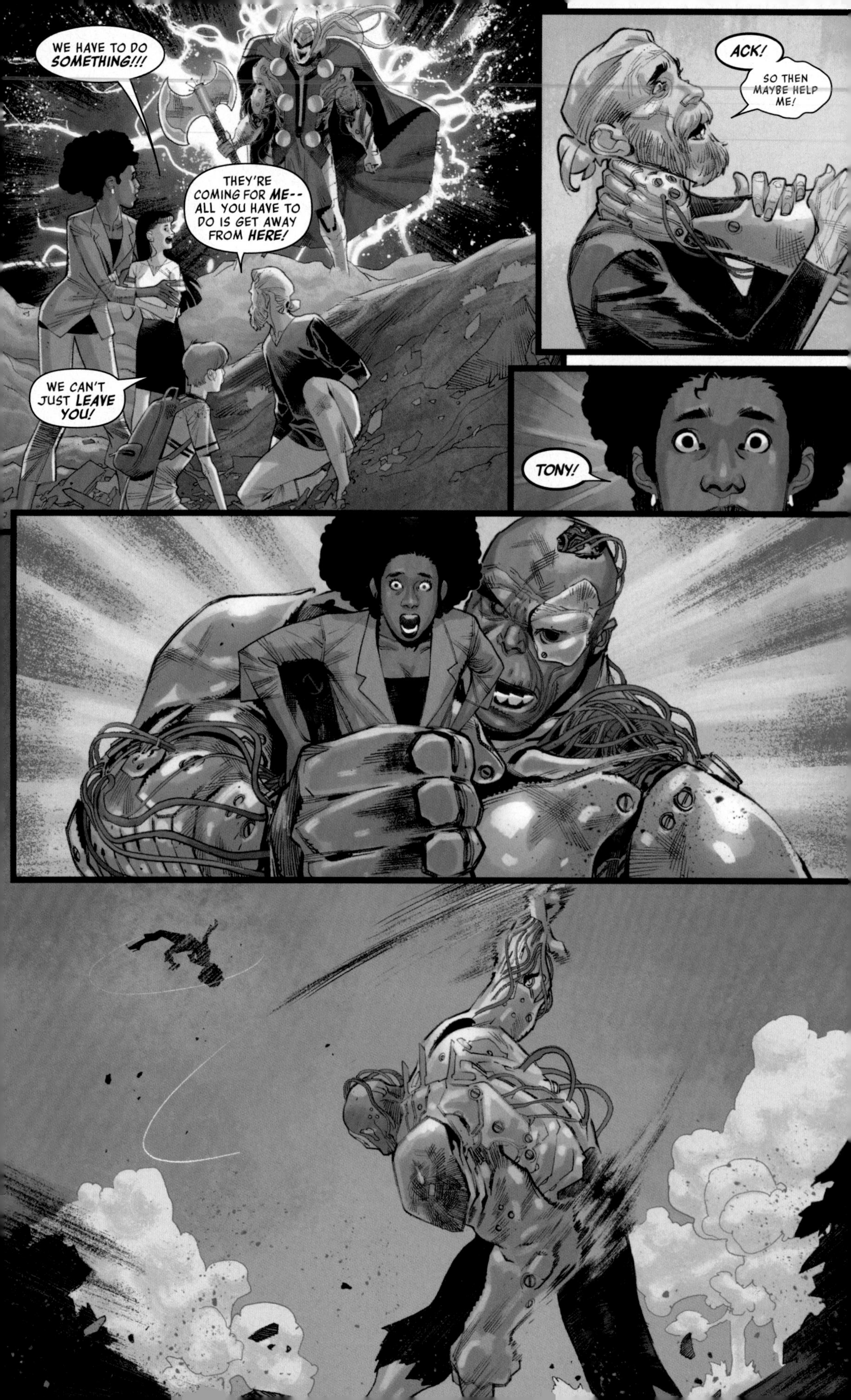
WE HAVE TO DO SOMETHING!!!
THEY'RE COMING FOR ME-- ALL YOU HAVE TO DO IS GET AWAY FROM HERE!
WE CAN'T JUST LEAVE YOU!
ACK!
SO THEN MAYBE HELP ME!
TONY!

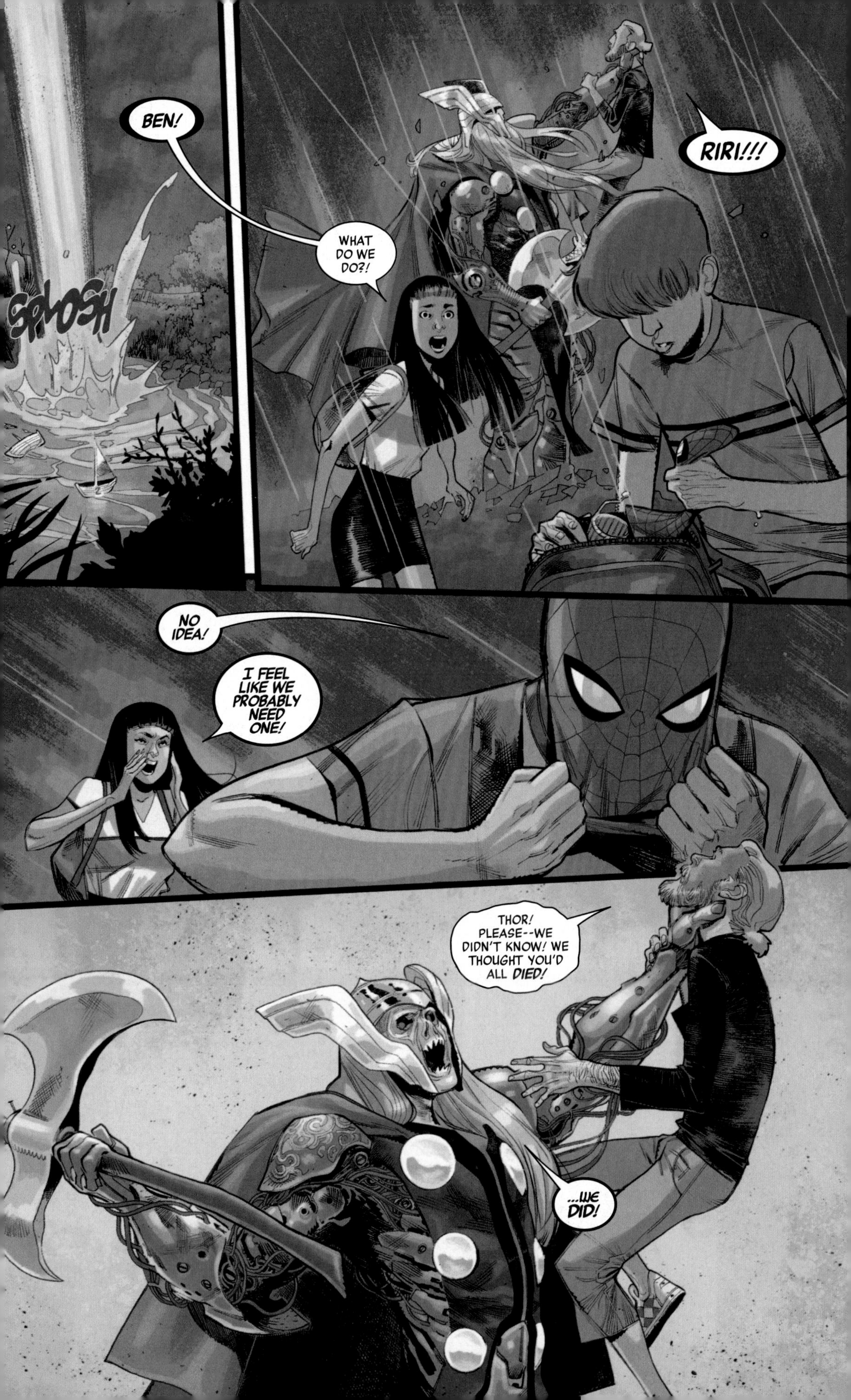
SPLOSH
BEN!
WHAT DO WE DO?!
RIRI!!!
NO IDEA!
I FEEL LIKE WE PROBABLY NEED ONE!
THOR! PLEASE--WE DIDN'T KNOW! WE THOUGHT YOU'D ALL DIED!
...WE DID!

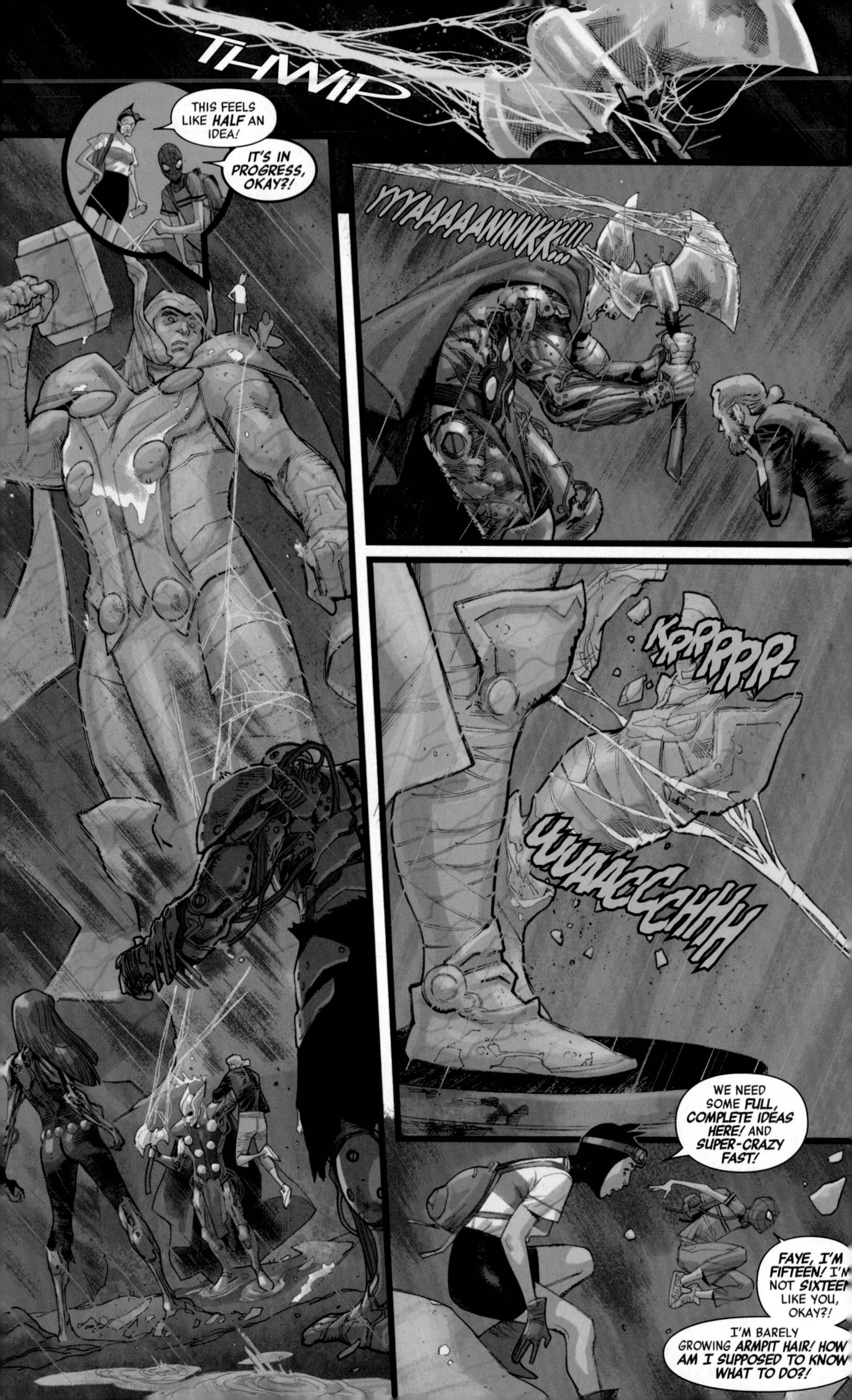
THWIP
THIS FEELS LIKE HALF AN IDEA!
IT'S IN PROGRESS, OKAY?!
YYYAAAAANNNKK!!!
KRRRRR
WWAACCHHH
WE NEED SOME FULL, COMPLETE IDEAS HERE! AND SUPER-CRAZY FAST!
FAYE, I'M FIFTEEN! I'M NOT SIXTEEN LIKE YOU, OKAY?!
I'M BARELY GROWING ARMPIT HAIR! HOW AM I SUPPOSED TO KNOW WHAT TO DO?!

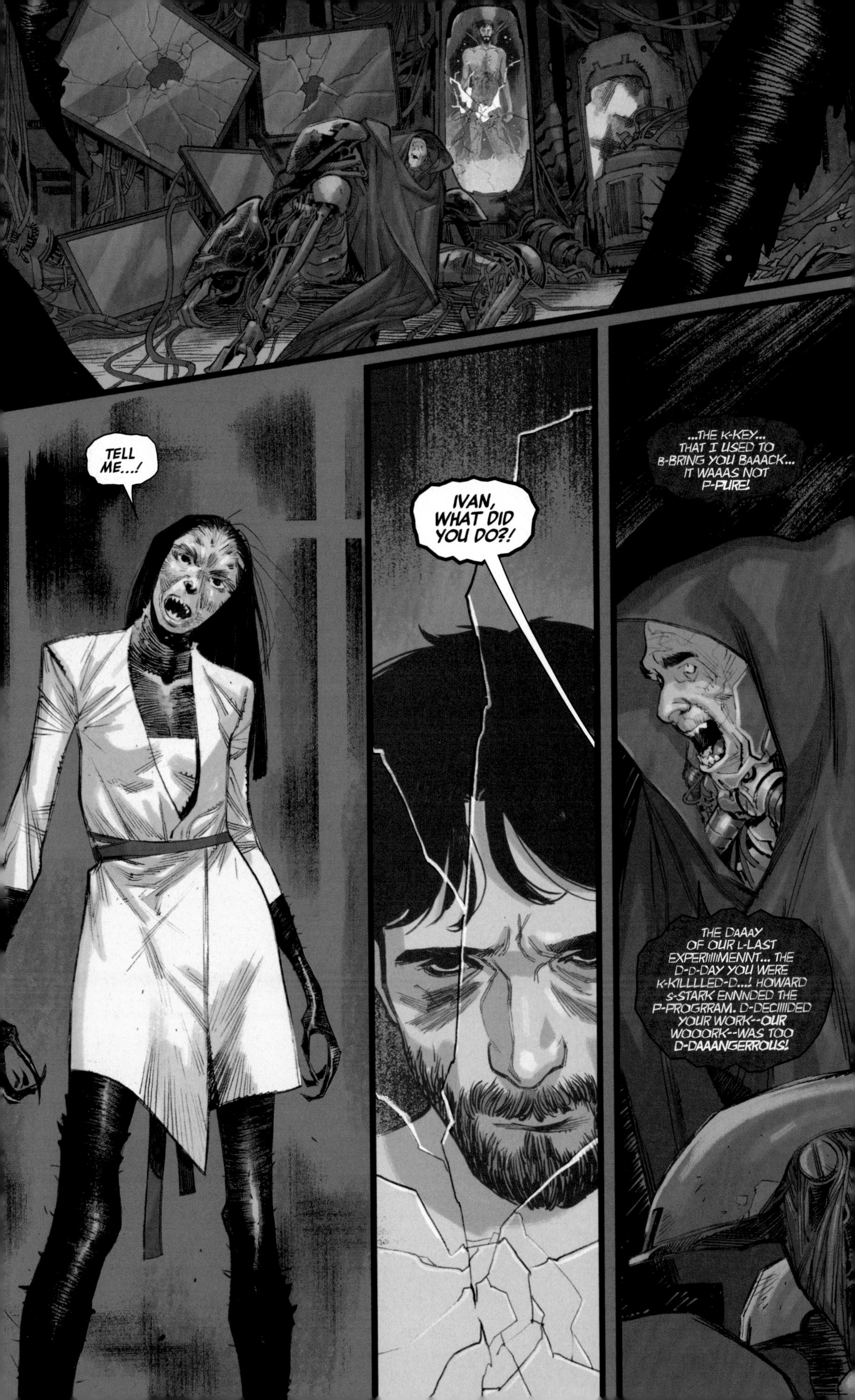
TELL ME...!
IVAN, WHAT DID YOU DO?!
...THE K-KEY... THAT I USED TO B-BRING YOU BAAACK... IT WAAAS NOT P-PURE!
THE DAAAY OF OUR L-LAST EXPERIIIIIMENNT... THE D-D-DAY YOU WERE K-KILLLLED-D...! HOWARD S-STARK ENNNDED THE P-PROGRAM. D-DECIIIIDED YOUR WORK--OUR WOOORK--WAS TOO D-DAAANGERROUS!

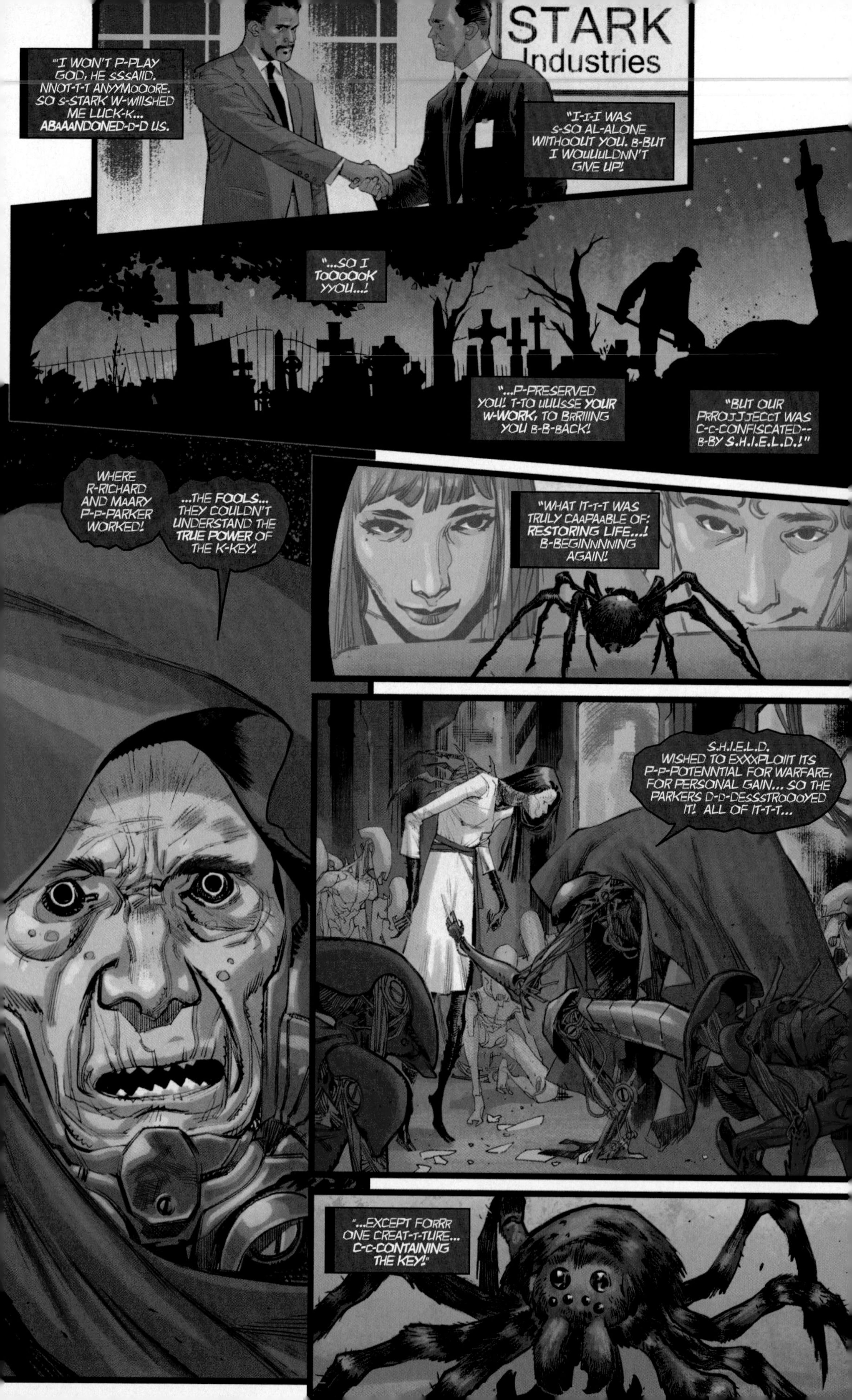
STARK Industries
"I WON'T P-PLAY GOD, HE SSSAIID. NNOT-T-T ANYYMOOORE. SO S-STARK W-WIIISHED ME LUCK-K... ABAAANDONED-D-D US.
"I-I-I WAS S-SO AL-ALONE WITHOOUT YOU. B-BUT I WOUUULDNN'T GIVE UP!
"...SO I TOOOOOK YYOU...!
"...P-PRESERVED YOU! T-TO UUUSSE YOUR W-WORK, TO BRRIIING YOU B-B-BACK!
"BUT OUR PRROJJJECCT WAS C-C-CONFISCATED-- B-BY S.H.I.E.L.D.!"
WHERE R-RICHARD AND MAARY P-P-PARKER WORKED!
...THE FOOLS... THEY COULDN'T UNDERSTAND THE TRUE POWER OF THE K-KEY!
"WHAT IT-T-T WAS TRULY CAAPAABLE OF: RESTORING LIFE...! B-BEGINNNNING AGAIN!
S.H.I.E.L.D. WISHED TO EXXXPLOIIT ITS P-P-POTENNTIAL FOR WARFARE, FOR PERSONAL GAIN... SO THE PARKERS D-D-DESSSTROOOYED IT! ALL OF IT-T-T...
"...EXCEPT FORRR ONE CREAT-T-TURE... C-C-CONTAINING THE KEY!"

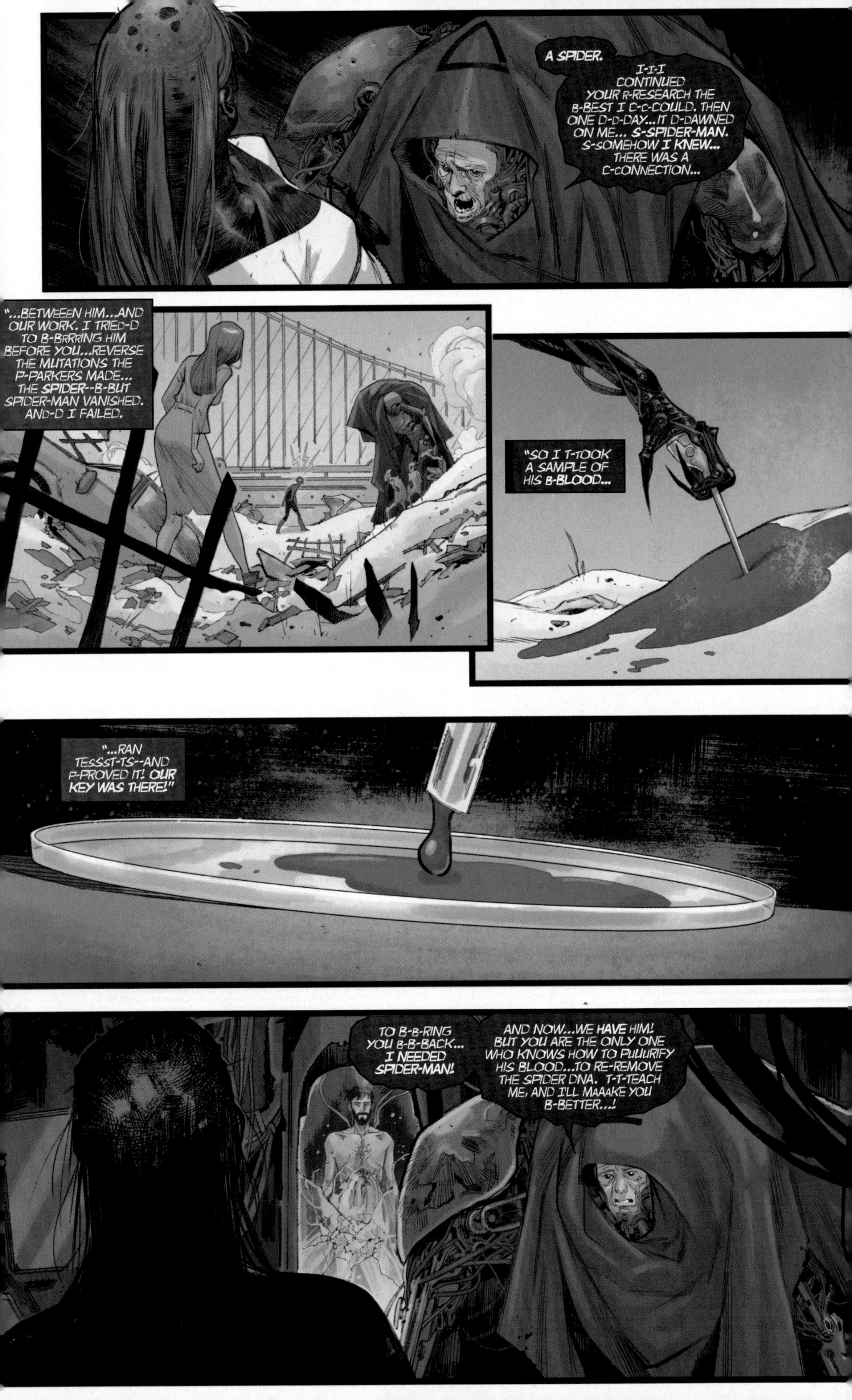
A SPIDER.
I-I-I CONTINUED YOUR R-RESEARCH THE B-BEST I C-C-COULD. THEN ONE D-D-DAY...IT D-DAWNED ON ME... S-SPIDER-MAN. S-SOMEHOW I KNEW... THERE WAS A C-CONNECTION...
"...BETWEEEN HIM...AND OUR WORK. I TRIED-D TO B-BRRRING HIM BEFORE YOU...REVERSE THE MUTATIONS THE P-PARKERS MADE... THE SPIDER--B-BUT SPIDER-MAN VANISHED. AND-D I FAILED.
"SO I T-TOOK A SAMPLE OF HIS B-BLOOD...
"...RAN TESSST-TS--AND P-PROVED IT! OUR KEY WAS THERE!"
TO B-B-RING YOU B-B-BACK... I NEEDED SPIDER-MAN!
AND NOW...WE HAVE HIM! BUT YOU ARE THE ONLY ONE WHO KNOWS HOW TO PUUURIFY HIS BLOOD...TO RE-REMOVE THE SPIDER DNA. T-T-TEACH ME, AND I'LL MAAAKE YOU B-BETTER...!

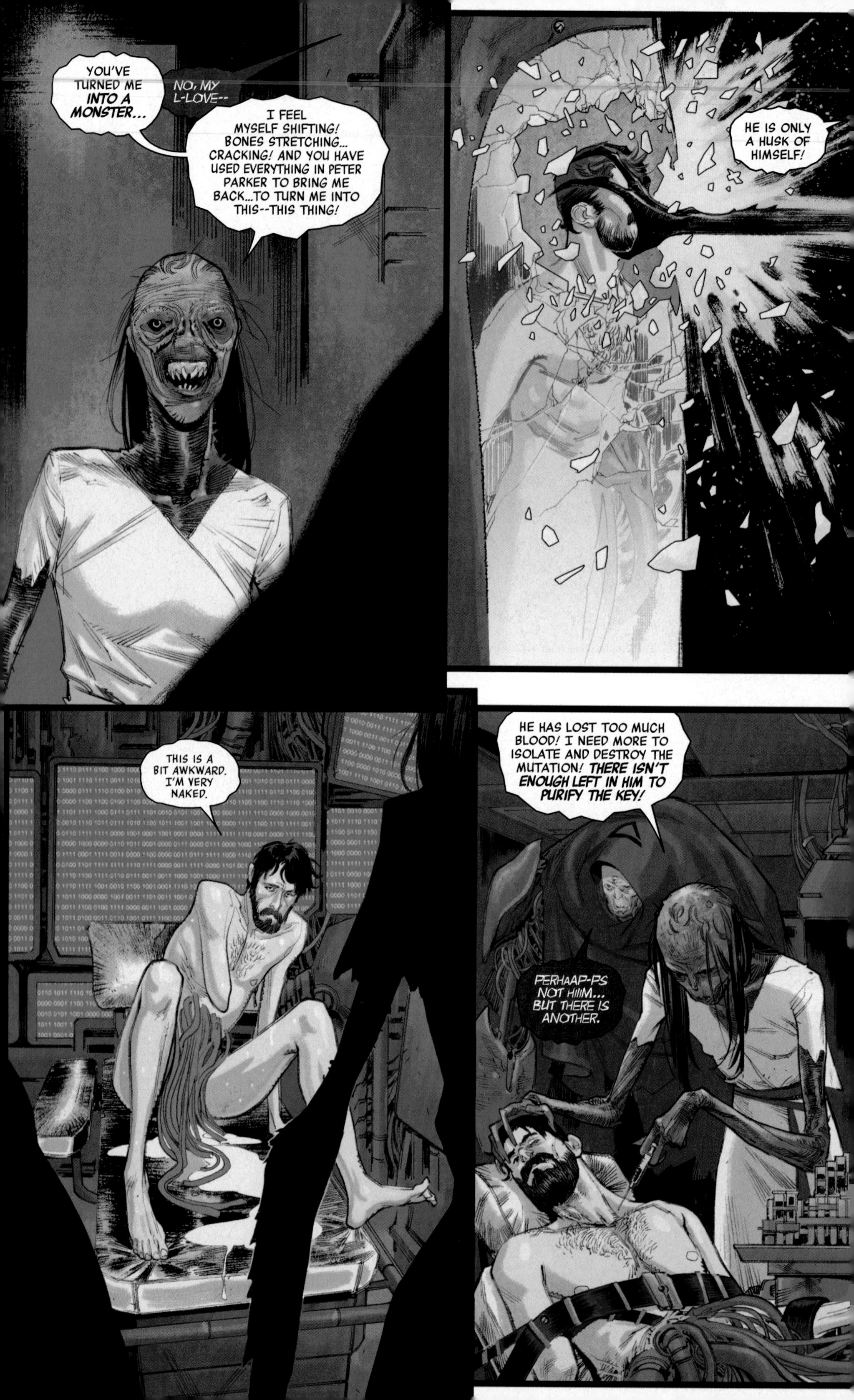
YOU'VE TURNED ME INTO A MONSTER...
NO, MY L-LOVE--
I FEEL MYSELF SHIFTING! BONES STRETCHING... CRACKING! AND YOU HAVE USED EVERYTHING IN PETER PARKER TO BRING ME BACK...TO TURN ME INTO THIS--THIS THING!
HE IS ONLY A HUSK OF HIMSELF!
THIS IS A BIT AWKWARD. I'M VERY NAKED.
HE HAS LOST TOO MUCH BLOOD! I NEED MORE TO ISOLATE AND DESTROY THE MUTATION! THERE ISN'T ENOUGH LEFT IN HIM TO PURIFY THE KEY!
PERHAAP-PS NOT HIIIM... BUT THERE IS ANOTHER.

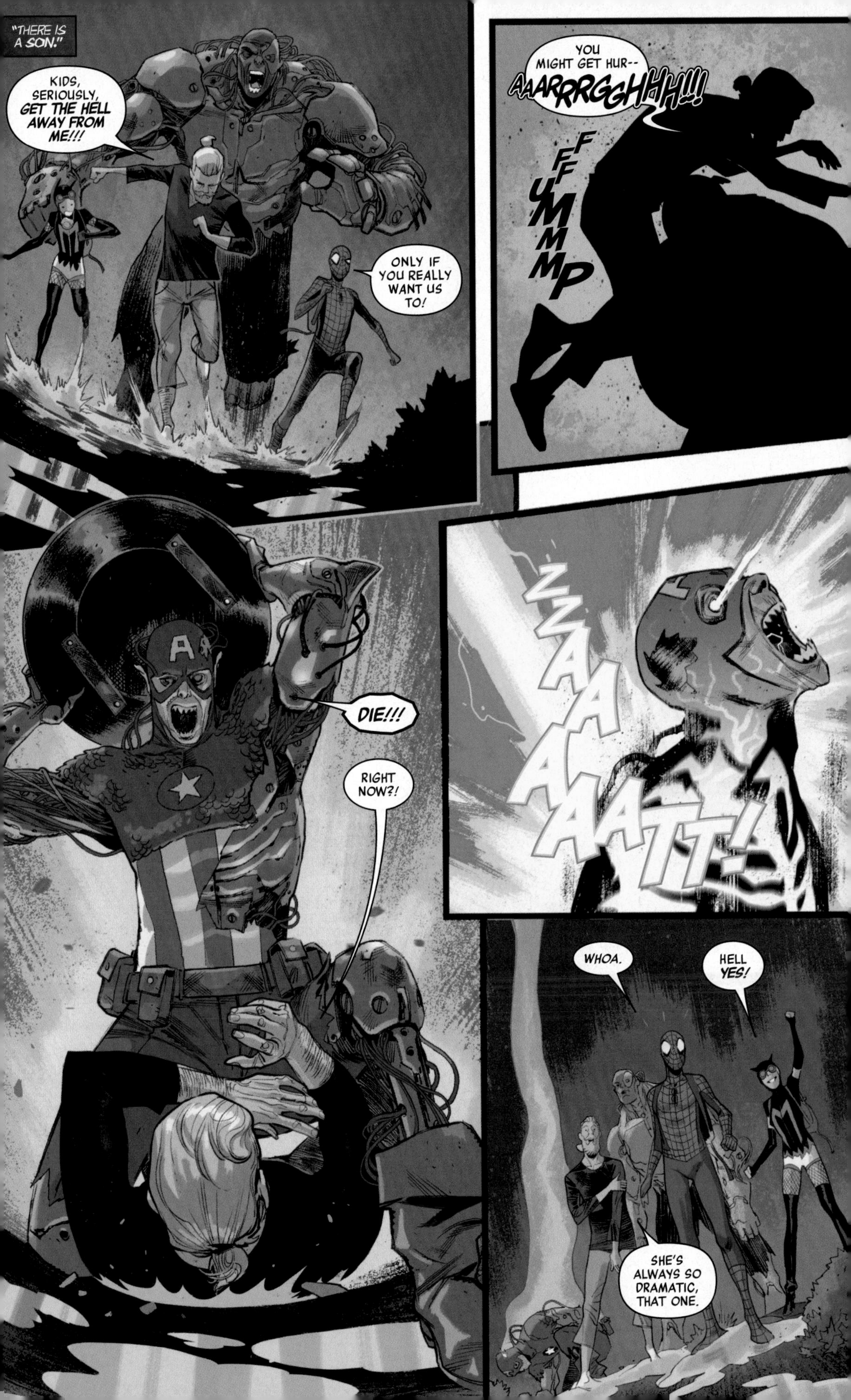
"THERE IS A SON."
KIDS, SERIOUSLY, GET THE HELL AWAY FROM ME!!!
ONLY IF YOU REALLY WANT US TO!
YOU MIGHT GET HUR--
AAARRRGGHHH!!!
FFFUMMMP
DIE!!!
RIGHT NOW?!
ZZAAAAAATT!
WHOA.
HELL YES!
SHE'S ALWAYS SO DRAMATIC, THAT ONE.

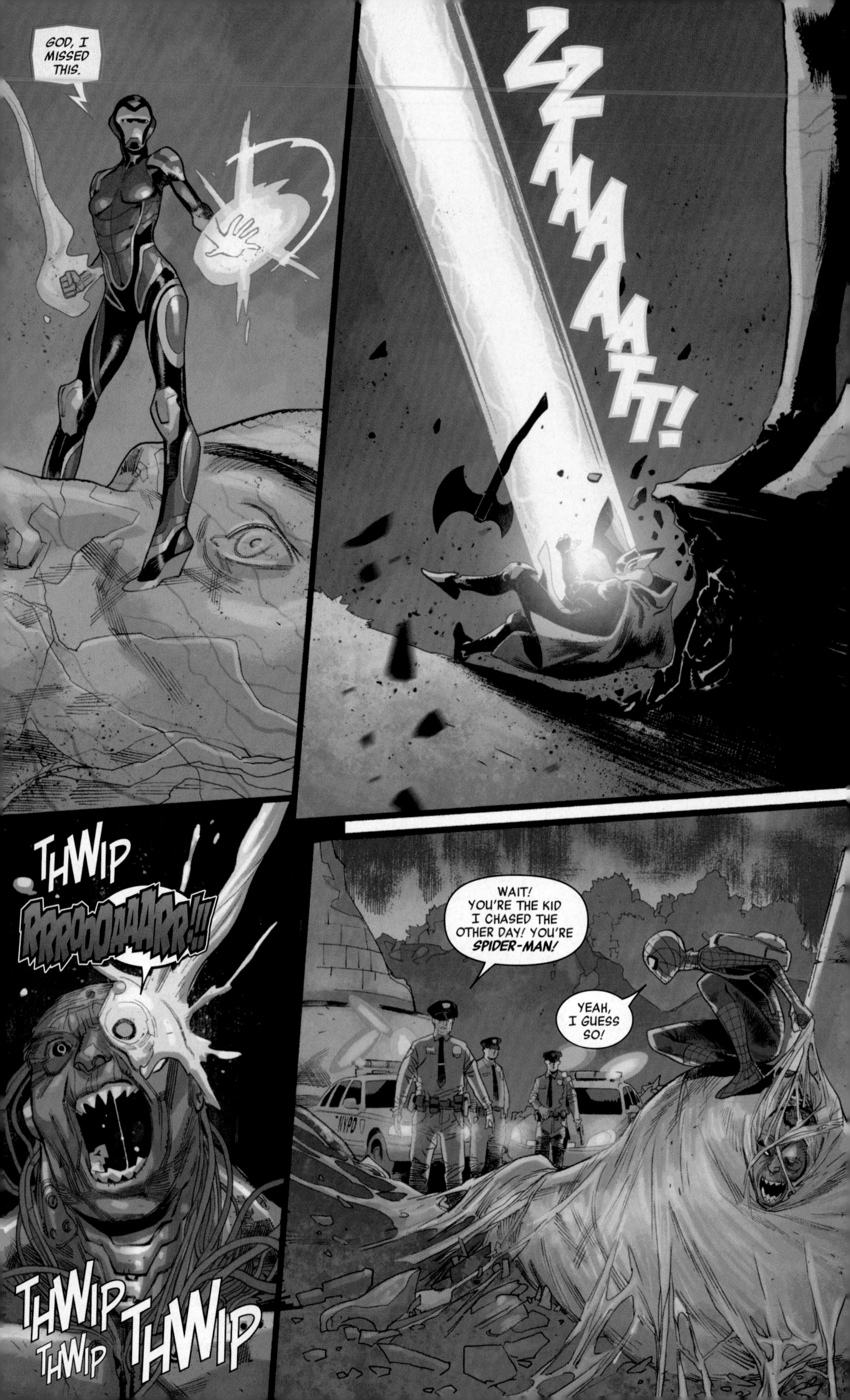
GOD, I MISSED THIS.
ZZZAAAAAAAFFT!
THWIP
RRROOOAAARR!!!
THWIP THWIP THWIP
WAIT! YOU'RE THE KID I CHASED THE OTHER DAY! YOU'RE SPIDER-MAN!
YEAH, I GUESS SO!
NYPD

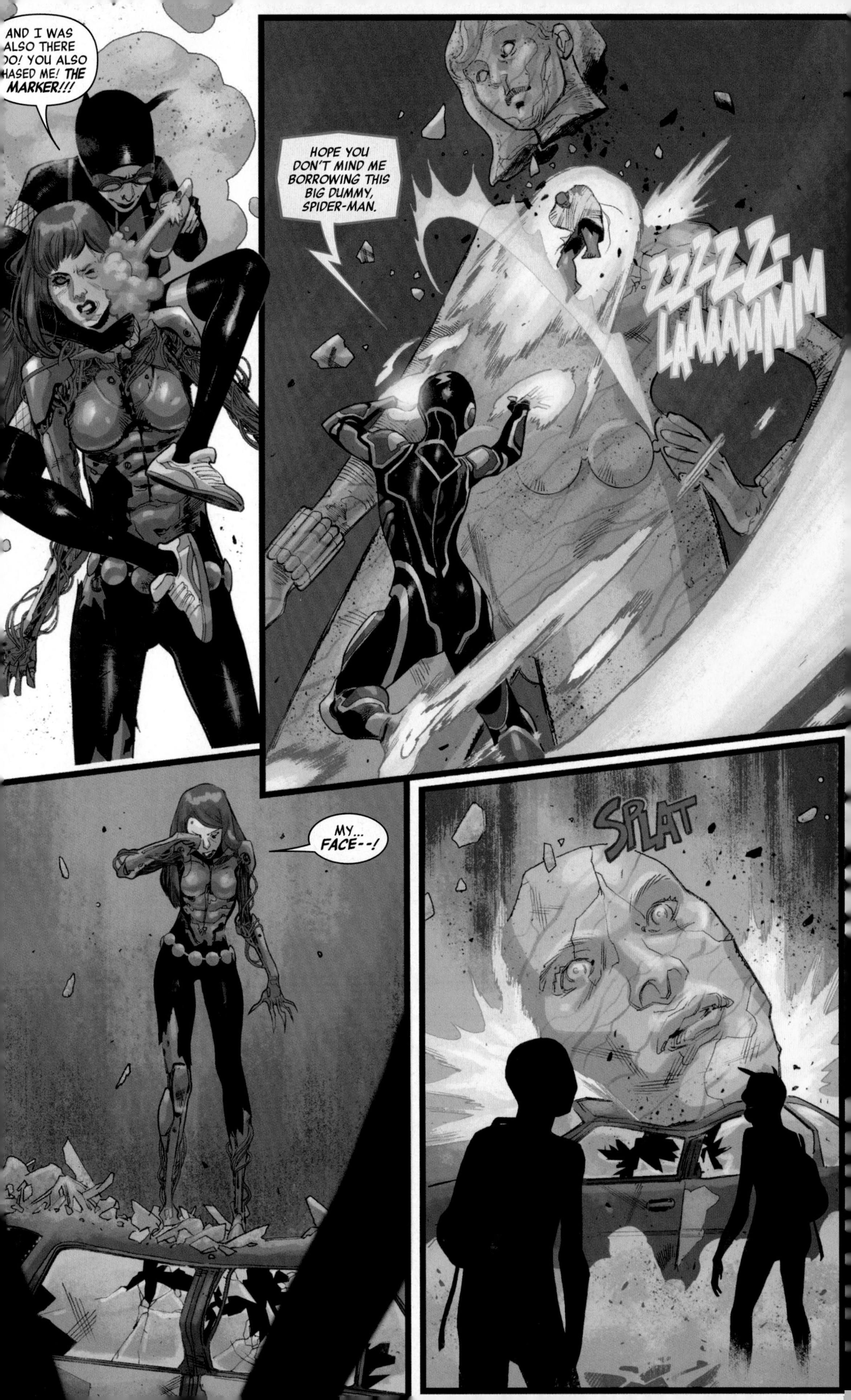

AND I WAS ALSO THERE TOO! YOU ALSO CHASED ME! THE MARKER!!!
HOPE YOU DON'T MIND ME BORROWING THIS BIG DUMMY, SPIDER-MAN.
ZZZZZ-LAAAAMMM
MY... FACE--!
SPLAT

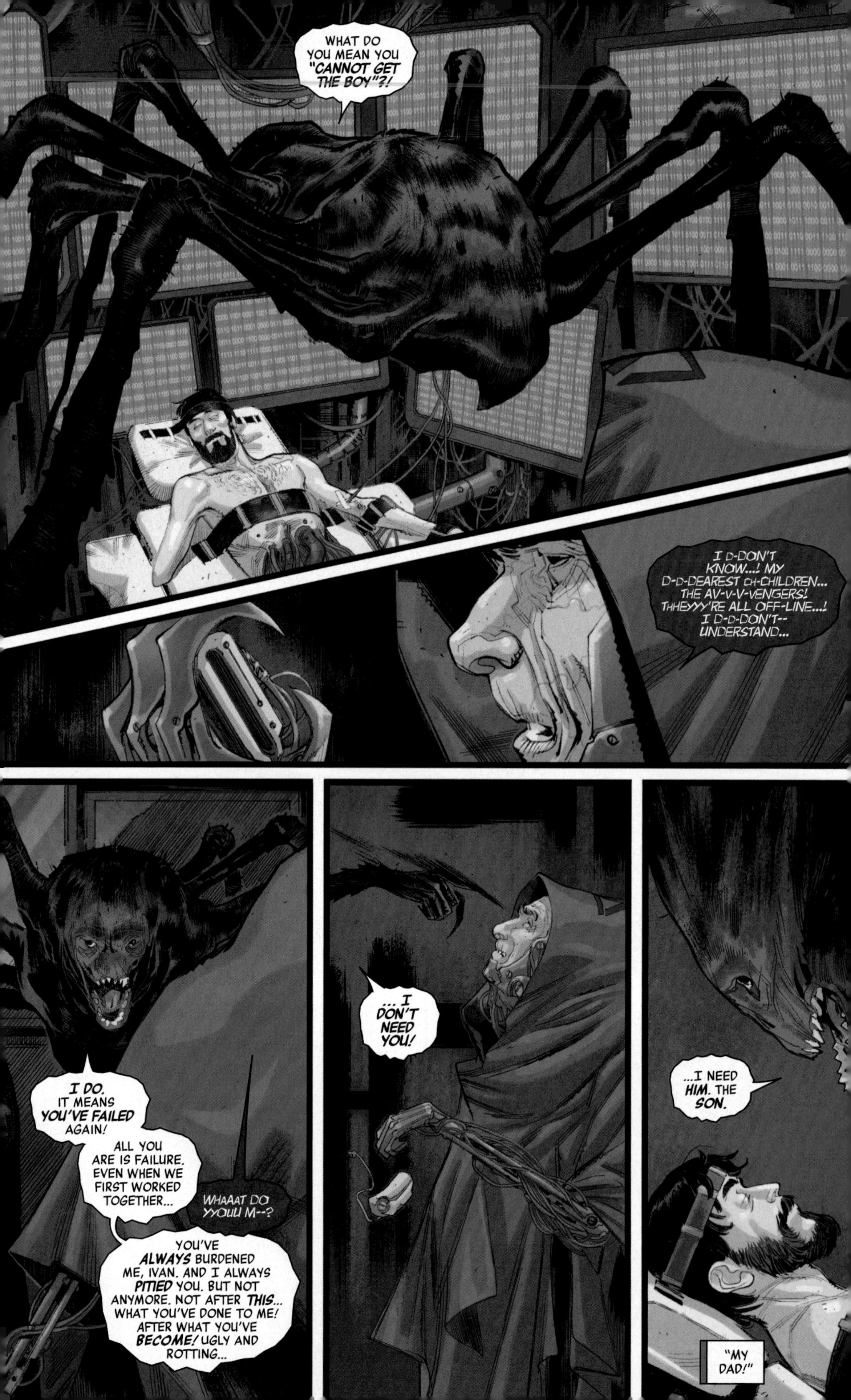

WHAT DO YOU MEAN YOU "CANNOT GET THE BOY"?!
I D-DON'T KNOW...! MY D-D-DEAREST CH-CHILDREN... THE AV-V-V-VENGERS! THHEYYY'RE ALL OFF-LINE...! I D-D-DON'T-- UNDERSTAND...
I DO. IT MEANS YOU'VE FAILED AGAIN!
ALL YOU ARE IS FAILURE. EVEN WHEN WE FIRST WORKED TOGETHER...
WHAAAT DO YYOUU M--?
YOU'VE ALWAYS BURDENED ME, IVAN. AND I ALWAYS PITIED YOU. BUT NOT ANYMORE. NOT AFTER THIS... WHAT YOU'VE DONE TO ME! AFTER WHAT YOU'VE BECOME! UGLY AND ROTTING...
...I DON'T NEED YOU!
...I NEED HIM. THE SON.
"MY DAD!"

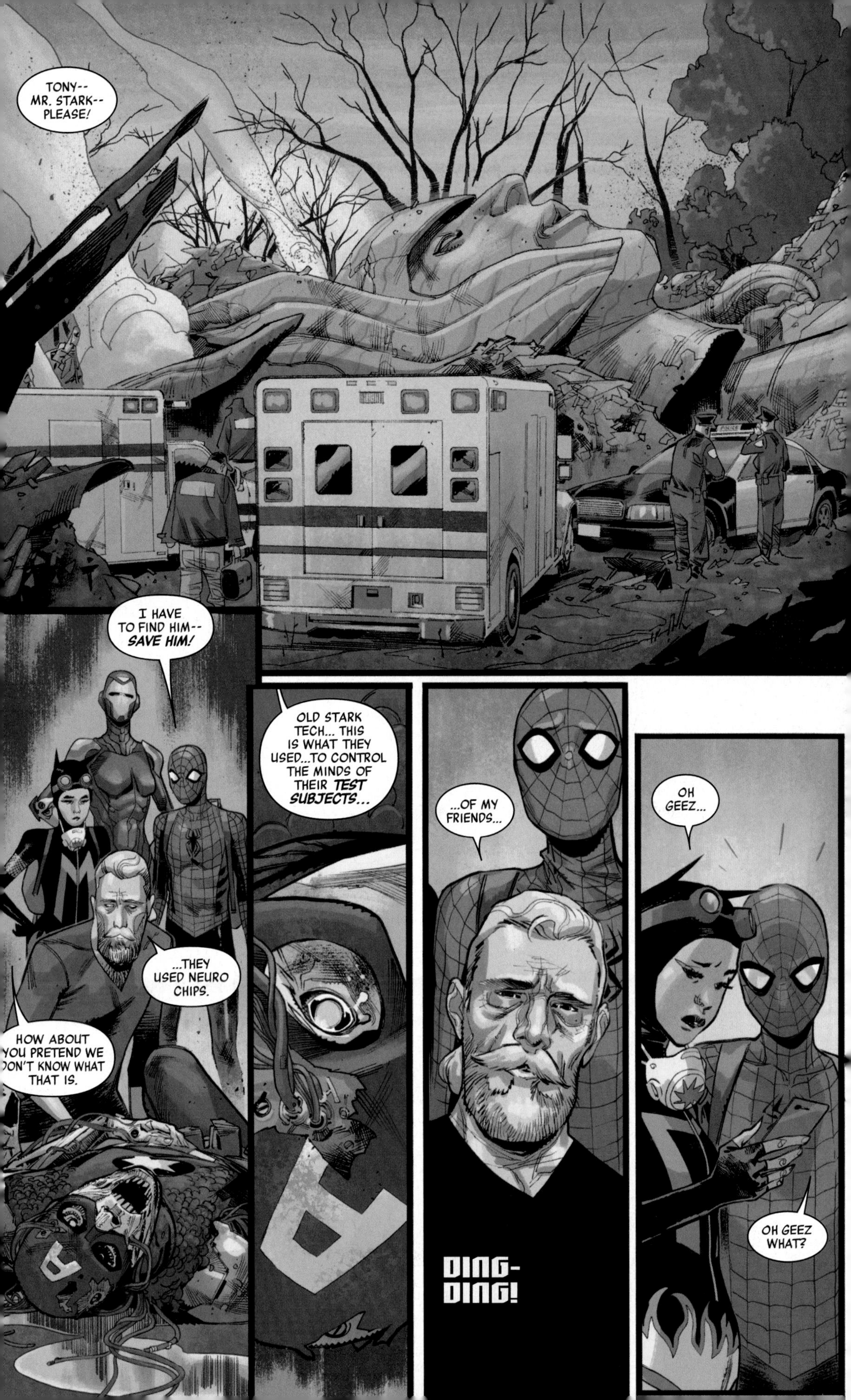
TONY-- MR. STARK-- PLEASE!
I HAVE TO FIND HIM-- SAVE HIM!
...THEY USED NEURO CHIPS.
HOW ABOUT YOU PRETEND WE DON'T KNOW WHAT THAT IS.
OLD STARK TECH... THIS IS WHAT THEY USED...TO CONTROL THE MINDS OF THEIR TEST SUBJECTS...
...OF MY FRIENDS...
DING-DING!
OH GEEZ...
OH GEEZ WHAT?

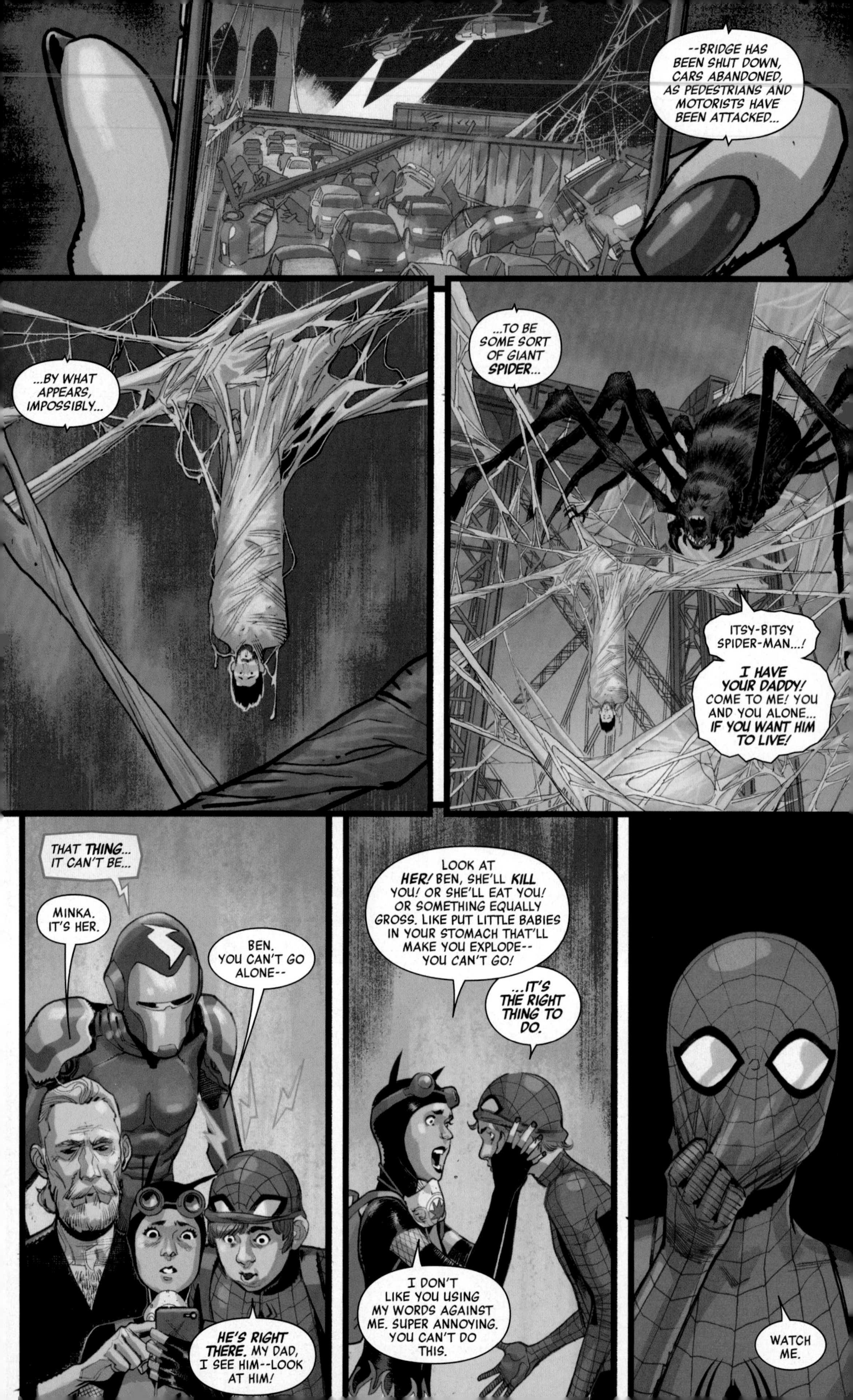

--BRIDGE HAS BEEN SHUT DOWN, CARS ABANDONED, AS PEDESTRIANS AND MOTORISTS HAVE BEEN ATTACKED...
...BY WHAT APPEARS, IMPOSSIBLY...
...TO BE SOME SORT OF GIANT SPIDER...
ITSY-BITSY SPIDER-MAN...!
I HAVE YOUR DADDY! COME TO ME! YOU AND YOU ALONE... IF YOU WANT HIM TO LIVE!
THAT THING... IT CAN'T BE...
MINKA. IT'S HER.
BEN. YOU CAN'T GO ALONE--
HE'S RIGHT THERE. MY DAD, I SEE HIM--LOOK AT HIM!
LOOK AT HER! BEN, SHE'LL KILL YOU! OR SHE'LL EAT YOU! OR SOMETHING EQUALLY GROSS. LIKE PUT LITTLE BABIES IN YOUR STOMACH THAT'LL MAKE YOU EXPLODE-- YOU CAN'T GO!
...IT'S THE RIGHT THING TO DO.
I DON'T LIKE YOU USING MY WORDS AGAINST ME. SUPER ANNOYING. YOU CAN'T DO THIS.
WATCH ME.

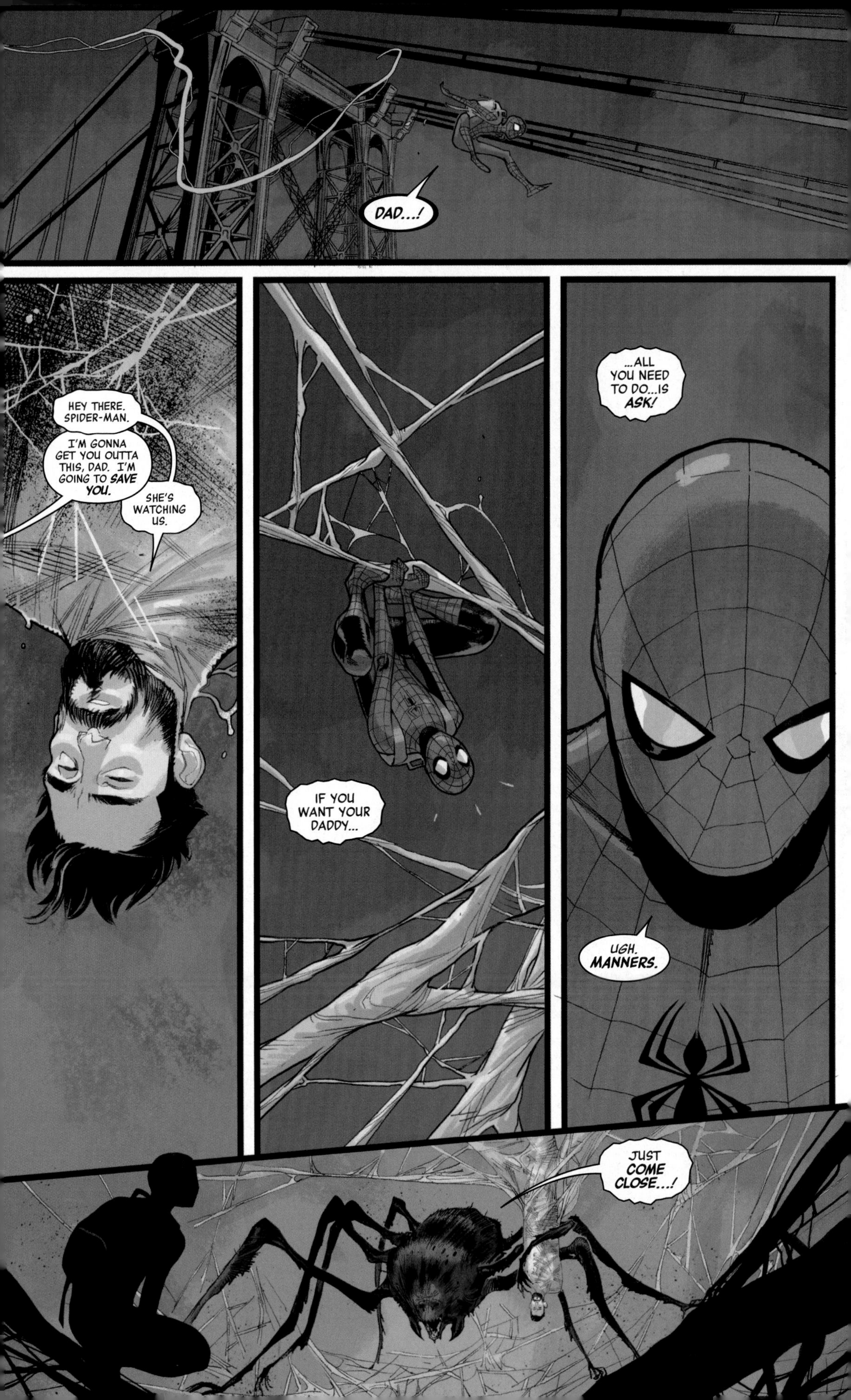
DAD...!
HEY THERE. SPIDER-MAN.
I'M GONNA GET YOU OUTTA THIS, DAD. I'M GOING TO SAVE YOU.
SHE'S WATCHING US.
IF YOU WANT YOUR DADDY...
...ALL YOU NEED TO DO...IS ASK!
UGH. MANNERS.
JUST COME CLOSE...!

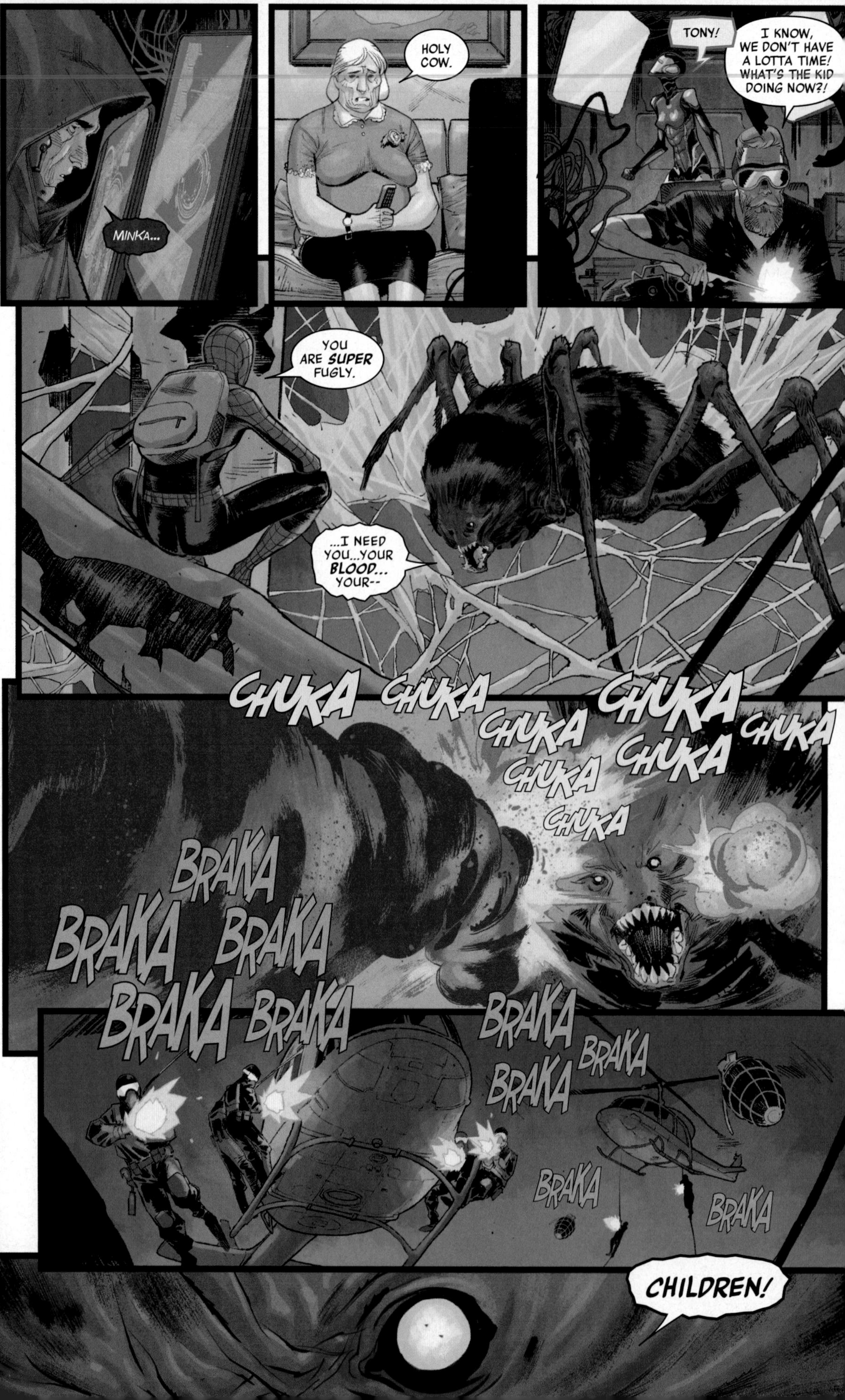
MINKA...
HOLY COW.
TONY!
I KNOW, WE DON'T HAVE A LOTTA TIME! WHAT'S THE KID DOING NOW?!
YOU ARE SUPER FUGLY.
...I NEED YOU...YOUR BLOOD... YOUR--
CHUKA CHUKA CHUKA CHUKA CHUKA CHUKA CHUKA CHUKA
BRAKA BRAKA BRAKA BRAKA BRAKA
BRAKA BRAKA BRAKA BRAKA BRAKA
CHILDREN!

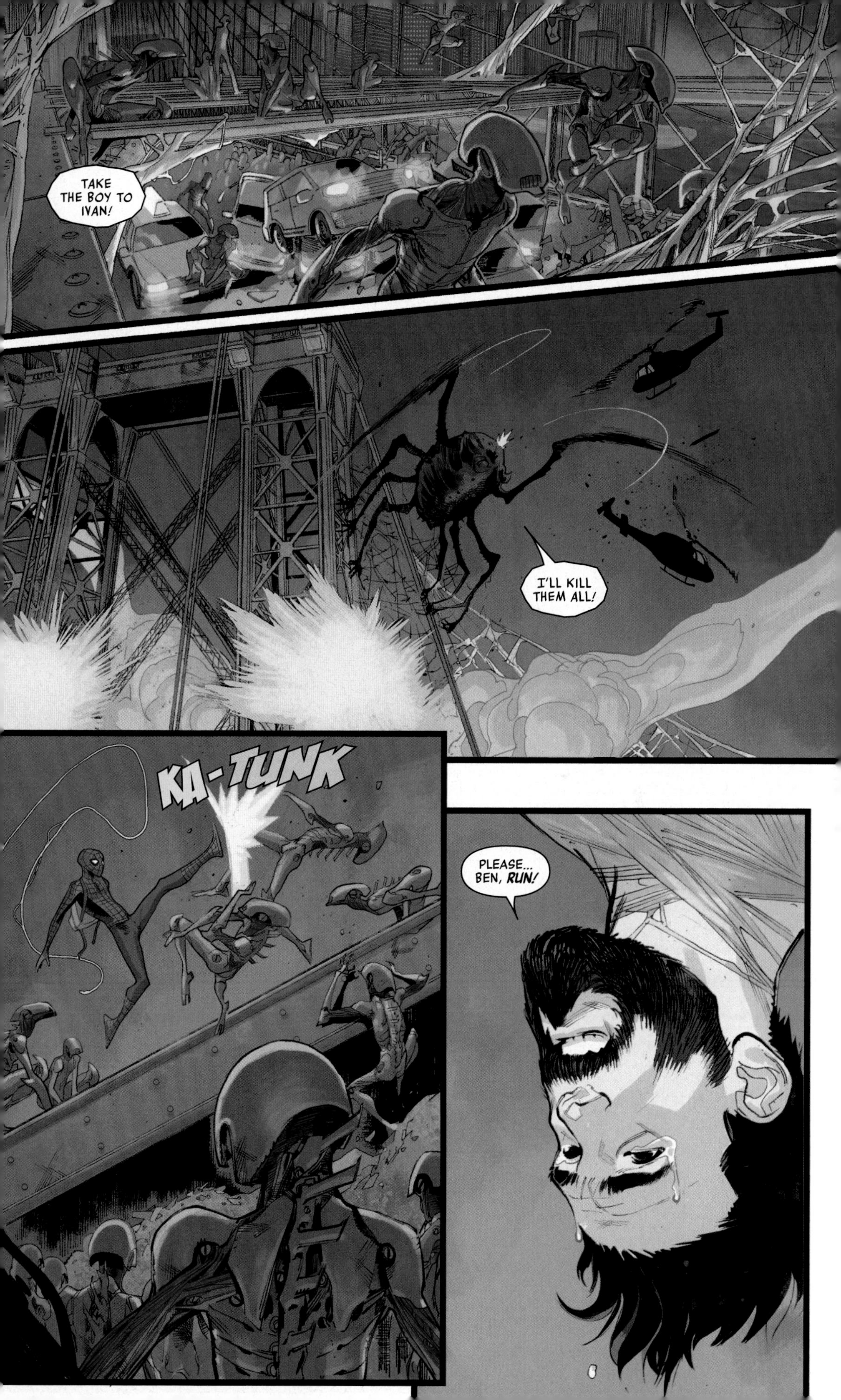
TAKE THE BOY TO IVAN!
I'LL KILL THEM ALL!
KA-TUNK
PLEASE... BEN, RUN!

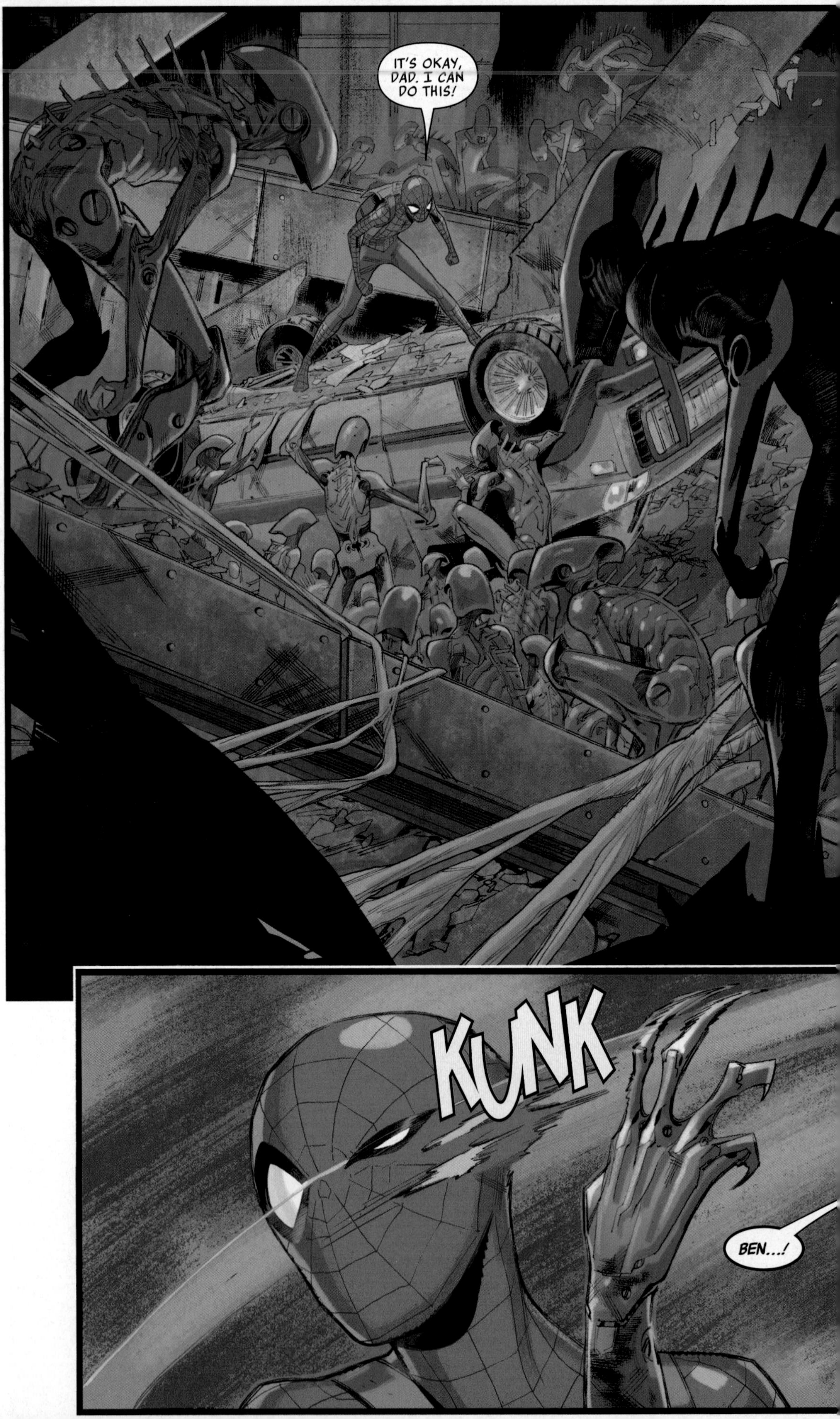
IT'S OKAY, DAD. I CAN DO THIS!
KUNK
BEN...!

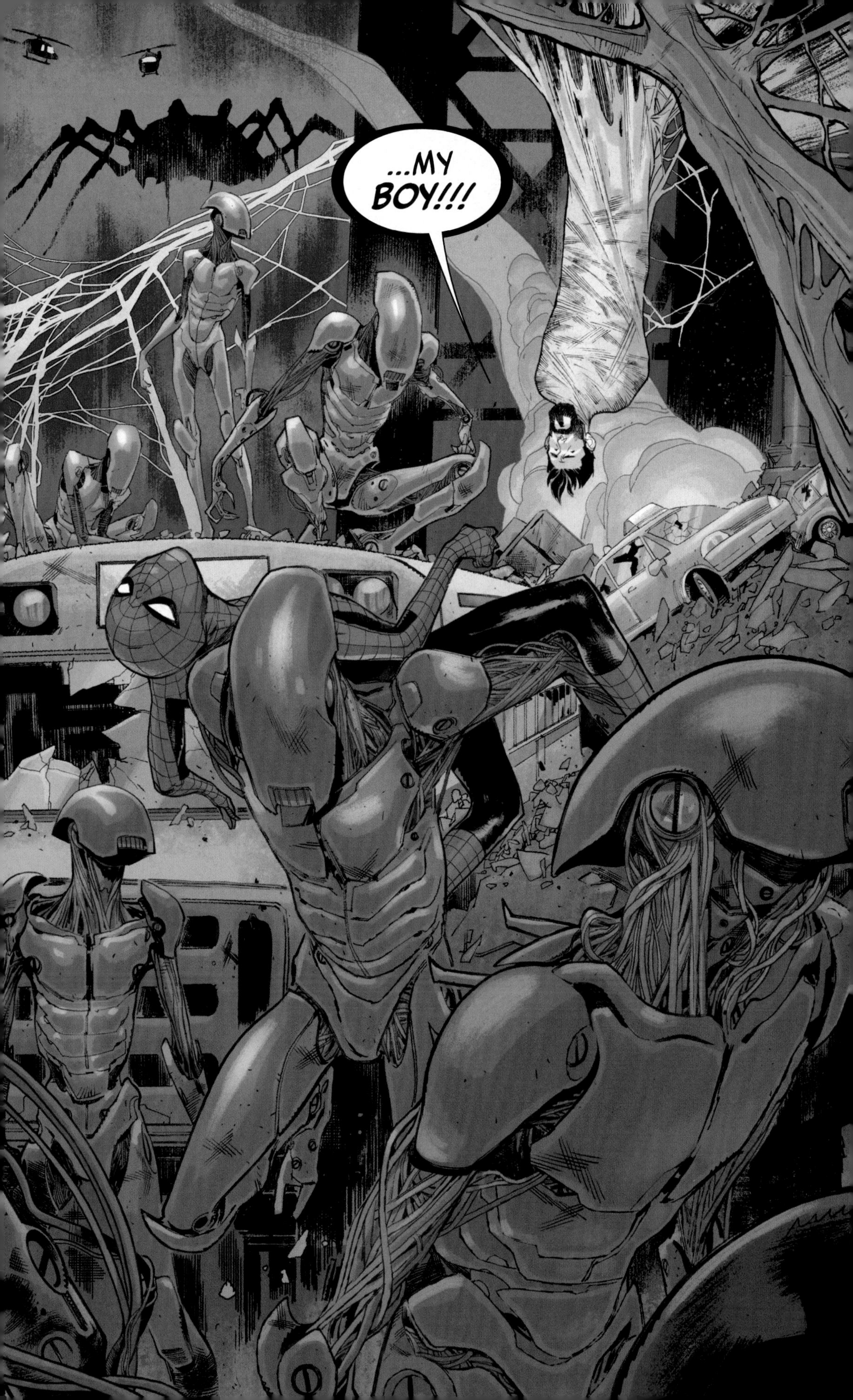
...MY BOY!!!

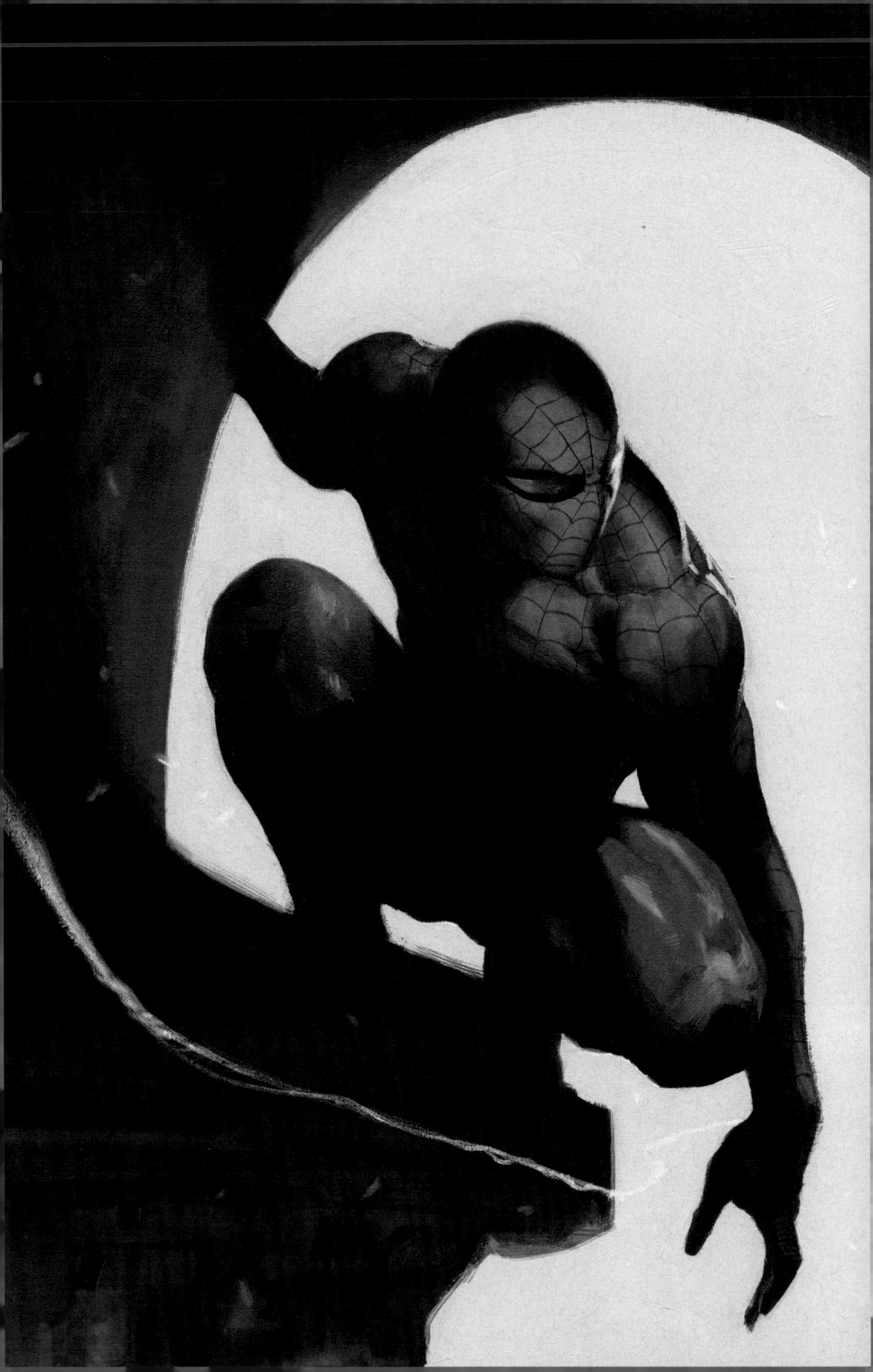

5

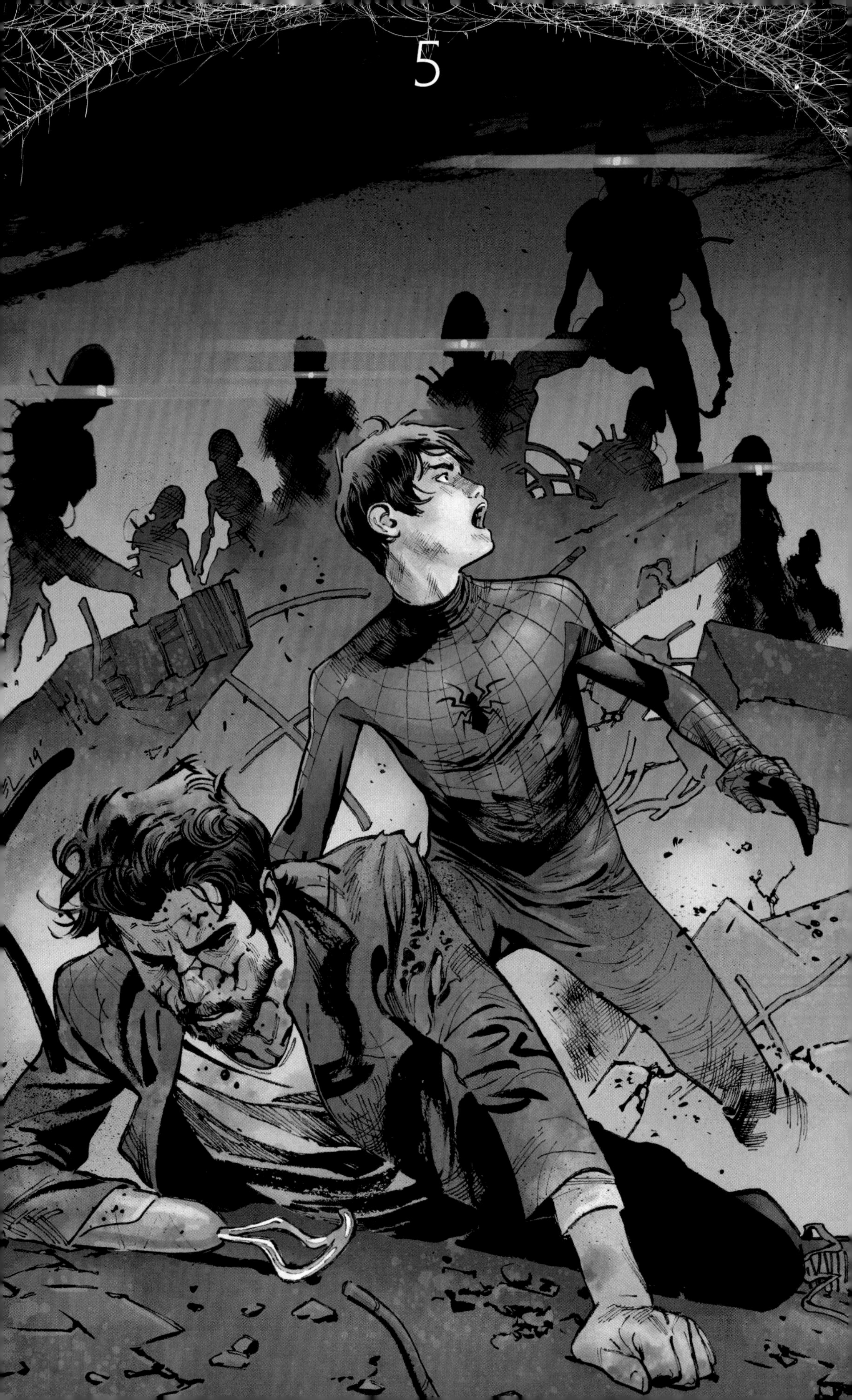

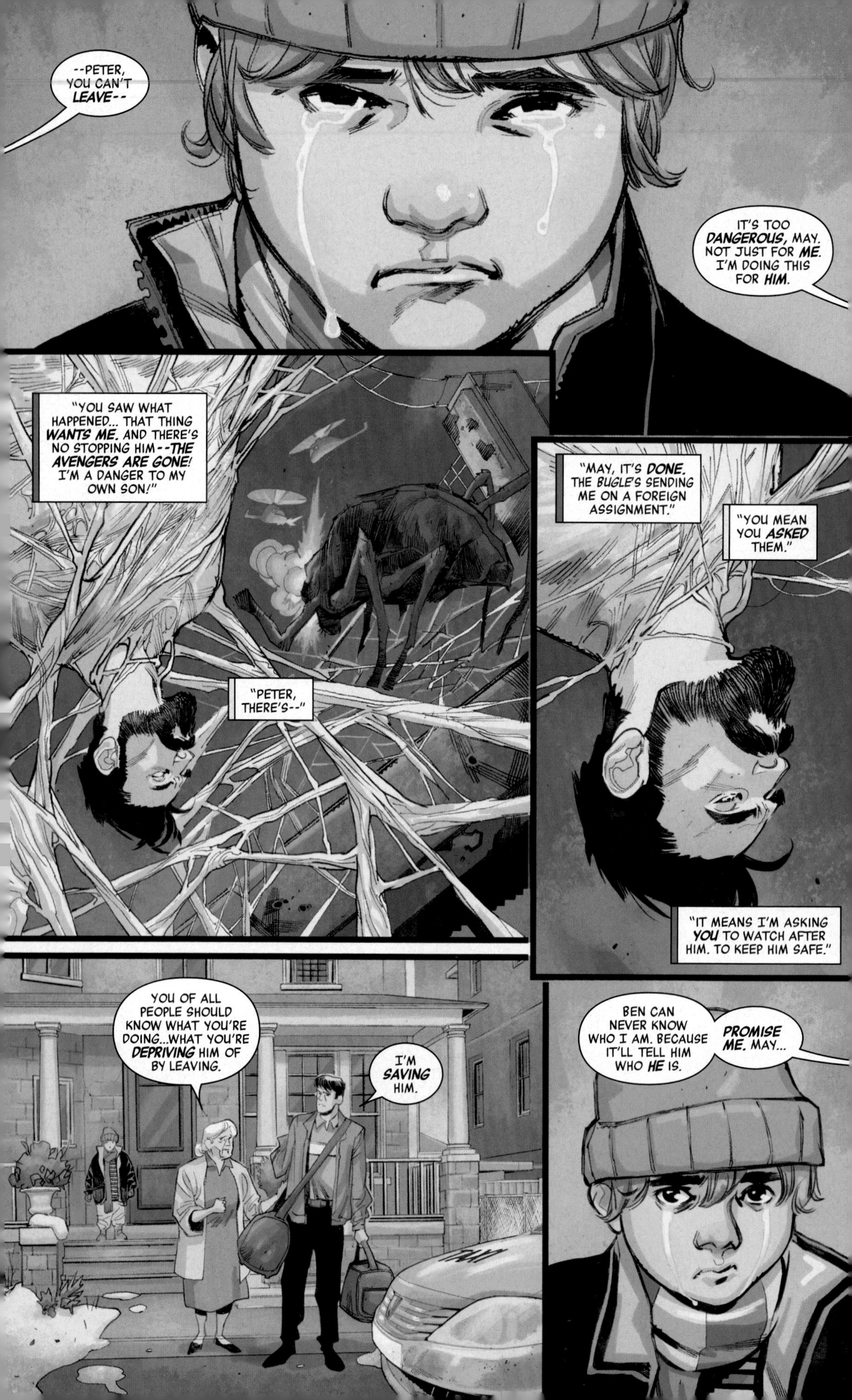
--PETER, YOU CAN'T LEAVE--
IT'S TOO DANGEROUS, MAY. NOT JUST FOR ME. I'M DOING THIS FOR HIM.
"YOU SAW WHAT HAPPENED... THAT THING WANTS ME. AND THERE'S NO STOPPING HIM--THE AVENGERS ARE GONE! I'M A DANGER TO MY OWN SON!"
"PETER, THERE'S--"
"MAY, IT'S DONE. THE BUGLE'S SENDING ME ON A FOREIGN ASSIGNMENT."
"YOU MEAN YOU ASKED THEM."
"IT MEANS I'M ASKING YOU TO WATCH AFTER HIM. TO KEEP HIM SAFE."
YOU OF ALL PEOPLE SHOULD KNOW WHAT YOU'RE DOING...WHAT YOU'RE DEPRIVING HIM OF BY LEAVING.
I'M SAVING HIM.
BEN CAN NEVER KNOW WHO I AM. BECAUSE IT'LL TELL HIM WHO HE IS.
PROMISE ME. MAY...

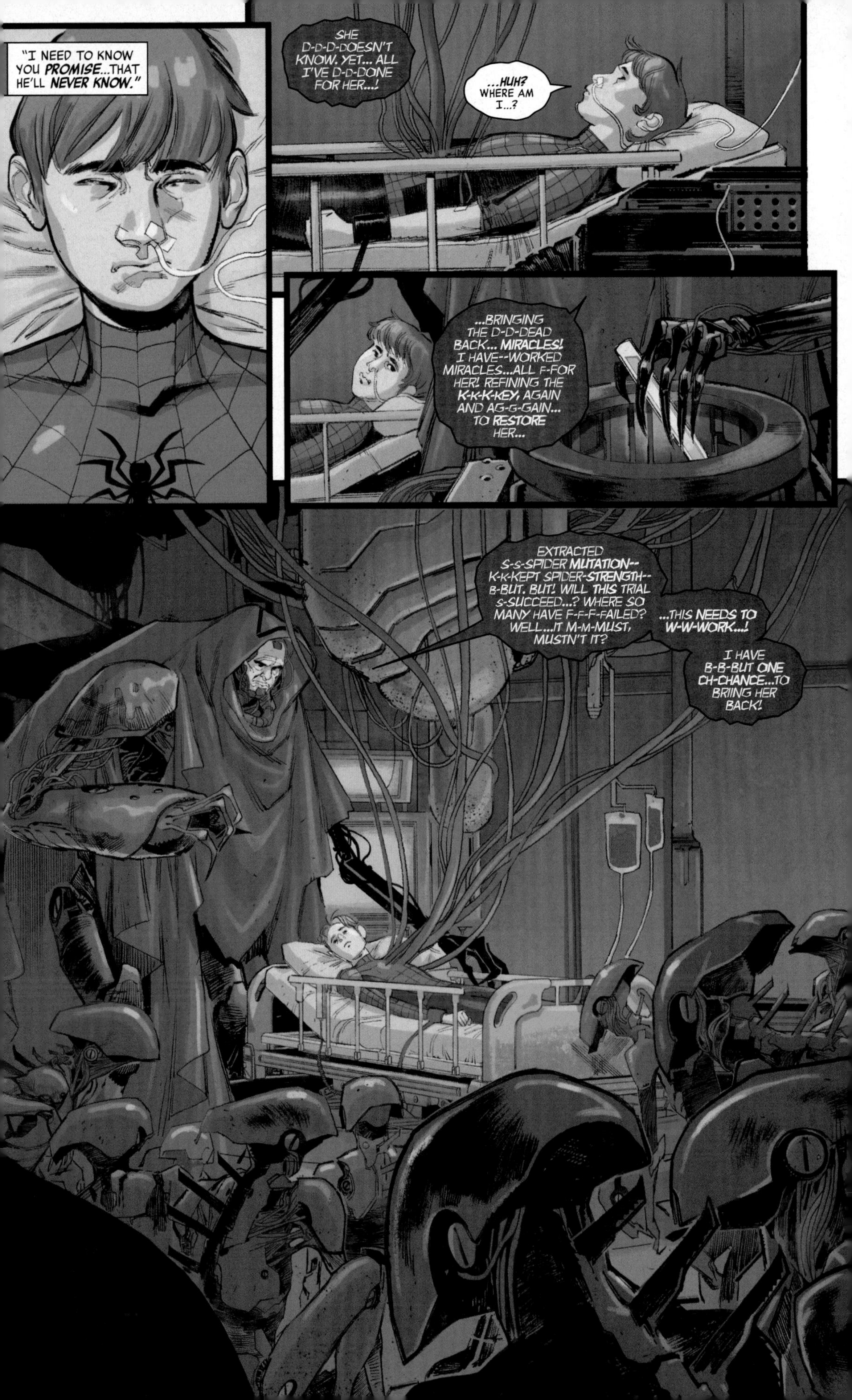
"I NEED TO KNOW YOU PROMISE...THAT HE'LL NEVER KNOW."
SHE D-D-D-DOESN'T KNOW. YET... ALL I'VE D-D-DONE FOR HER...!
...HUH? WHERE AM I...?
...BRINGING THE D-D-DEAD BACK... MIRACLES! I HAVE--WORKED MIRACLES...ALL F-FOR HER! REFINING THE K-K-K-KEY, AGAIN AND AG-G-GAIN... TO RESTORE HER...
EXTRACTED S-S-SPIDER MUTATION-- K-K-KEPT SPIDER-STRENGTH-- B-BUT. BUT! WILL THIS TRIAL S-SUCCEED...? WHERE SO MANY HAVE F-F-F-FAILED? WELL...IT M-M-MUST, MUSTN'T IT?
...THIS NEEDS TO W-W-WORK...!
I HAVE B-B-BUT ONE CH-CHANCE...TO BRIING HER BACK!

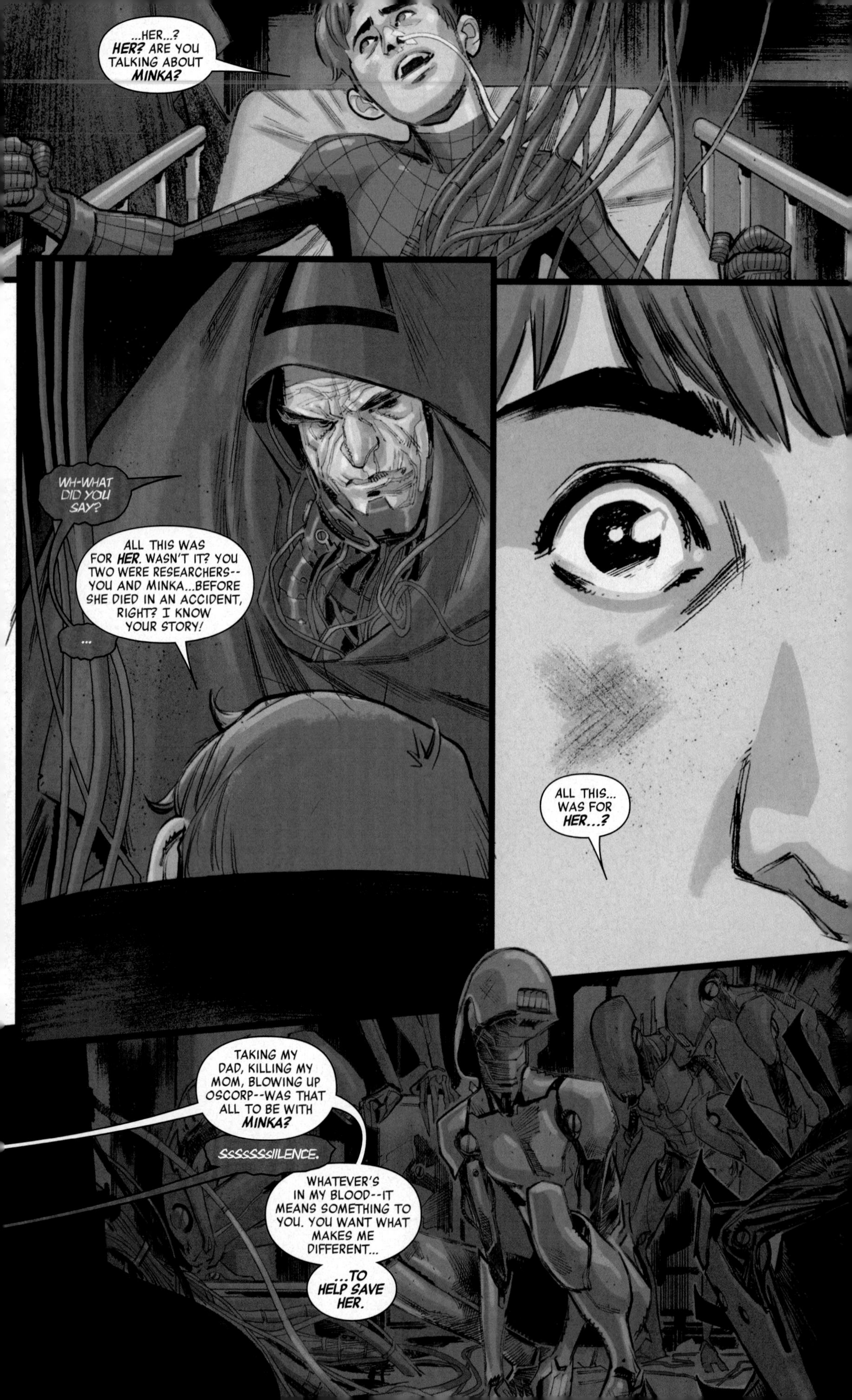
...HER...? HER? ARE YOU TALKING ABOUT MINKA?
WH-WHAT DID YOU SAY?
ALL THIS WAS FOR HER. WASN'T IT? YOU TWO WERE RESEARCHERS--YOU AND MINKA...BEFORE SHE DIED IN AN ACCIDENT, RIGHT? I KNOW YOUR STORY!
...
ALL THIS... WAS FOR HER...?
TAKING MY DAD, KILLING MY MOM, BLOWING UP OSCORP--WAS THAT ALL TO BE WITH MINKA?
SSSSSSSSIILENCE.
WHATEVER'S IN MY BLOOD--IT MEANS SOMETHING TO YOU. YOU WANT WHAT MAKES ME DIFFERENT...
...TO HELP SAVE HER.

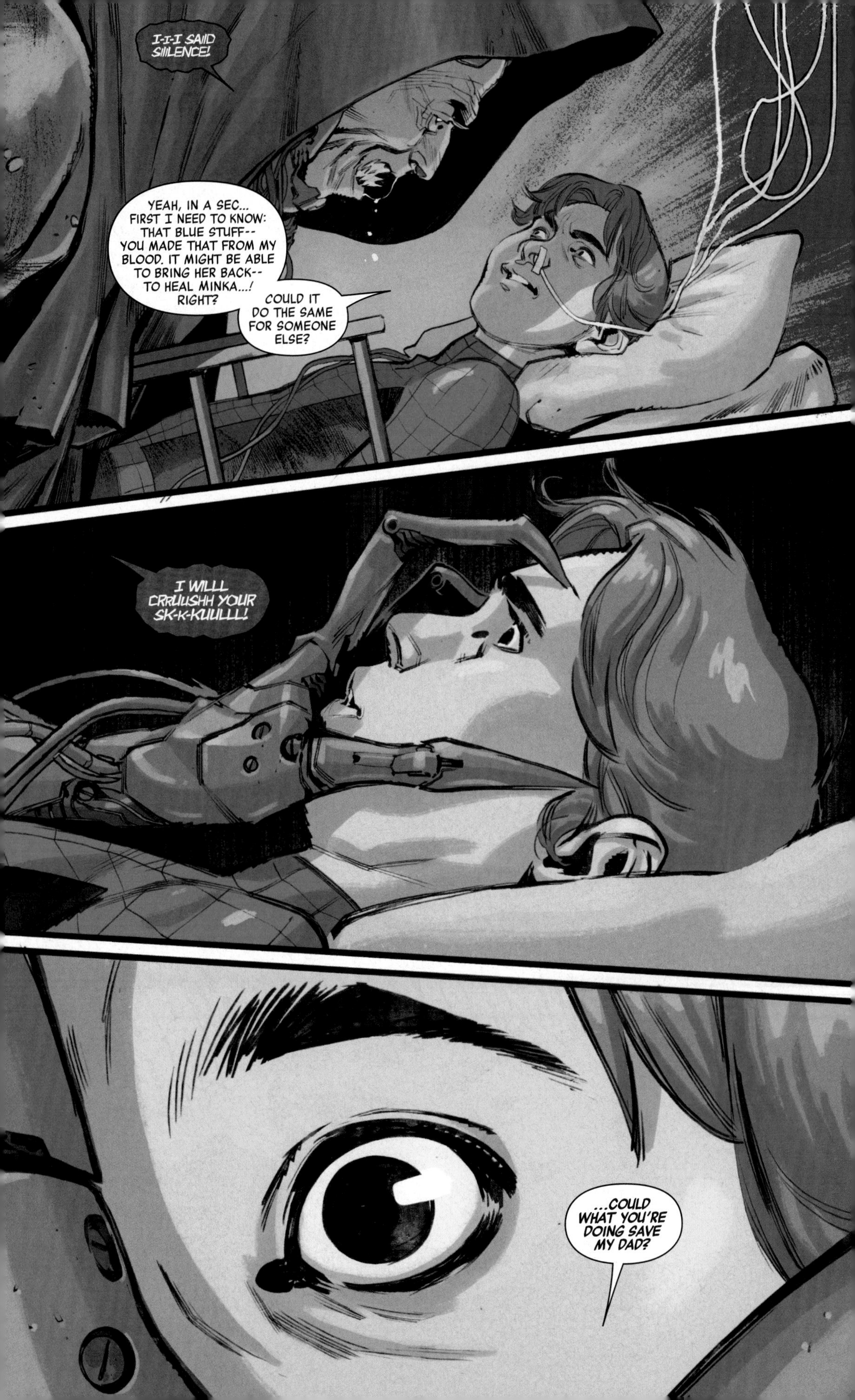
I-I-I SAIID SIIILENCE!
YEAH, IN A SEC... FIRST I NEED TO KNOW: THAT BLUE STUFF-- YOU MADE THAT FROM MY BLOOD. IT MIGHT BE ABLE TO BRING HER BACK-- TO HEAL MINKA...! RIGHT?
COULD IT DO THE SAME FOR SOMEONE ELSE?
I WILLL CRRUUSHH YOUR SK-K-KUULLL!
...COULD WHAT YOU'RE DOING SAVE MY DAD?

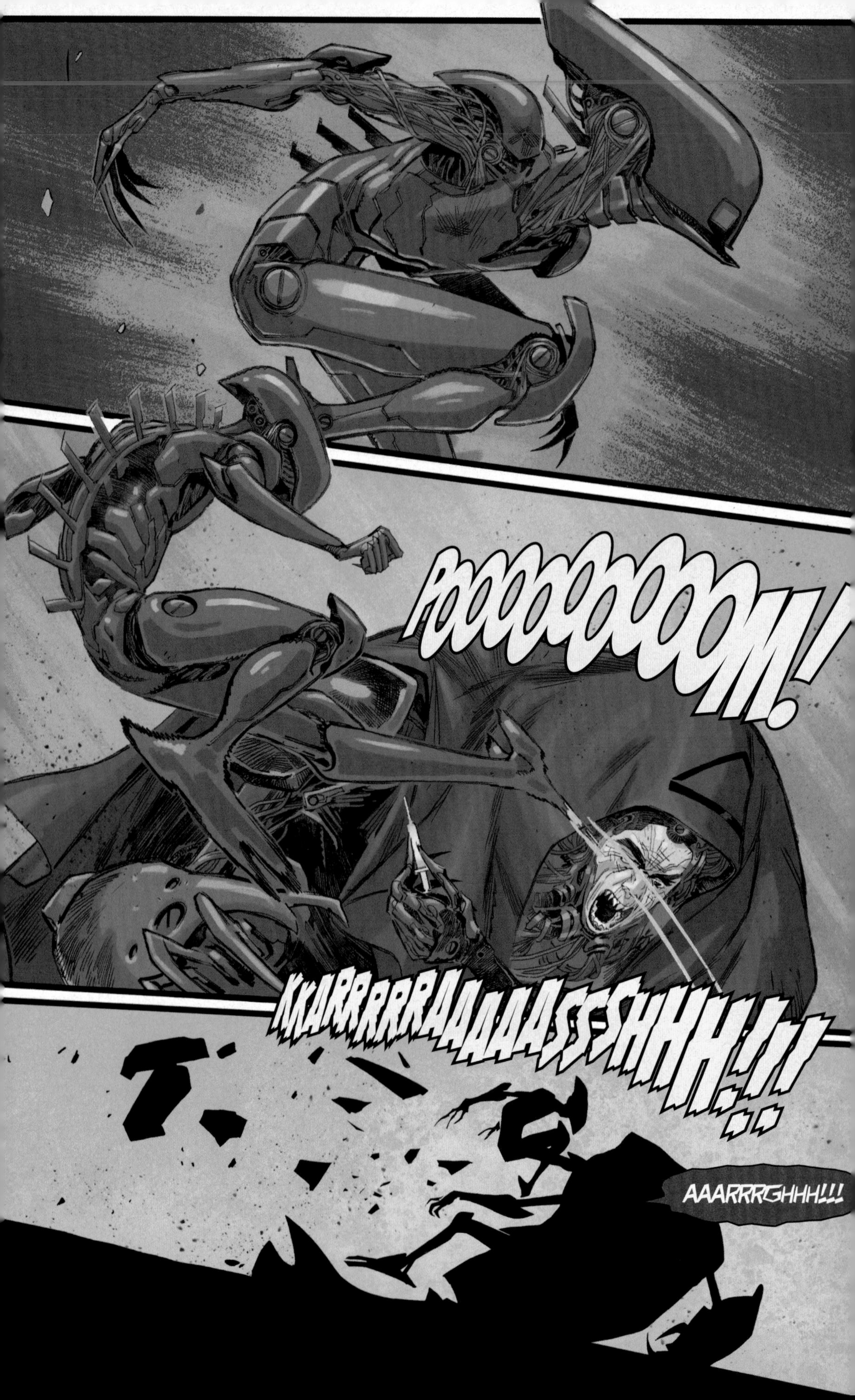
POOOOOOOOOM!
KKARRRRRRAAAAASSHHH!!!
AAARRRGHHH!!!

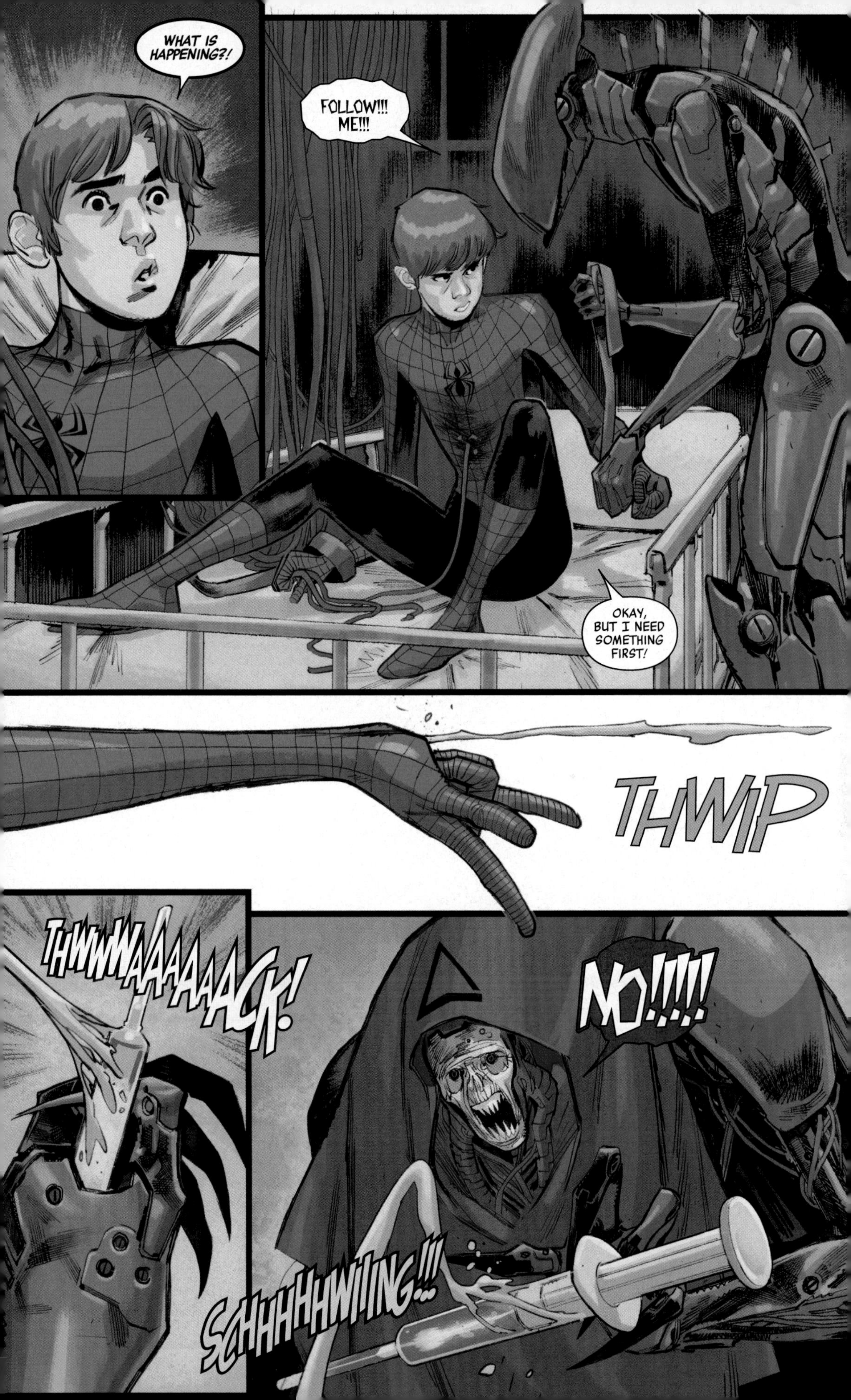
WHAT IS HAPPENING?!
FOLLOW!!! ME!!!
OKAY, BUT I NEED SOMETHING FIRST!
THWIP
THWWAAAAAACK!
NO!!!!!
SCHHHHWIIING!!!

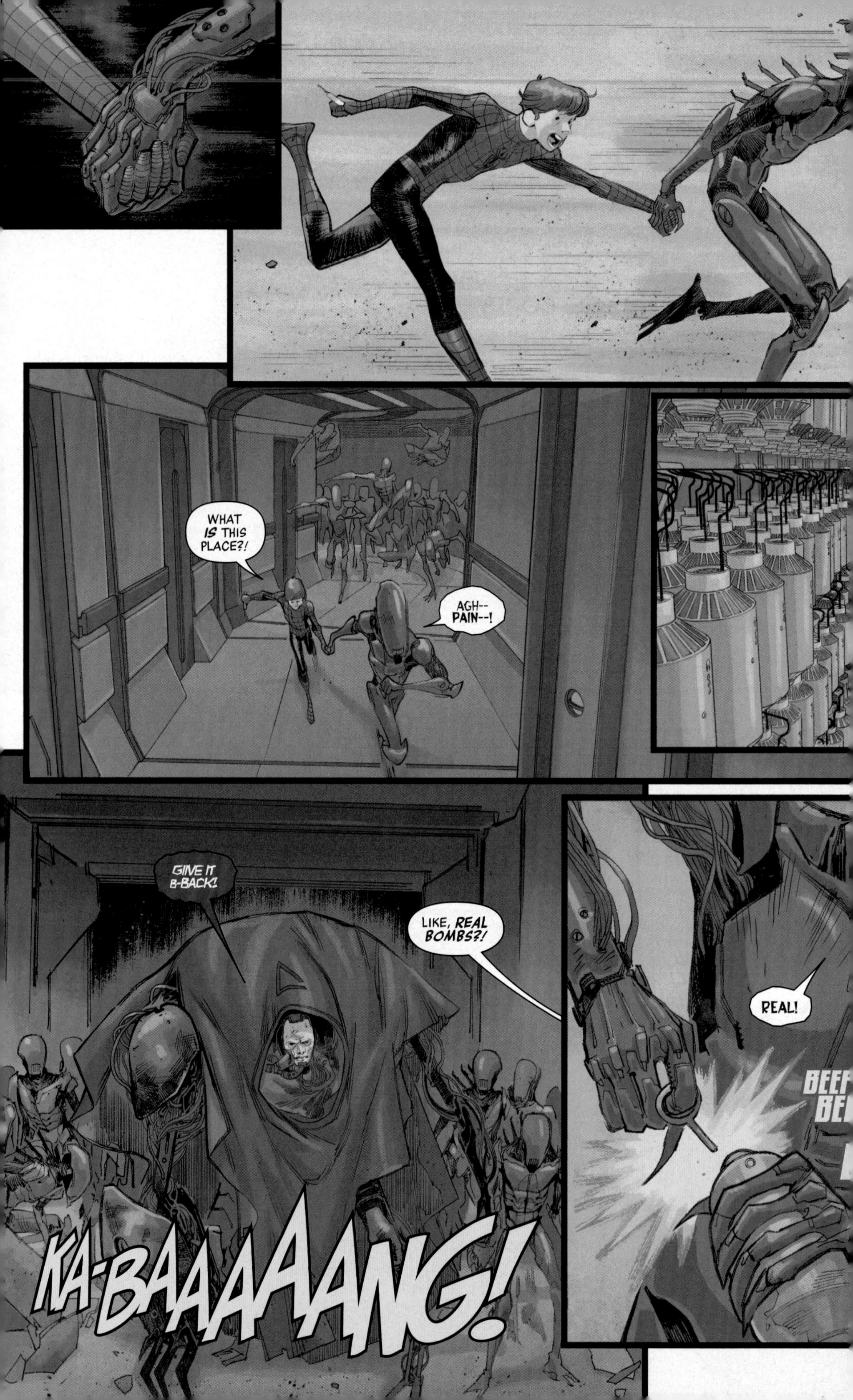
WHAT IS THIS PLACE?!
AGH-- PAIN--!
GIVE IT B-BACK!
LIKE, REAL BOMBS?!
REAL!
KA-BAAAAANG!

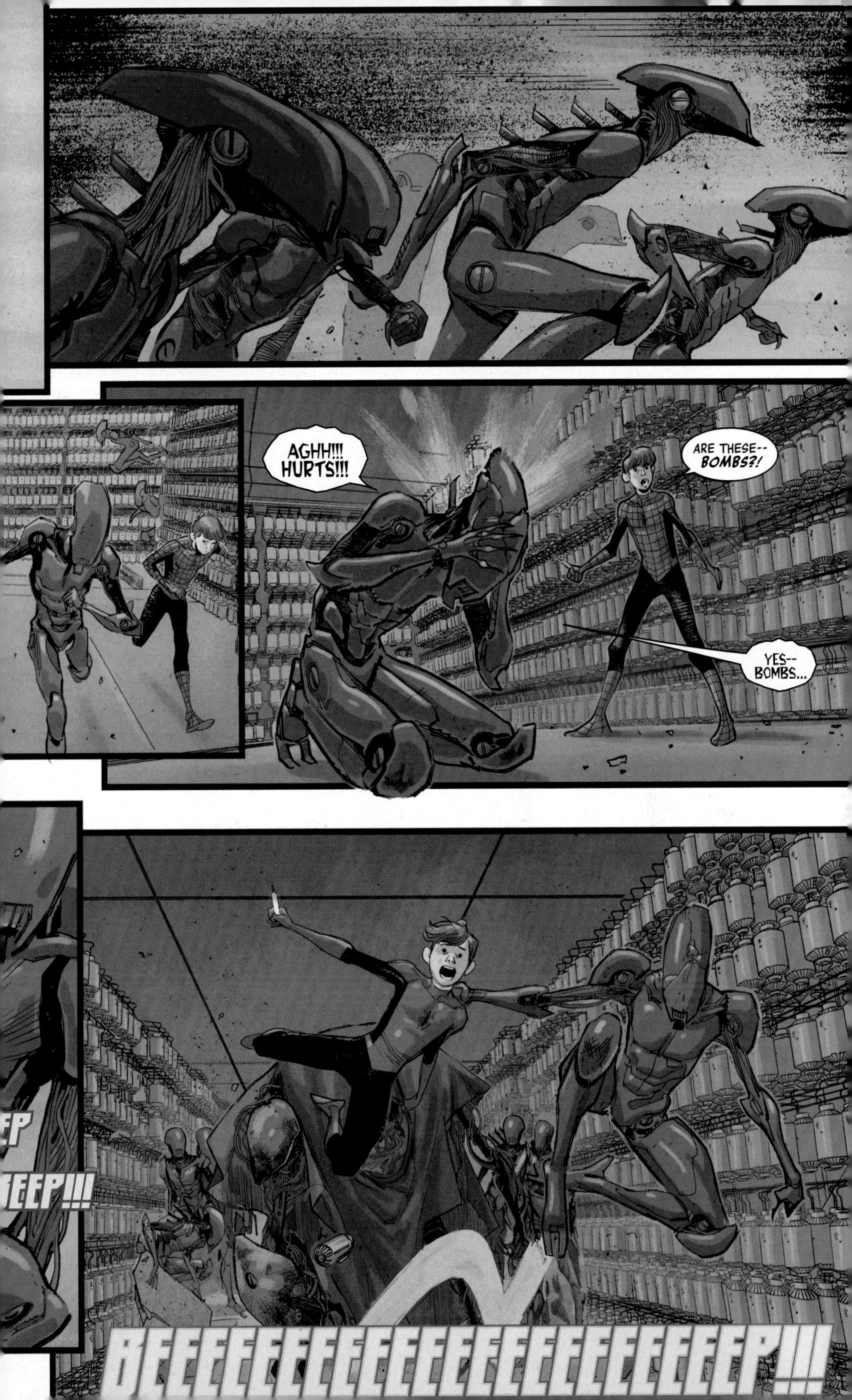
AGHH!!! HURTS!!!
ARE THESE-- BOMBS?!
YES-- BOMBS...
BEEEEEEEEEEEEEEEEEEEEEEEEEEEP!!!

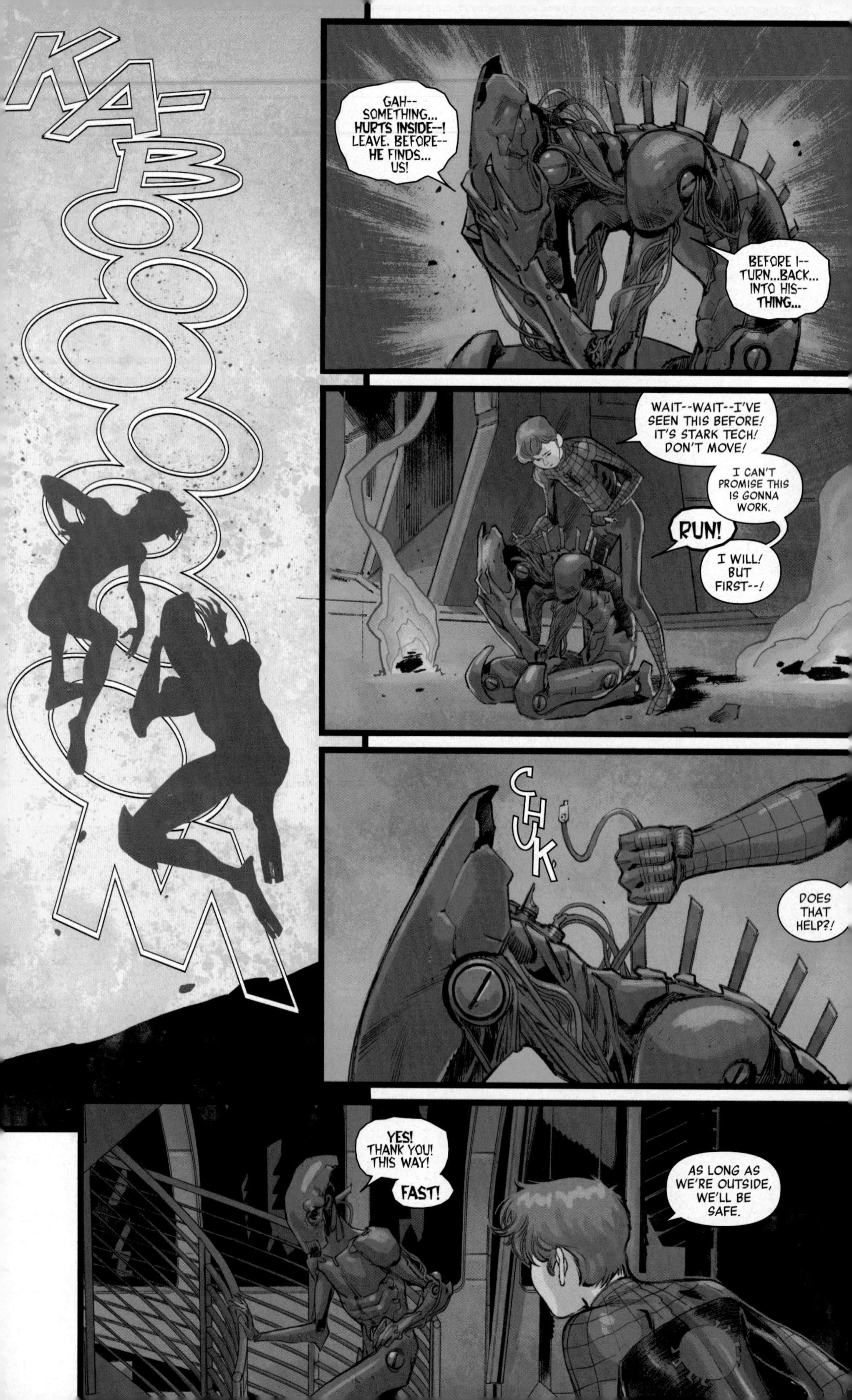
KA-BOOOOOOM
GAH--
SOMETHING...
HURTS INSIDE--!
LEAVE. BEFORE--
HE FINDS...
US!
BEFORE I--
TURN...BACK...
INTO HIS--
THING...
WAIT--WAIT--I'VE
SEEN THIS BEFORE!
IT'S STARK TECH!
DON'T MOVE!
I CAN'T
PROMISE THIS
IS GONNA
WORK.
RUN!
I WILL!
BUT
FIRST--!
CHUK
DOES
THAT
HELP?!
YES!
THANK YOU!
THIS WAY!
FAST!
AS LONG AS
WE'RE OUTSIDE,
WE'LL BE
SAFE.

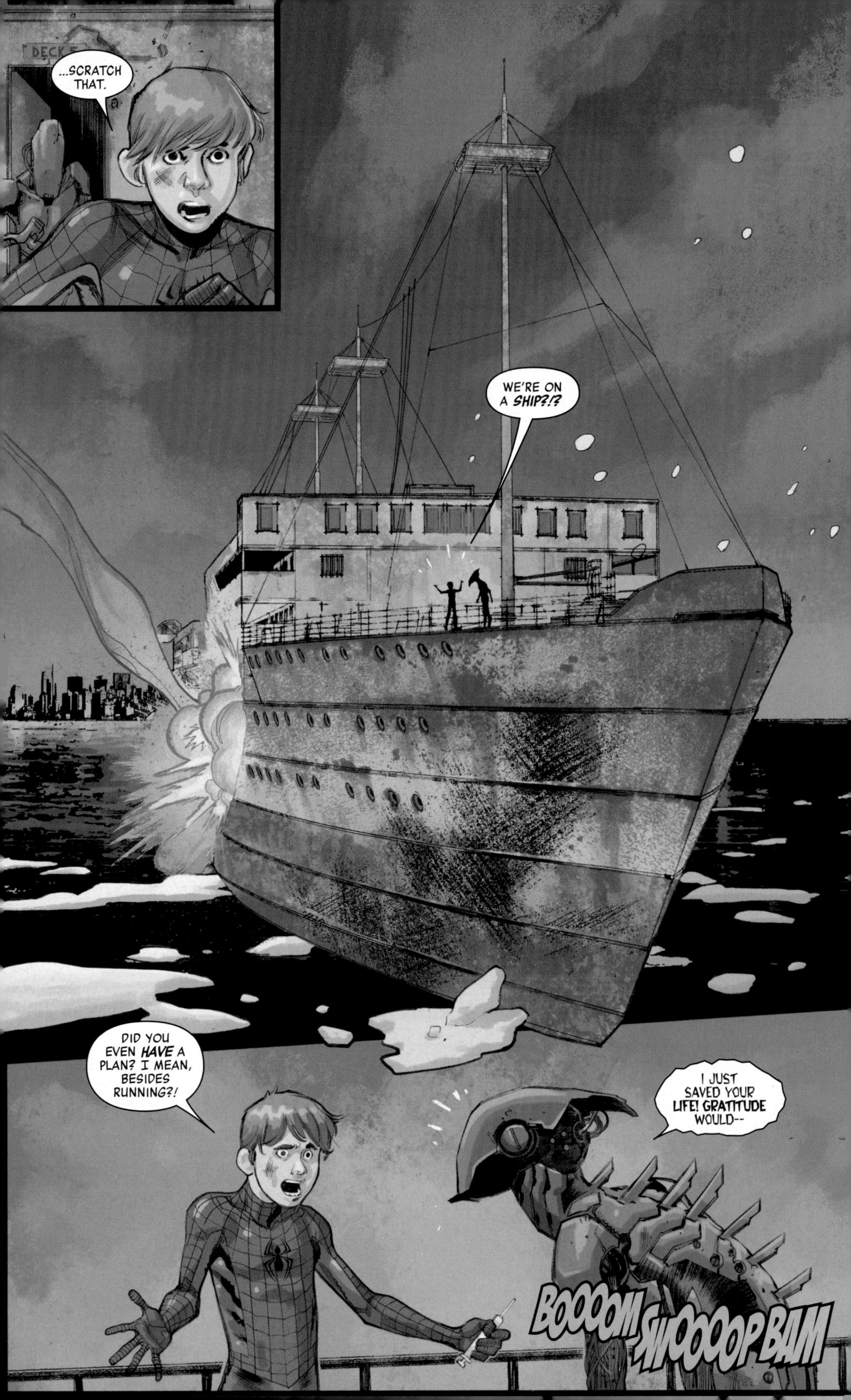
DECK
...SCRATCH THAT.
WE'RE ON A SHIP?!?
DID YOU EVEN HAVE A PLAN? I MEAN, BESIDES RUNNING?!
I JUST SAVED YOUR LIFE! GRATITUDE WOULD--
BOOOOM
SWOOOOP BAM

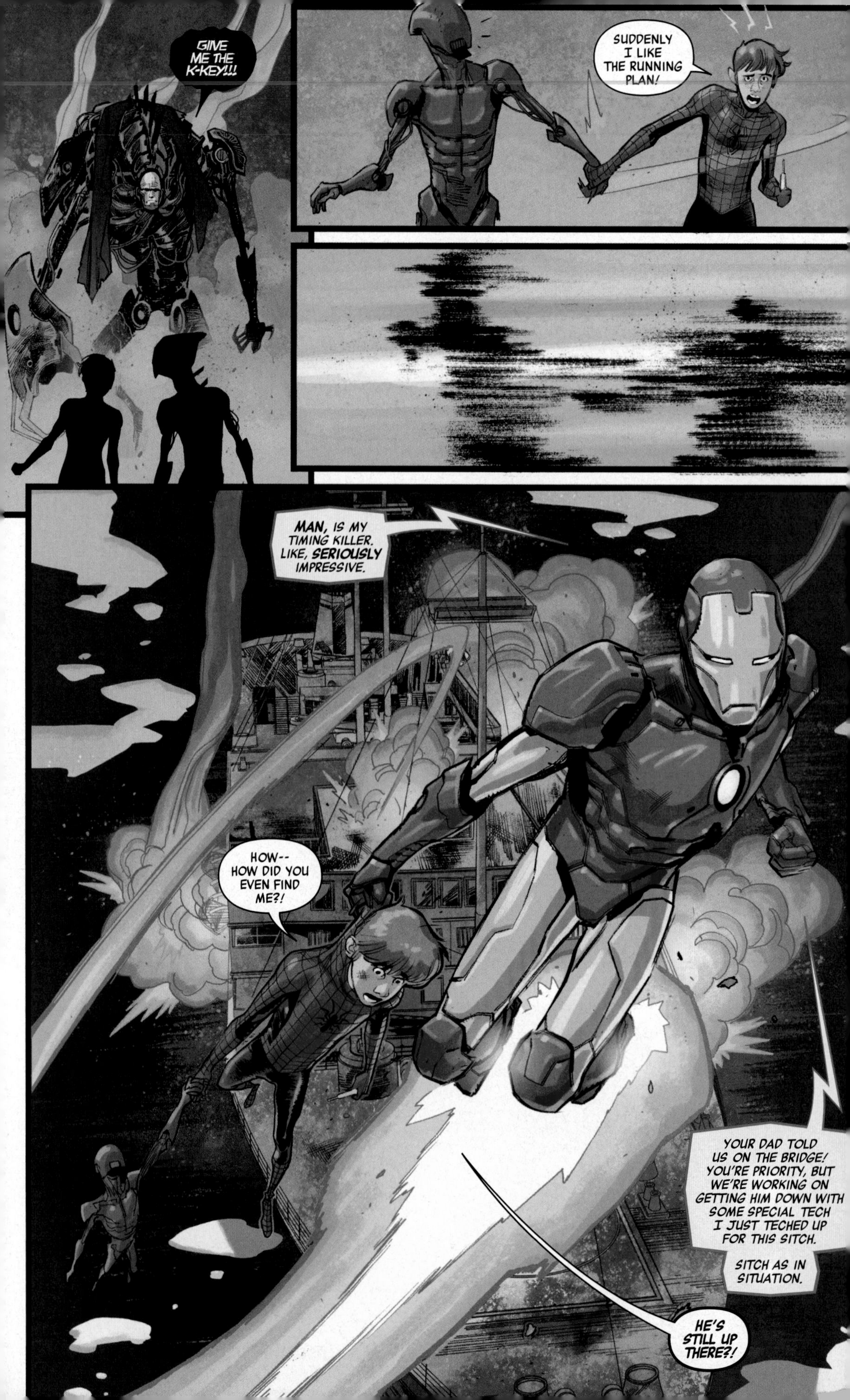
GIVE ME THE K-KEY!!!
SUDDENLY I LIKE THE RUNNING PLAN!
MAN, IS MY TIMING KILLER. LIKE, SERIOUSLY IMPRESSIVE.
HOW-- HOW DID YOU EVEN FIND ME?!
YOUR DAD TOLD US ON THE BRIDGE! YOU'RE PRIORITY, BUT WE'RE WORKING ON GETTING HIM DOWN WITH SOME SPECIAL TECH I JUST TECHED UP FOR THIS SITCH.
SITCH AS IN SITUATION.
HE'S STILL UP THERE?!

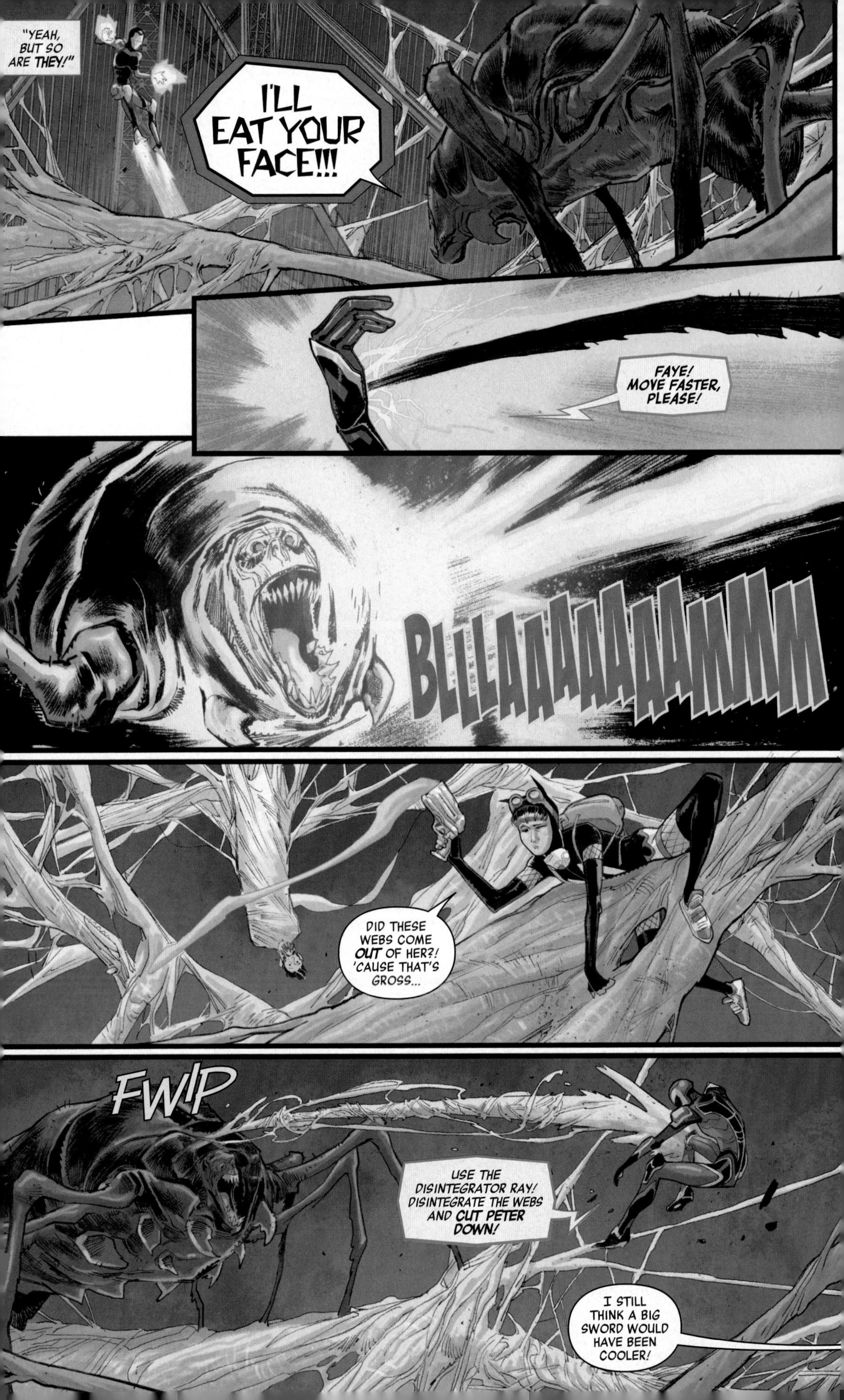
"YEAH, BUT SO ARE THEY!"
I'LL EAT YOUR FACE!!!
FAYE! MOVE FASTER, PLEASE!
BLLLAAAAAAAMMM
DID THESE WEBS COME OUT OF HER?! 'CAUSE THAT'S GROSS...
FWIP
USE THE DISINTEGRATOR RAY! DISINTEGRATE THE WEBS AND CUT PETER DOWN!
I STILL THINK A BIG SWORD WOULD HAVE BEEN COOLER!

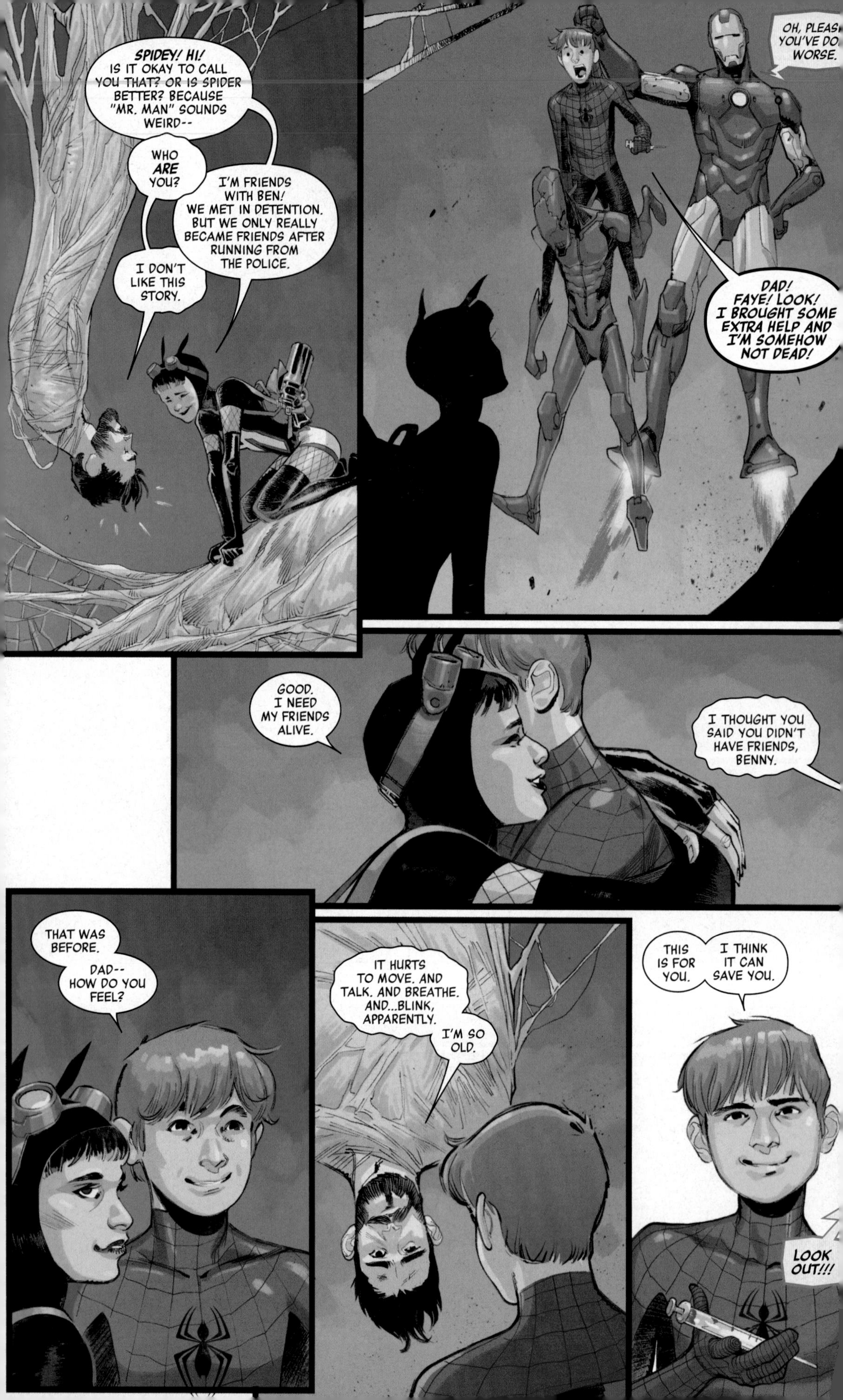
SPIDEY! HI! IS IT OKAY TO CALL YOU THAT? OR IS SPIDER BETTER? BECAUSE "MR. MAN" SOUNDS WEIRD--
WHO ARE YOU?
I'M FRIENDS WITH BEN! WE MET IN DETENTION. BUT WE ONLY REALLY BECAME FRIENDS AFTER RUNNING FROM THE POLICE.
I DON'T LIKE THIS STORY.
OH, PLEAS YOU'VE DO WORSE.
DAD! FAYE! LOOK! I BROUGHT SOME EXTRA HELP AND I'M SOMEHOW NOT DEAD!
GOOD. I NEED MY FRIENDS ALIVE.
I THOUGHT YOU SAID YOU DIDN'T HAVE FRIENDS, BENNY.
THAT WAS BEFORE.
DAD-- HOW DO YOU FEEL?
IT HURTS TO MOVE. AND TALK. AND BREATHE. AND...BLINK, APPARENTLY.
I'M SO OLD.
THIS IS FOR YOU.
I THINK IT CAN SAVE YOU.
LOOK OUT!!!

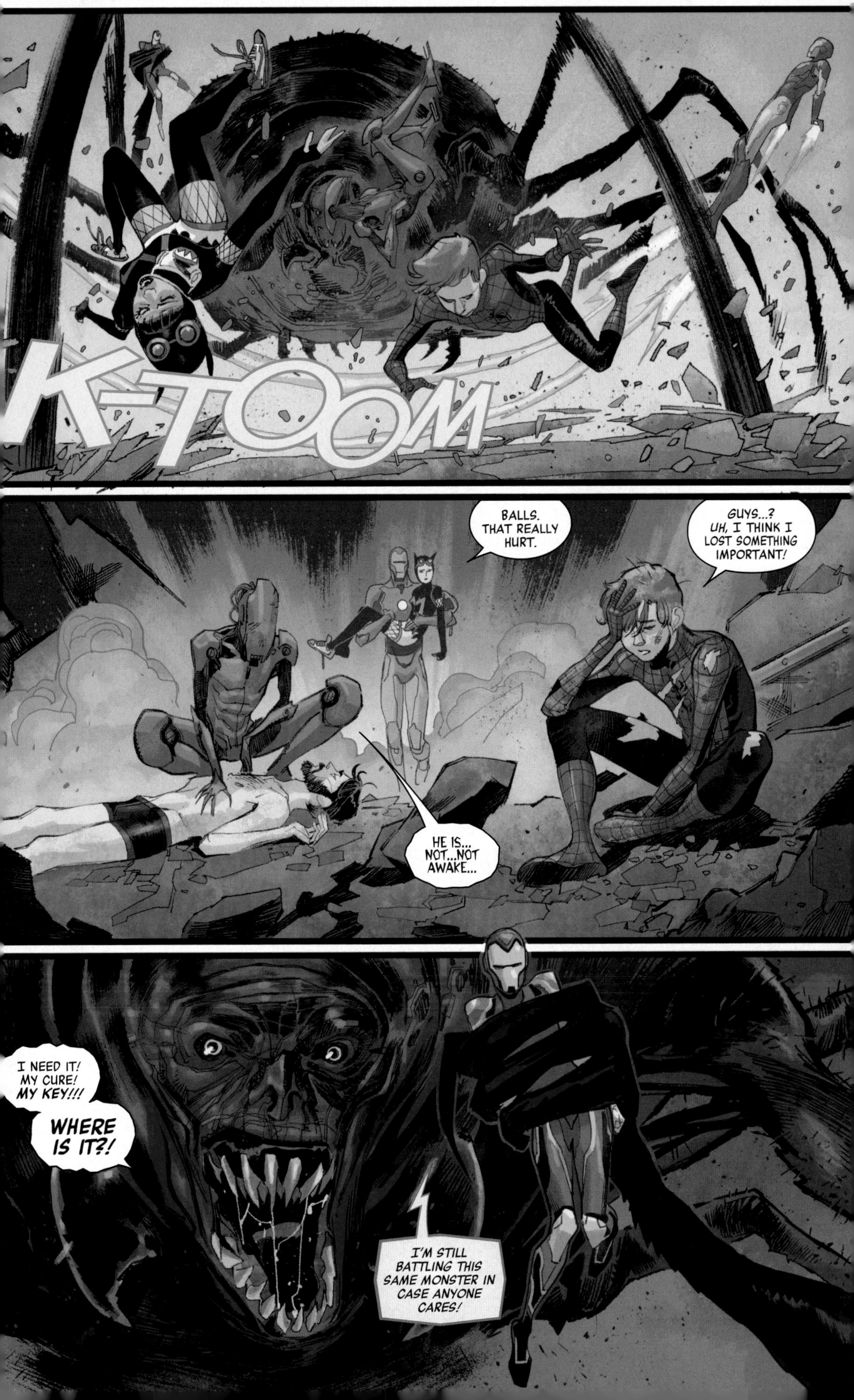
K-TOOM
BALLS. THAT REALLY HURT.
GUYS...? UH, I THINK I LOST SOMETHING IMPORTANT!
HE IS... NOT...NOT AWAKE...
I NEED IT! MY CURE! MY KEY!!!
WHERE IS IT?!
I'M STILL BATTLING THIS SAME MONSTER IN CASE ANYONE CARES!

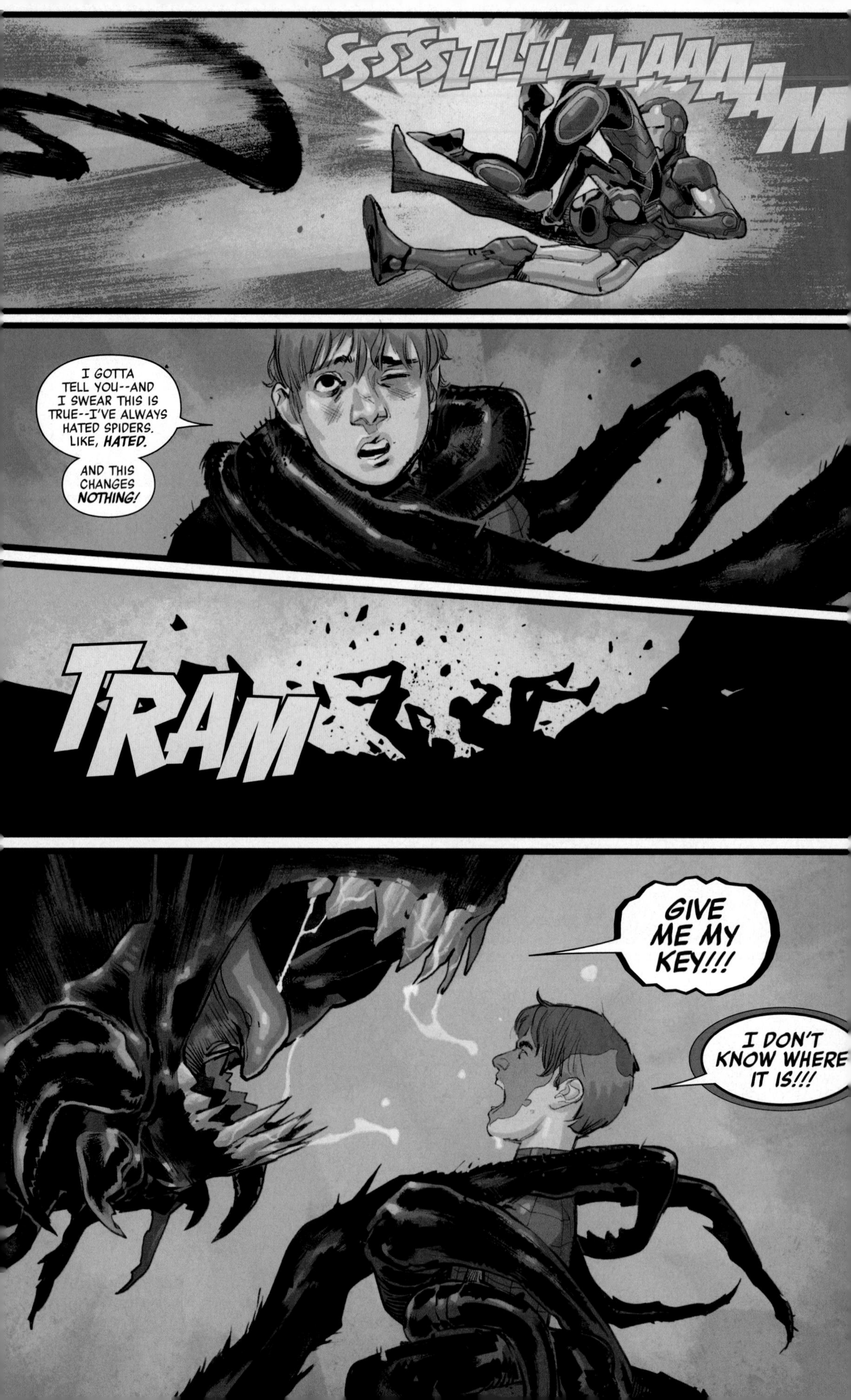
SSSSLLLLLAAAAAAAM
I GOTTA TELL YOU--AND I SWEAR THIS IS TRUE--I'VE ALWAYS HATED SPIDERS. LIKE, *HATED.*
AND THIS CHANGES *NOTHING!*
TRAM
GIVE ME MY KEY!!!
I DON'T KNOW WHERE IT IS!!!

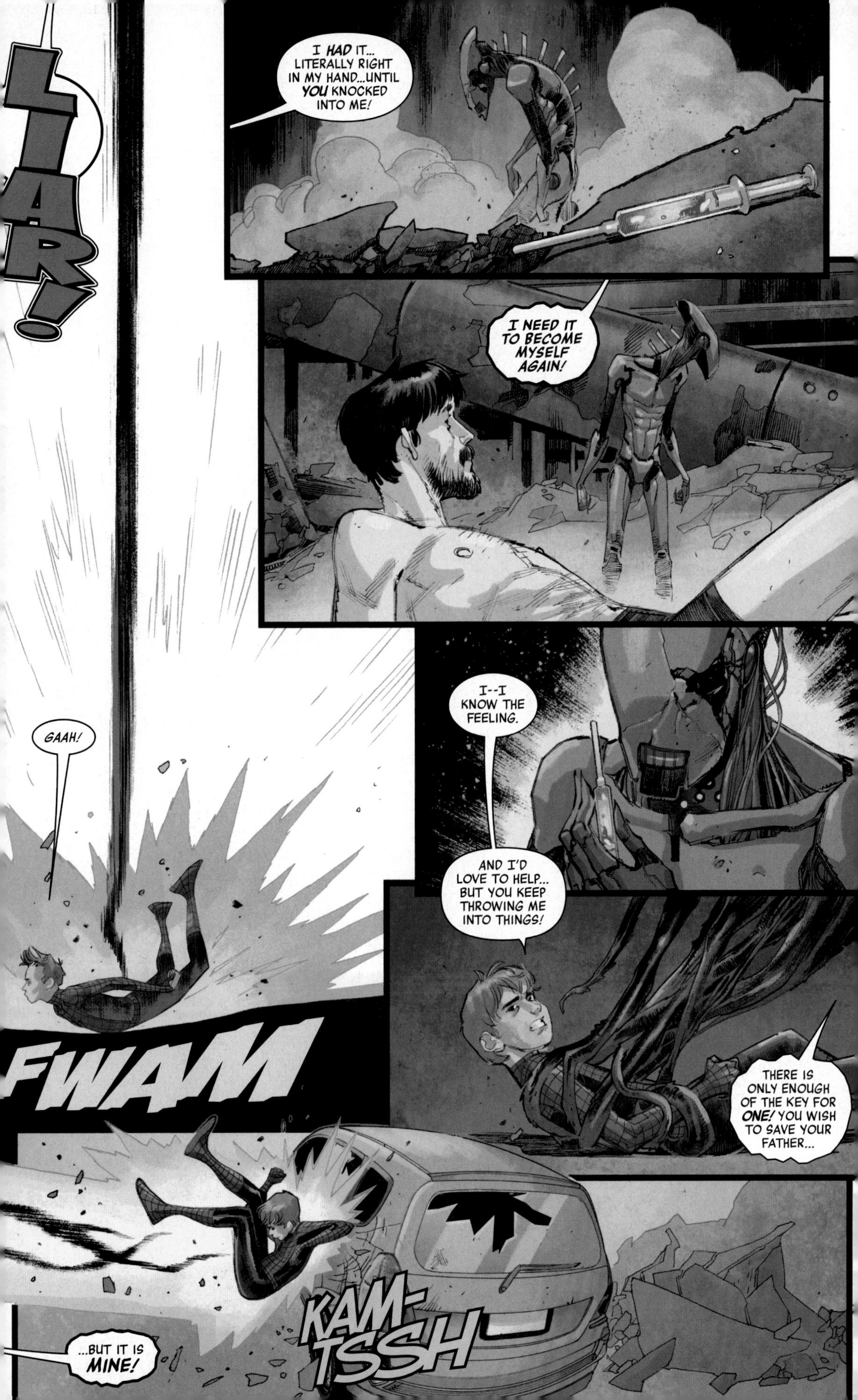
LIAR!
I HAD IT... LITERALLY RIGHT IN MY HAND...UNTIL YOU KNOCKED INTO ME!
I NEED IT TO BECOME MYSELF AGAIN!
GAAH!
FWAM
I--I KNOW THE FEELING.
AND I'D LOVE TO HELP... BUT YOU KEEP THROWING ME INTO THINGS!
THERE IS ONLY ENOUGH OF THE KEY FOR ONE! YOU WISH TO SAVE YOUR FATHER...
...BUT IT IS MINE!
KAM-TSSH

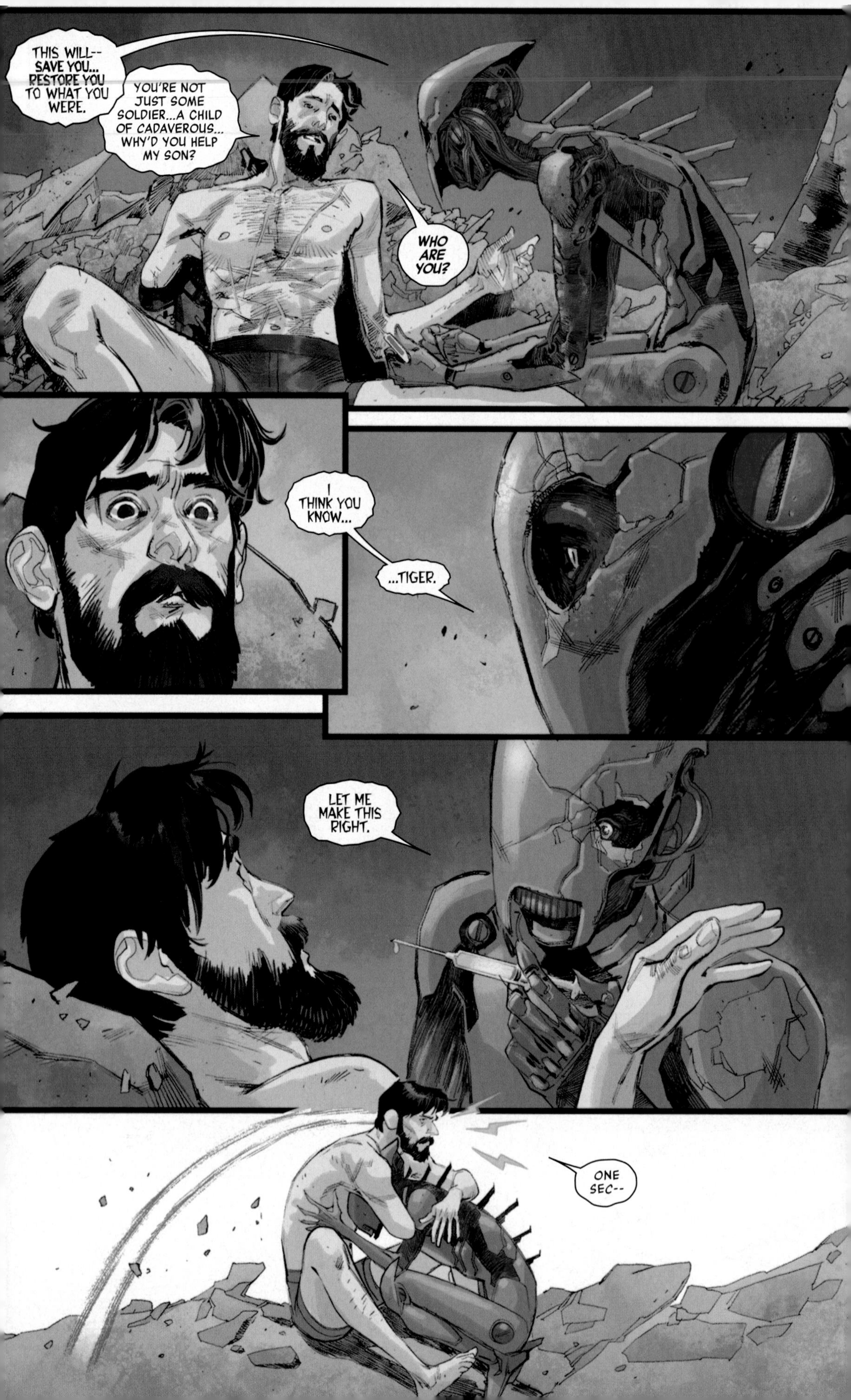
THIS WILL--
SAVE YOU...
RESTORE YOU
TO WHAT YOU
WERE.
YOU'RE NOT JUST SOME SOLDIER...A CHILD OF CADAVEROUS... WHY'D YOU HELP MY SON?
WHO ARE YOU?
I THINK YOU KNOW...
...TIGER.
LET ME MAKE THIS RIGHT.
ONE SEC--

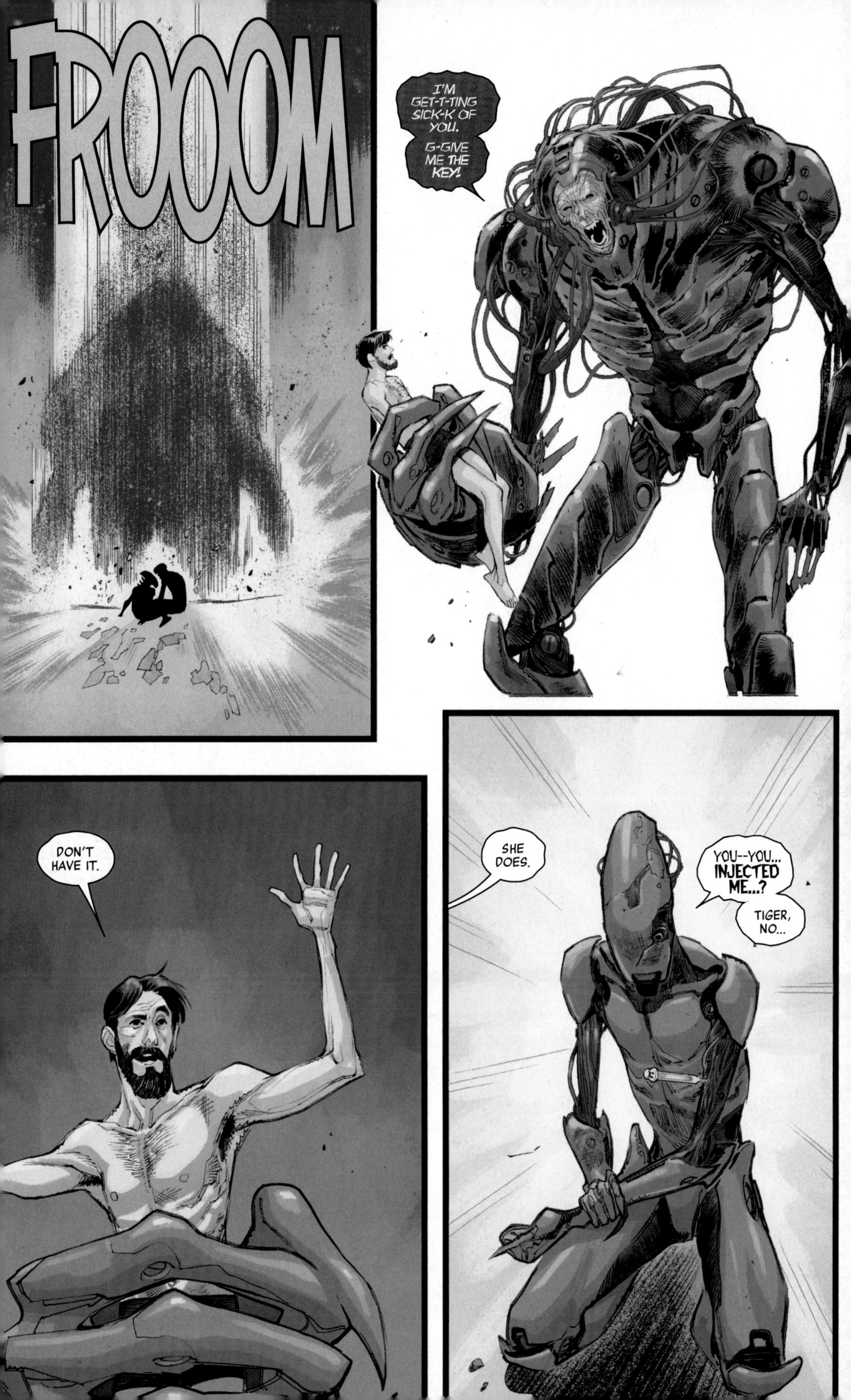
FROOOM
I'M GET-T-TING SICK-K OF YOU.
G-GIVE ME THE KEY!
DON'T HAVE IT.
SHE DOES.
YOU--YOU... INJECTED ME...?
TIGER, NO...

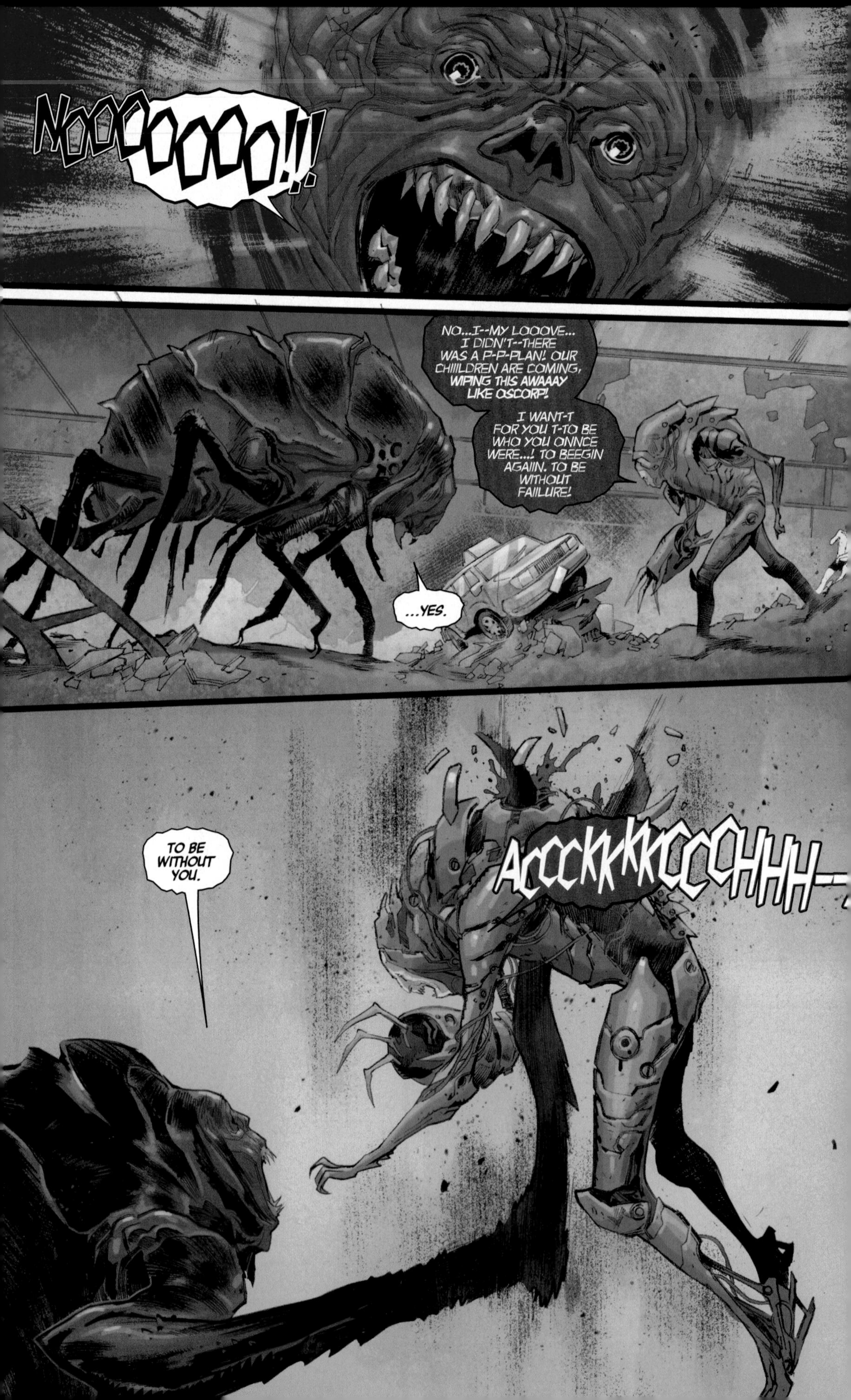
NOOOOOOOO!!!
NO...I--MY LOOOVE... I DIDN'T--THERE WAS A P-P-PLAN! OUR CHIIILDREN ARE COMING, WIPING THIS AWAAAY LIKE OSCORP!
I WANT-T FOR YOU T-TO BE WHO YOU ONNCE WERE...! TO BEEGIN AGAIIN. TO BE WITHOUT FAILURE!
...YES.
TO BE WITHOUT YOU.
ACCCKKKKCCCHHH--

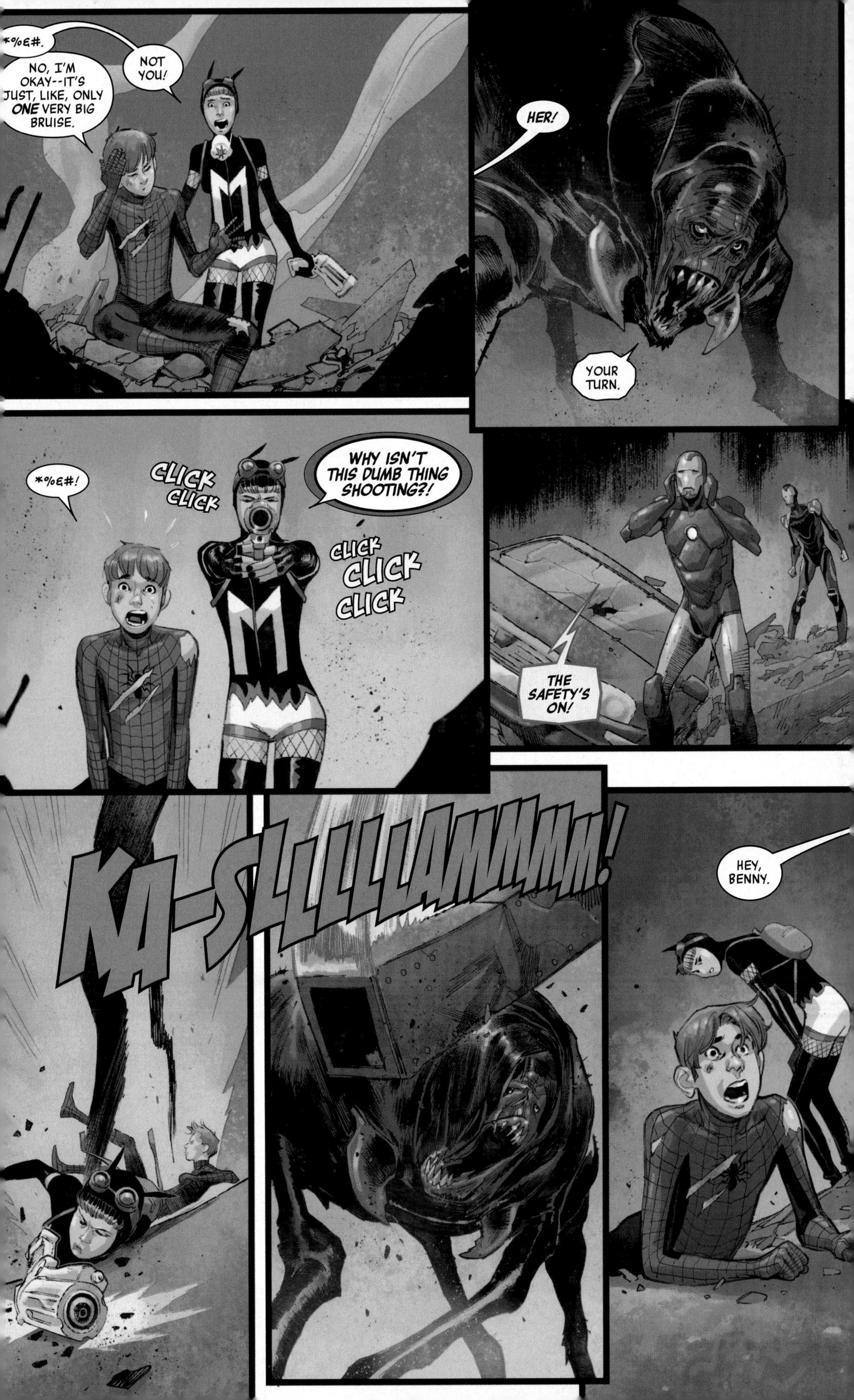
*%&#.
NO, I'M OKAY--IT'S JUST, LIKE, ONLY ONE VERY BIG BRUISE.
NOT YOU!
HER!
YOUR TURN.
*%&#!
CLICK CLICK
WHY ISN'T THIS DUMB THING SHOOTING?!
CLICK CLICK CLICK
THE SAFETY'S ON!
KA-SLLLLLAMMMMM!
HEY, BENNY.

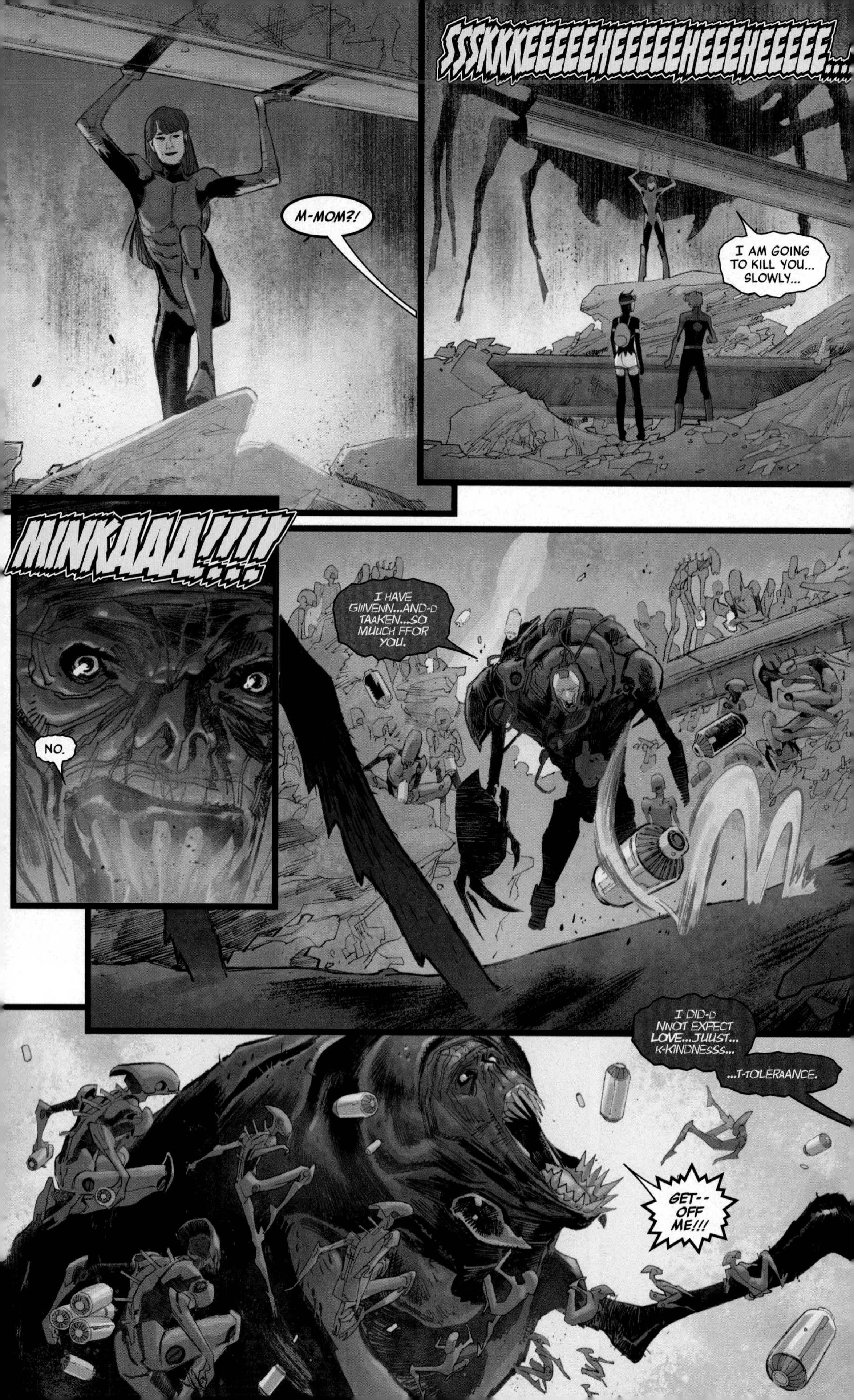
M-MOM?!
SSSKKKEEEEEHEEEEEHEEEHEEEEE...!
I AM GOING TO KILL YOU... SLOWLY...
MINKAAA!!!!
NO.
I HAVE GIIIVENN...AND-D TAAKEN...SO MUUCH FFOR YOU.
I DID-D NNOT EXPECT LOVE...JUUST... K-KINDNESSS...
...T-TOLERAANCE.
GET-- OFF ME!!!

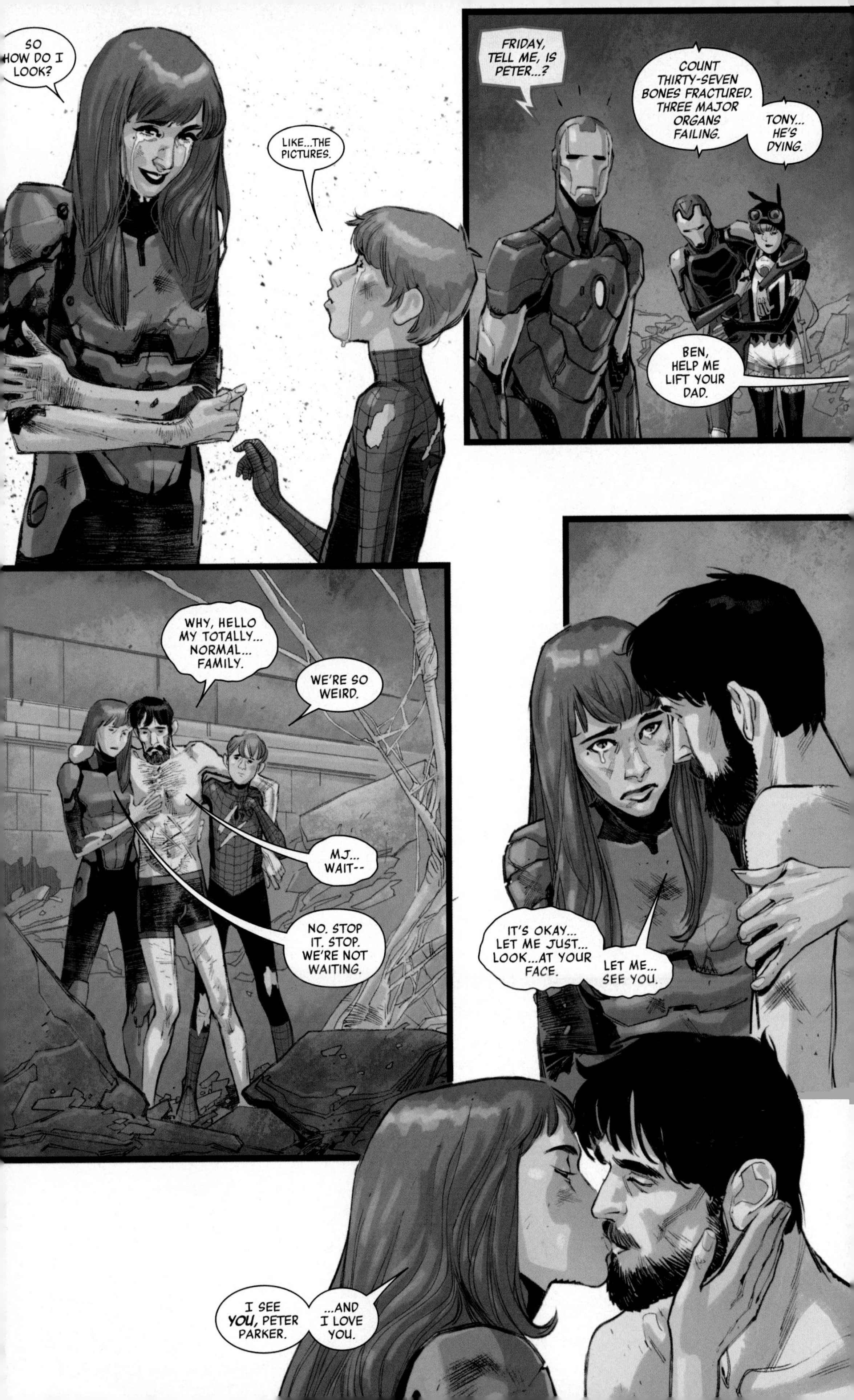
SO HOW DO I LOOK?
LIKE...THE PICTURES.
FRIDAY, TELL ME, IS PETER...?
COUNT THIRTY-SEVEN BONES FRACTURED. THREE MAJOR ORGANS FAILING.
TONY... HE'S DYING.
BEN, HELP ME LIFT YOUR DAD.
WHY, HELLO MY TOTALLY... NORMAL... FAMILY.
WE'RE SO WEIRD.
MJ... WAIT--
NO. STOP IT. STOP. WE'RE NOT WAITING.
IT'S OKAY... LET ME JUST... LOOK...AT YOUR FACE.
LET ME... SEE YOU.
I SEE YOU, PETER PARKER.
...AND I LOVE YOU.

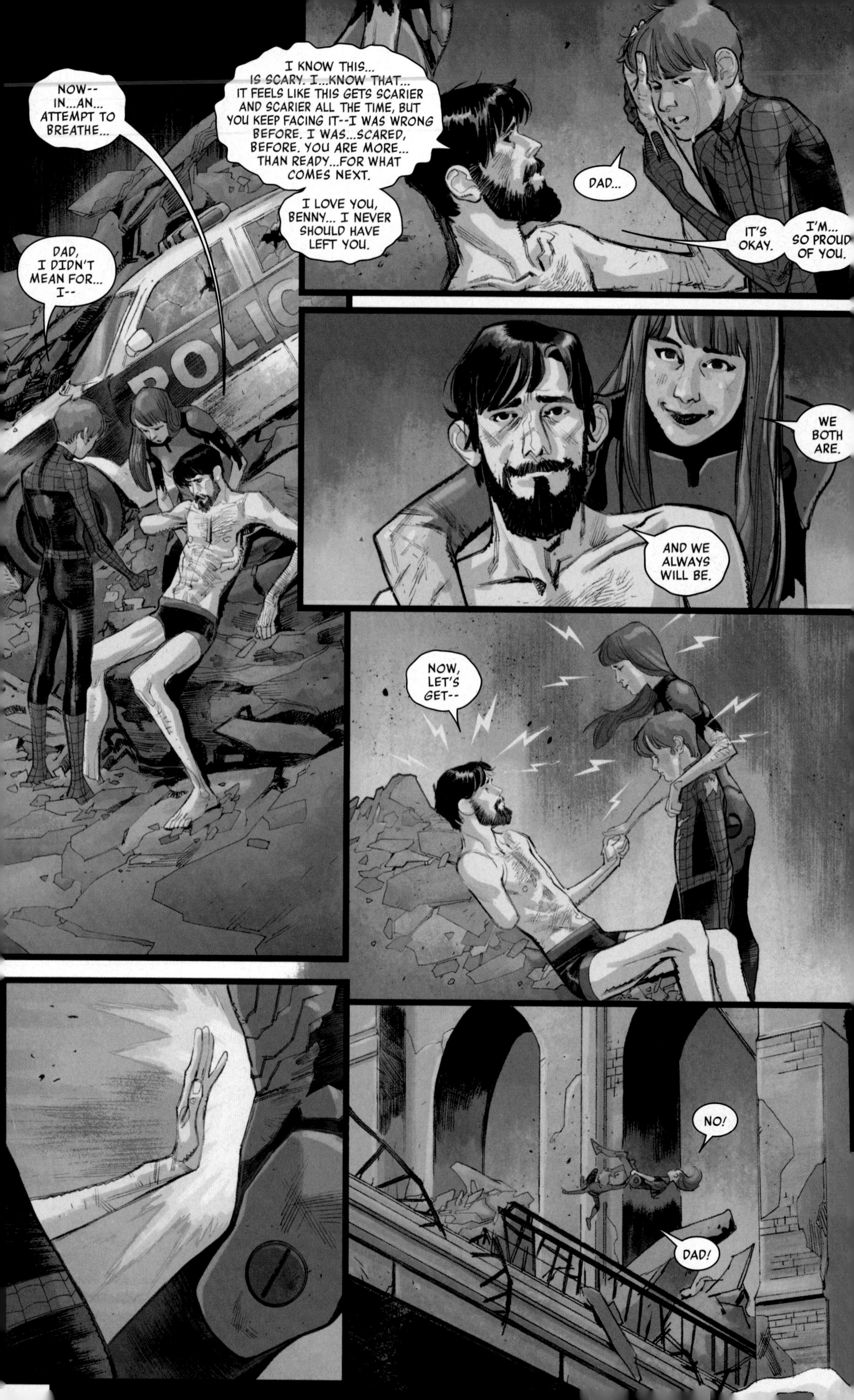
NOW-- IN...AN... ATTEMPT TO BREATHE...
I KNOW THIS... IS SCARY. I...KNOW THAT... IT FEELS LIKE THIS GETS SCARIER AND SCARIER ALL THE TIME, BUT YOU KEEP FACING IT--I WAS WRONG BEFORE. I WAS...SCARED, BEFORE. YOU ARE MORE... THAN READY...FOR WHAT COMES NEXT.
I LOVE YOU, BENNY... I NEVER SHOULD HAVE LEFT YOU.
DAD, I DIDN'T MEAN FOR... I--
DAD...
IT'S OKAY.
I'M... SO PROUD OF YOU.
WE BOTH ARE.
AND WE ALWAYS WILL BE.
NOW, LET'S GET--
NO!
DAD!

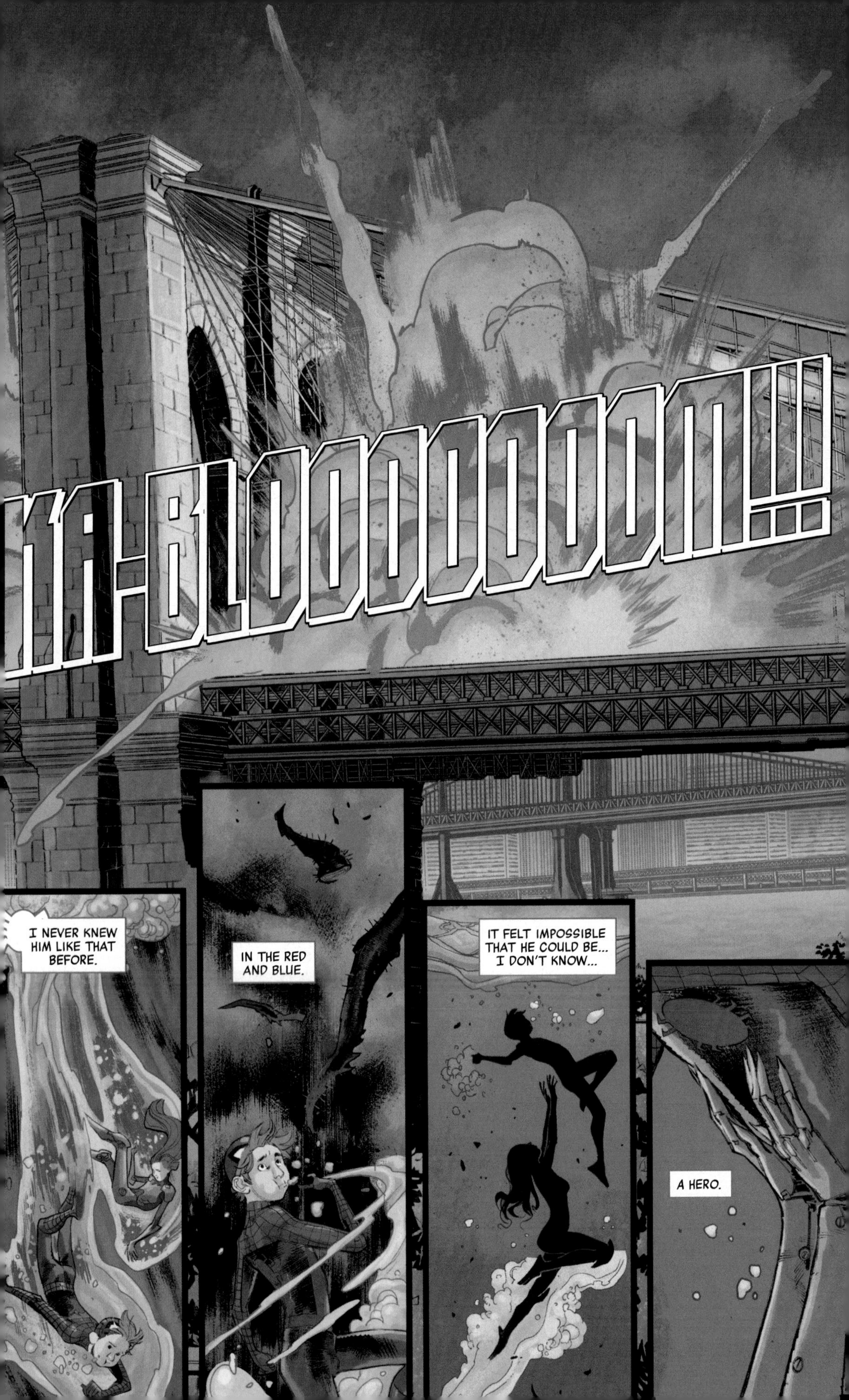
KA-BLOOOOOOM!!!
I NEVER KNEW HIM LIKE THAT BEFORE.
IN THE RED AND BLUE.
IT FELT IMPOSSIBLE THAT HE COULD BE... I DON'T KNOW...
A HERO.

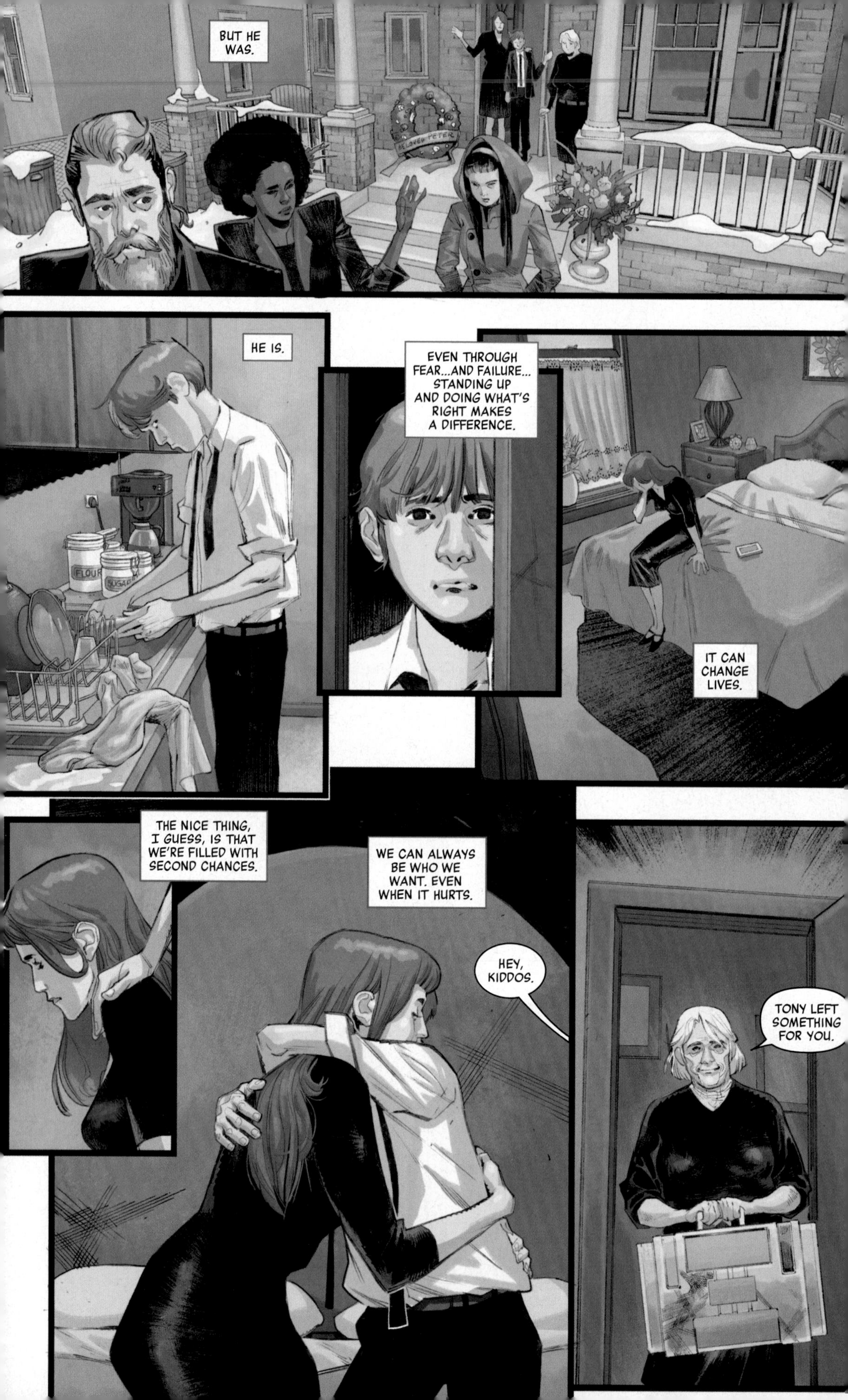
BUT HE WAS.
HE IS.
FLOUR
EVEN THROUGH FEAR...AND FAILURE... STANDING UP AND DOING WHAT'S RIGHT MAKES A DIFFERENCE.
IT CAN CHANGE LIVES.
THE NICE THING, I GUESS, IS THAT WE'RE FILLED WITH SECOND CHANCES.
WE CAN ALWAYS BE WHO WE WANT. EVEN WHEN IT HURTS.
HEY, KIDDOS.
TONY LEFT SOMETHING FOR YOU.

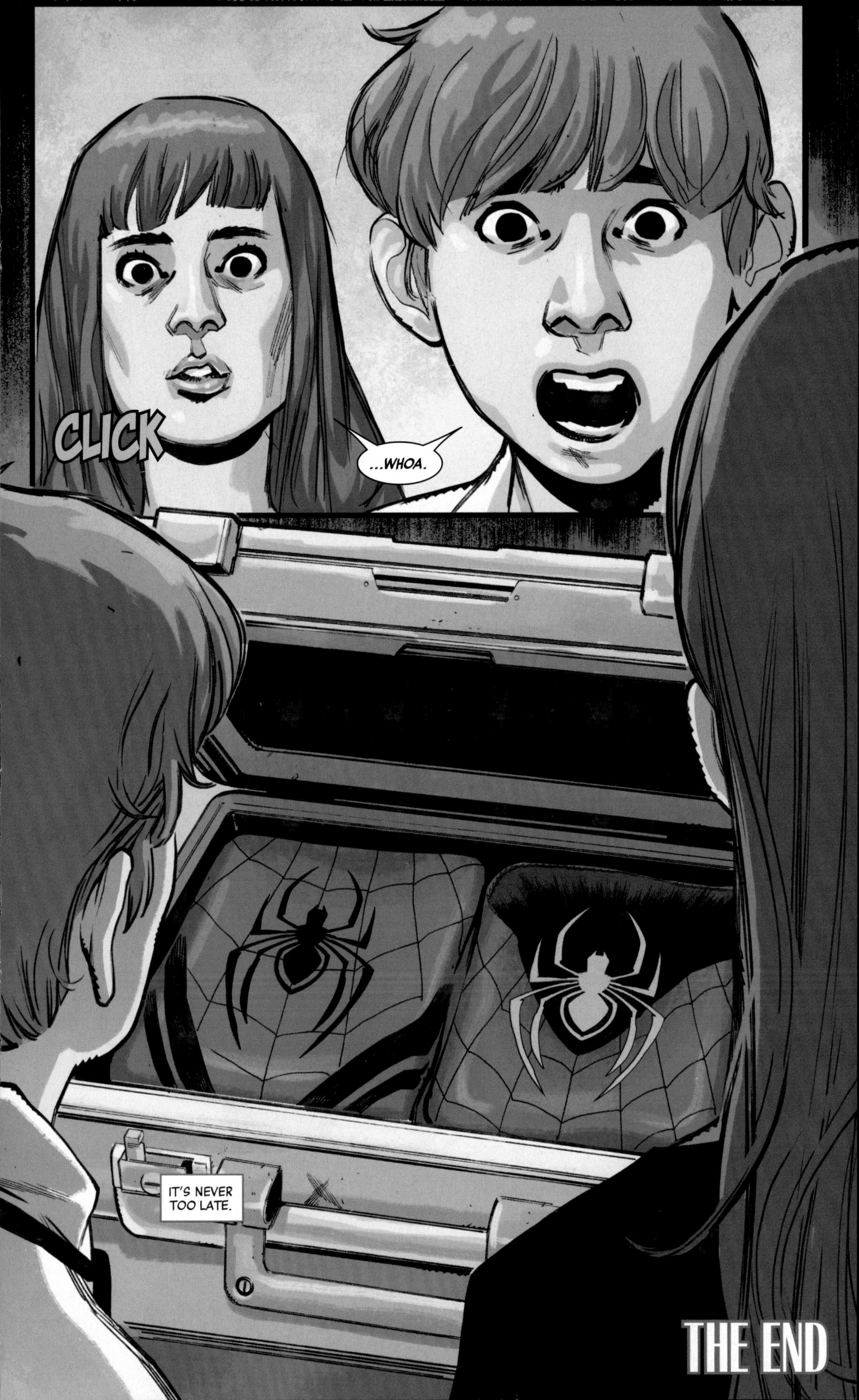
CLICK
...WHOA.
IT'S NEVER TOO LATE.
THE END

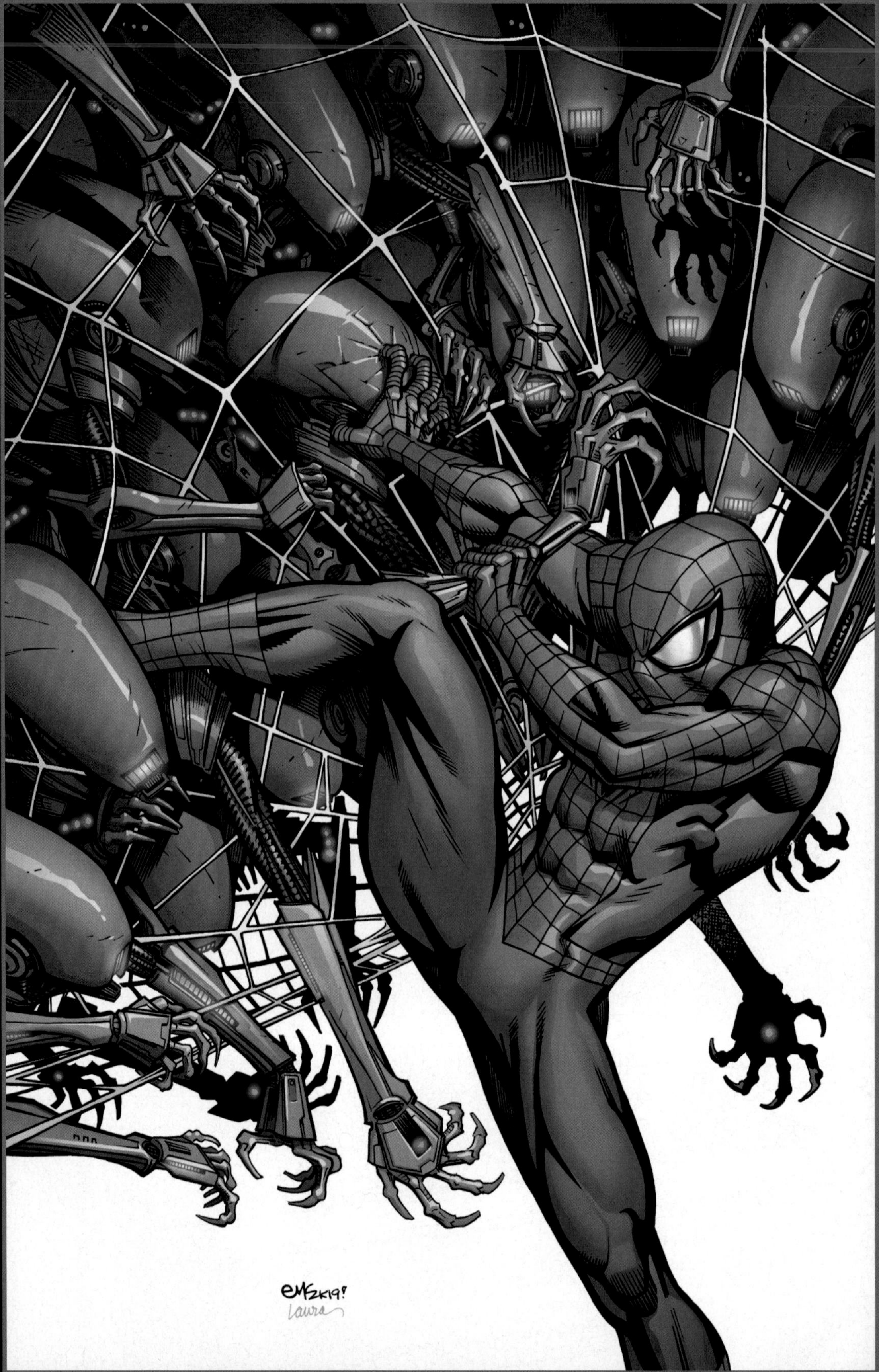

eMcG 2K19!
Laura

ED McGUINNESS & LAURA MARTIN

NO. 1 VARIANT

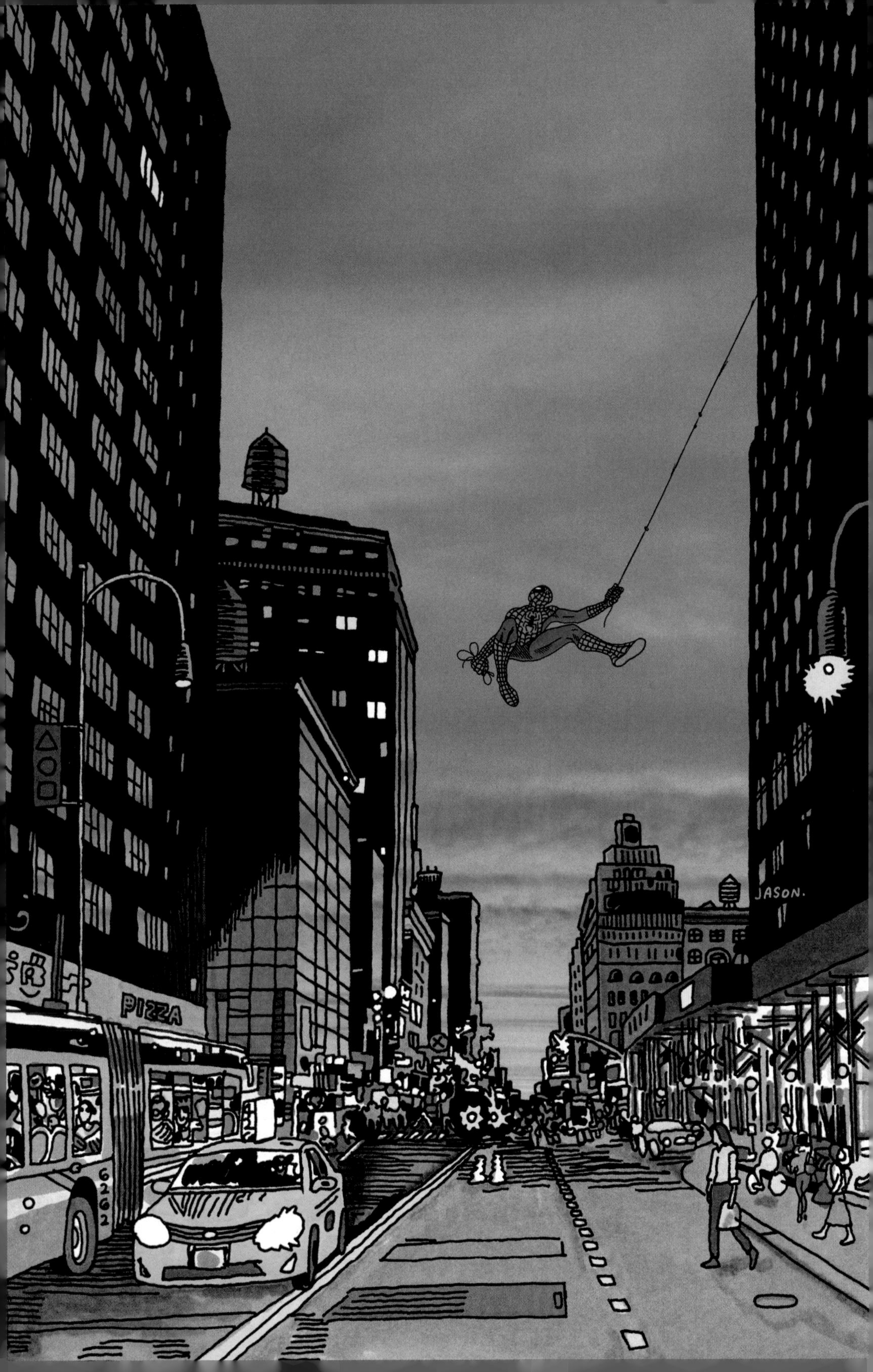
PIZZA
6262
JASON.

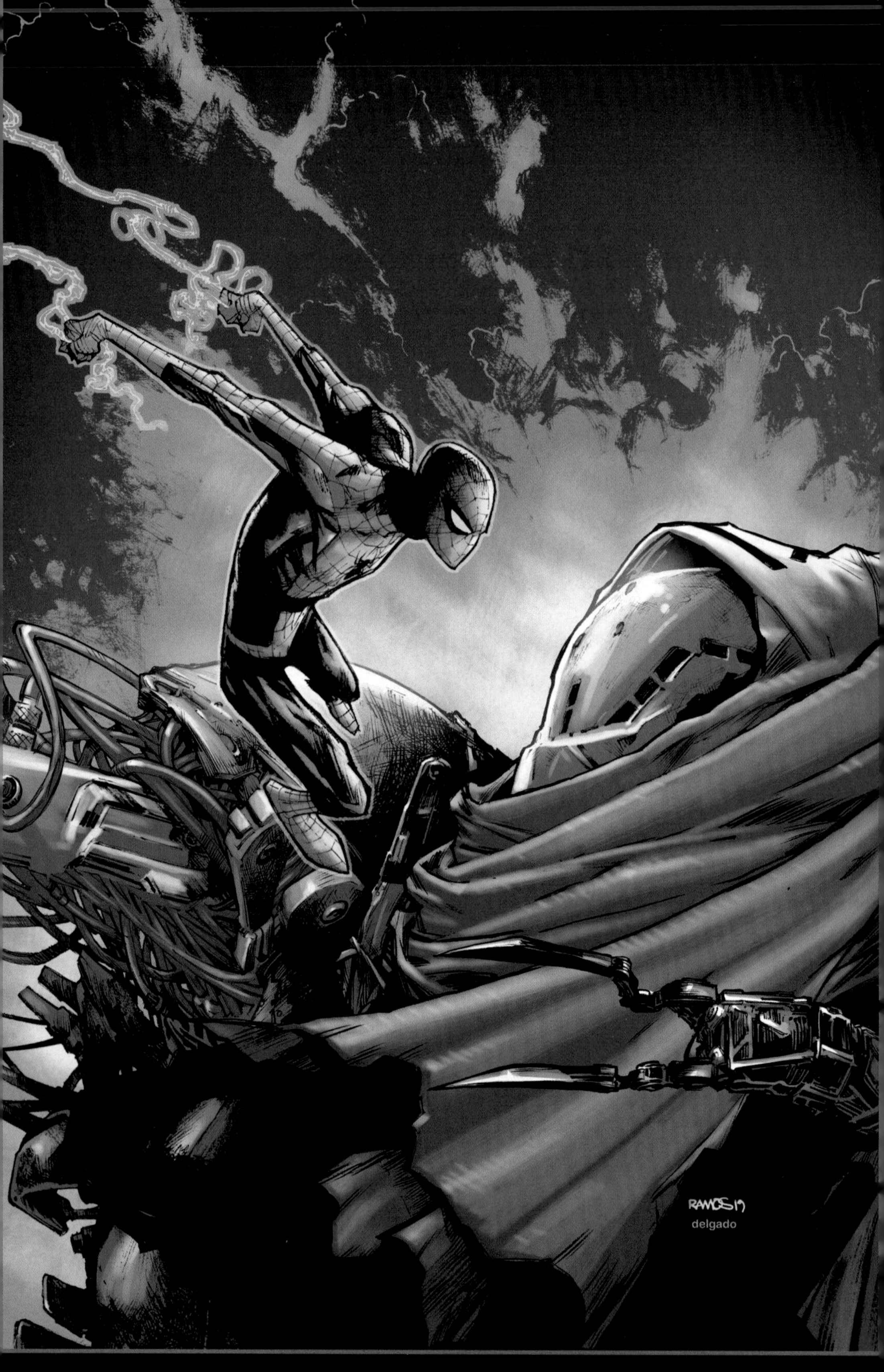
RAMOS19
delgado

HUMBERTO RAMOS – EDGAR DELGADO

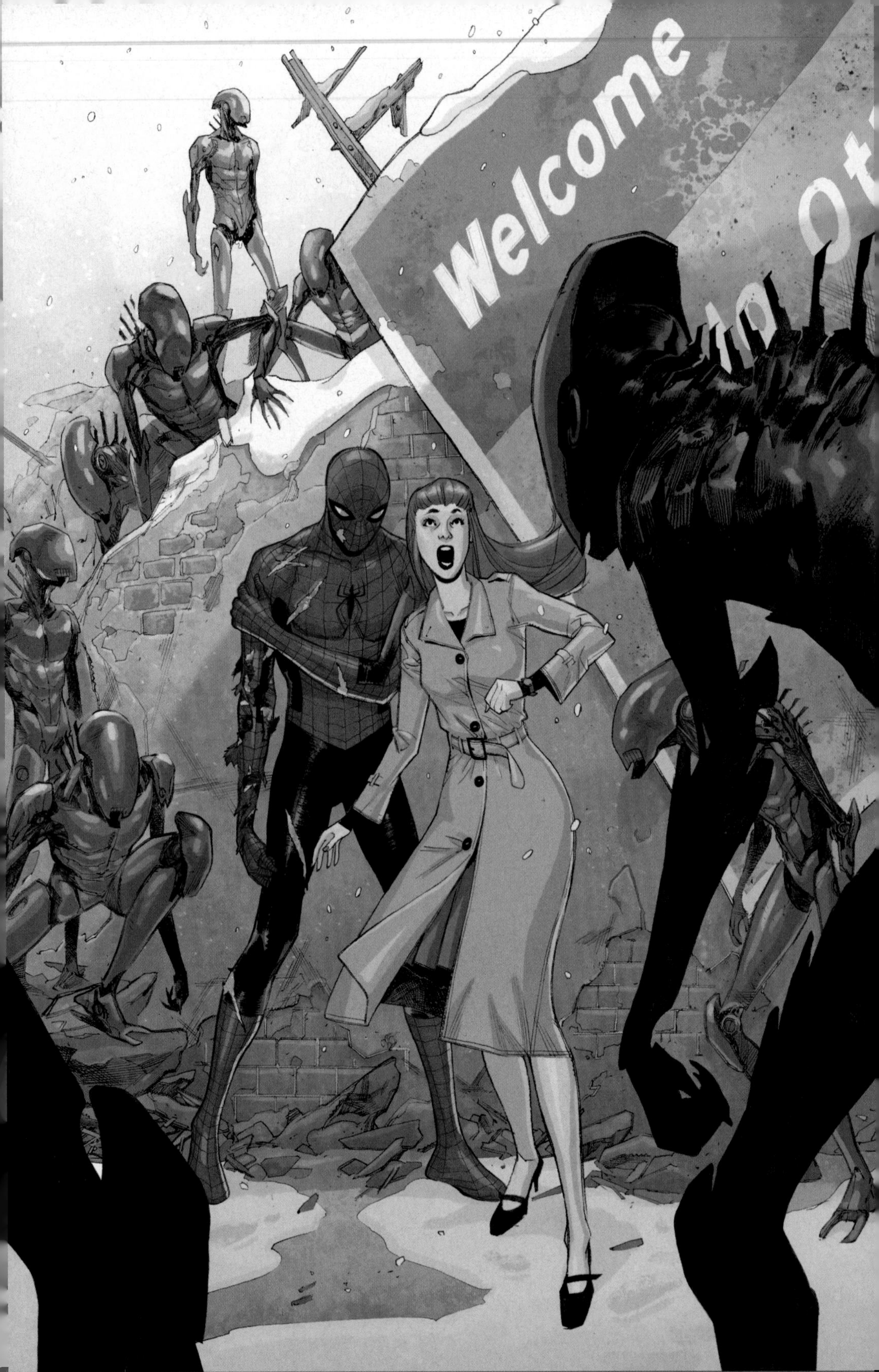
Welcome

SAR

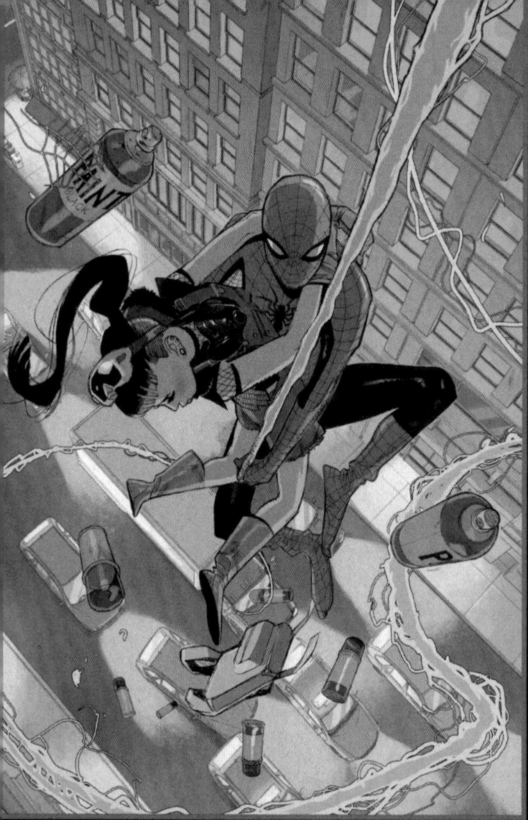
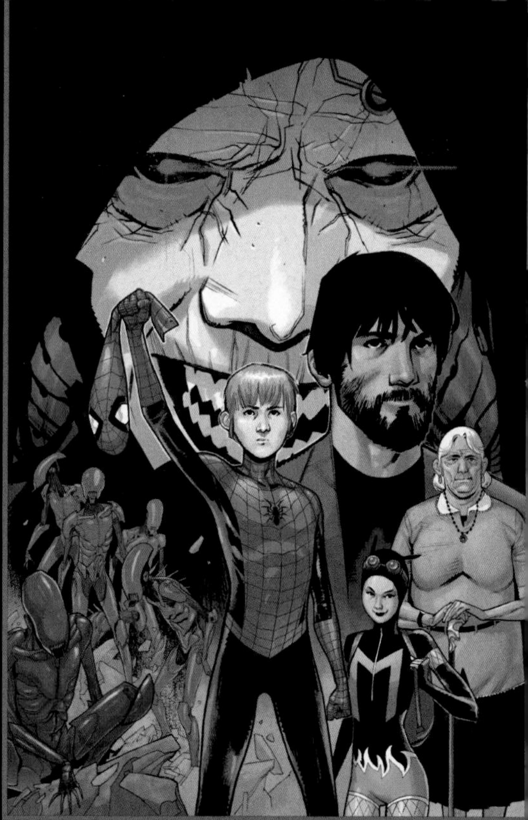
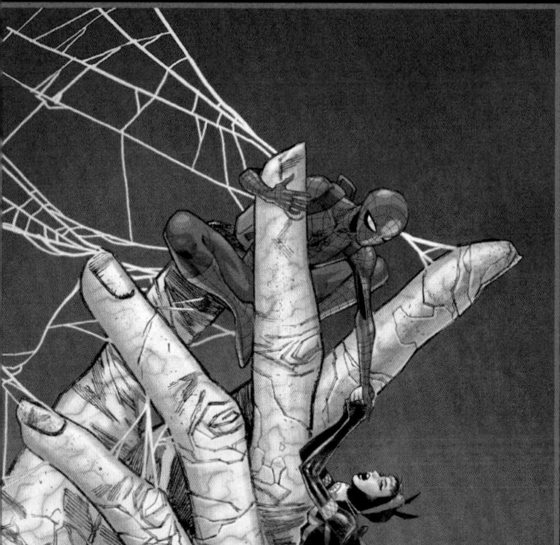
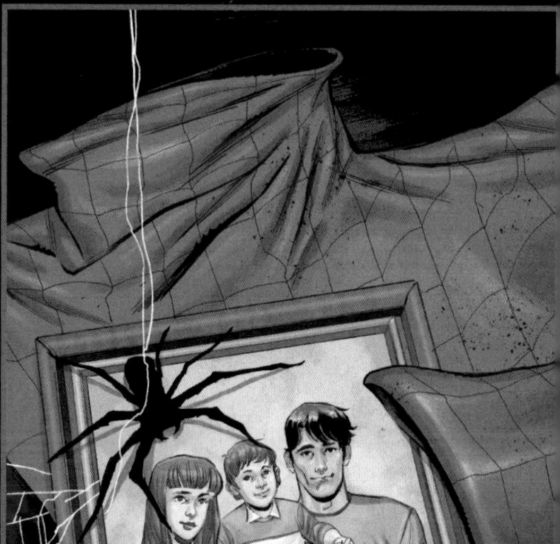

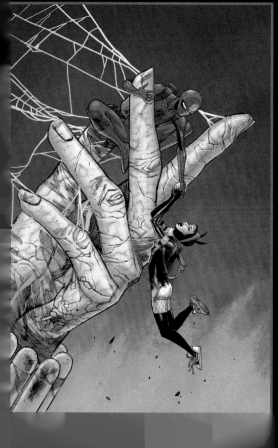

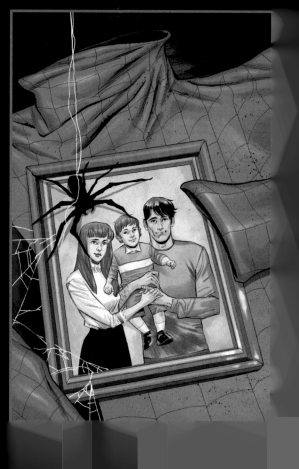

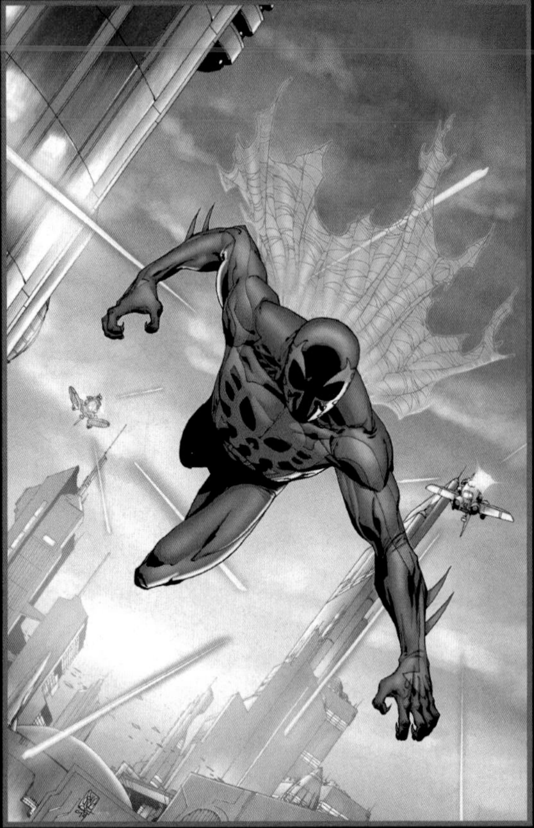

GIUSEPPE CAMUNCOLI & EDGAR DELGADO

NO.3 2099 VARIANT

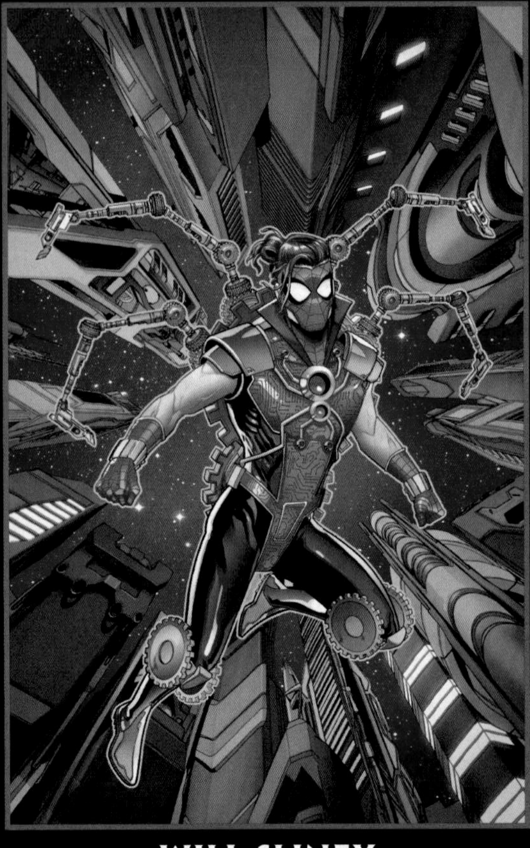

WILL SLINEY

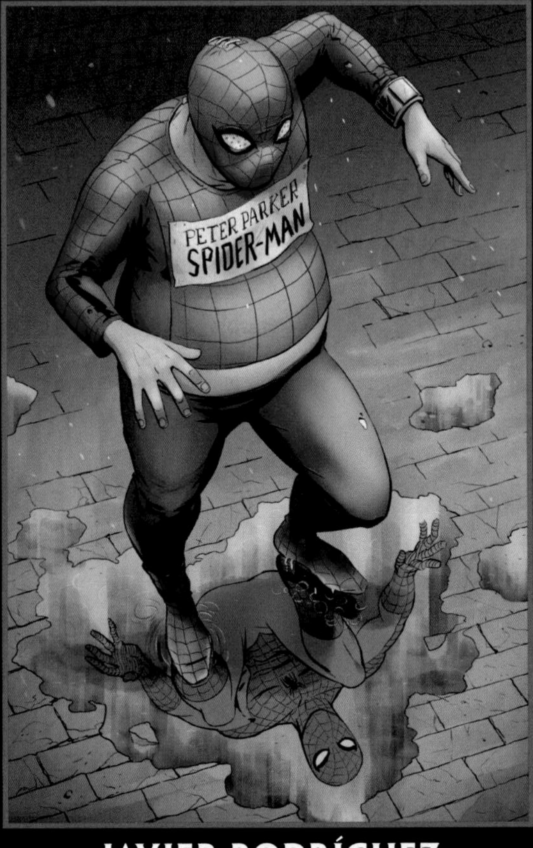
PETER PARKER
SPIDER-MAN

JAVIER RODRÍGUEZ